Approaches and Frameworks for HCI Research

This research textbook, designed for young human–computer interaction (HCI) researchers beginning their careers, surveys the research models and methods in use today and offers a general framework to bring together the disparate concepts. HCI spans many disciplines and professions, including information science, applied psychology, computer science, informatics, software engineering and social science, making it difficult for newcomers to get a good overview of the field and the available approaches. The book's rigorous 'approach-and-framework' response is to the challenge of retaining growth and diversification in HCI research by building up a general framework from approaches for innovation, art, craft, applied, science and engineering. This general framework is compared with other HCI frameworks and theories for completeness and coherence, all within a historical perspective of dissemination success. Readers can use this as a model to design and assess their own research frameworks and theories against those reported in the literature.

John Long is Emeritus Professor of Cognitive Engineering at University College London, where he was previously Professor of Cognitive Ergonomics and Director of the Ergonomics and HCI Unit. He has served as manager at Shell Oil International in Africa and Vietnam and as senior scientist at the Medical Research Council Applied Psychology Unit (MRC/APU), Cambridge. His research includes three co-authored books, more than 200 publications, and numerous presentations, grants and consultancies. He has received the Ergonomics Society (ES) Sir Frederick Bartlett medal, the International Ergonomics Association (IEA) Outstanding Educator's Award, and recently received the Athena Swan Award, being identified as a hero of Computer Science by the University of York. An avid cyclist, he has completed the Tour de France, Giro d'Italia and other major cycling tour routes elsewhere in Europe, Australia and Asia. He is also an expressive abstractionist painter. His 'Framed Approaches' from 1989 serves as the cover for this book. He is an unreconstructed existentialist.

T0201452

Approaches and Frameworks
for HCI Research

JOHN LONG
University College London

CAMBRIDGE
UNIVERSITY PRESS

CAMBRIDGE
UNIVERSITY PRESS

University Printing House, Cambridge CB2 8BS, United Kingdom

One Liberty Plaza, 20th Floor, New York, NY 10006, USA

477 Williamstown Road, Port Melbourne, VIC 3207, Australia

314–321, 3rd Floor, Plot 3, Splendor Forum, Jasola District Centre,
New Delhi – 110025, India

79 Anson Road, #06–04/06, Singapore 079906

Cambridge University Press is part of the University of Cambridge.

It furthers the University's mission by disseminating knowledge in the pursuit of
education, learning, and research at the highest international levels of excellence.

www.cambridge.org
Information on this title: www.cambridge.org/9781108719070
DOI: 10.1017/9781108754972

First published 2021

Printed in the United Kingdom by TJ Books Limited, Padstow Cornwall

A catalogue record for this publication is available from the British Library.

Library of Congress Cataloging-in-Publication Data
Names: Long, John (John B.), author.
Title: Approaches and frameworks for HCI research / John Long, University College
London.
Description: First edition. | Cambridge, United Kingdom ; New York, NY : Cambridge
University Press, 2021. | Includes bibliographical references and index.
Identifiers: LCCN 2020036010 (print) | LCCN 2020036011 (ebook) | ISBN 9781108719070
(paperback) | ISBN 9781108754972 (ebook)
Subjects: LCSH: Human-computer interaction – Research.
Classification: LCC QA76.9.H85 L67 2021 (print) | LCC QA76.9.H85 (ebook) | DDC
004.01/9–dc23
LC record available at https://lccn.loc.gov/2020036010
LC ebook record available at https://lccn.loc.gov/2020036011

ISBN 978-1-108-71907-0 Paperback

To Doris, Hadley and Ben.
And to Paola for listening.

Contents

Contents

Preface

About This Book

The title of this book, *Approaches and Frameworks for HCI Research*, makes clear its scope and content. The latter concerns both what it is and what it is not. It is about human–computer interaction (HCI) research, not just about HCI in general. However, both subjects are addressed. This distinguishes it from other attempts to address the two subjects, either as separate or as undifferentiated topics. Here, approaches are distinguished from frameworks. However, both are specified explicitly, including the relations between them.

The book presents an 'approach-and-framework' response to the HCI research challenge of addressing the increased growth and diversification of HCI. The response supports researchers building on and validating each other's work. The aim is to decrease theory fragmentation and so to increase HCI discipline progress. The contrast is with HCI community progress, which continues apace.

It is a book for researchers, especially young researchers, and so might properly be described as a research textbook. In this respect, it is unique and different from other textbooks, which are aimed primarily at supporting the HCI teaching of undergraduate and masters' students. This difference is reflected in its 'how to do research' aspects, exemplified by the research practice assignments and, in particular, the research design scenarios presented at the end of chapters. For this reason, the text is organised and written to support application of the approaches and frameworks proposed. Encouraging researchers to internalise the latter is part of that support. This is in addition to supporting researchers in their ability to understand and to reason about the approaches and frameworks.

Although intended primarily for researchers starting their careers in academia or industry, the textbook is also suitable for graduate and postgraduate students being introduced to the world of research. It also aims to support the supervisors teaching them about HCI research and its relation to HCI more generally. In particular, the textbook supports students in learning how approaches and frameworks contribute to the planning and conduct of research in practice.

It is a good time to publish such a research textbook. It offers a clear alternative to the current 'design-an-application-for-a-good-user-experience' line of design practice research. The latter, whatever its strengths, notably fails to address the HCI research challenge identified earlier concerning poor discipline progress. It might even be said to contribute to that challenge by the very number of frameworks and theories that it has helped to engender. Indeed, it is hard, on occasion, to distinguish such design practice research from HCI design practice itself. The textbook's strength lies in its recognition of the current differences between the many types of HCI approach to research appearing in the literature. Its strength also lies in the need for frameworks to apply to such approaches and so to support researchers building on and validating each other's work.

About the Author

The author feels able to write such a research textbook. The conception underlying the proposed relationship between approaches and frameworks for HCI research was developed by colleagues, PhD students and himself during their time at University College London. The conception has been used, then and since, for MSc and PhD student teaching, also for both academic and commercial research. The latter provides an extensive source of illustrations for the book together with the HCI research literature more generally.

About the Readership

As indicated, the textbook is primarily for young HCI researchers and their supervisors, from both engineering and science academics to research and development innovators. The book is also for researchers in related disciplines seeking ways to contribute to HCI research. Such disciplines include information science, applied psychology, computer science, informatics, software engineering and social science. Researchers are expected to use the textbook for detailed and ongoing reference in support of their work.

Acknowledgements

The book is offered as an affectionate, if somewhat belated, *festschrift* for colleagues and PhD students at the Ergonomics and HCI Unit/University College London (EU/UCL Unit) from 1979 to 2001. Their invaluable research contributions, and in particular my work with John Dowell, have made it possible.

I wish to acknowledge the journal *Interacting with Computers* and its erstwhile editor Dianne Murray for publishing in 2010 a Special Issue, entitled 'Festschrift for John Long'. The idea originated with the guest editors, Alistair Sutcliffe and Ann Blandford.

1

Approaches and Frameworks for HCI Research

This chapter introduces human–computer interaction (HCI) and HCI research and describes their current states. Challenges to HCI research are identified and the aims of the book presented. The concepts of 'approach' and 'framework' are outlined, together with their relations. The chapter sets the scene for the following two chapters, which address respectively approaches and frameworks separately and in greater depth.

1.1 Why HCI?

HCI, as a description of the field of human–computer interaction, is more established and general than alternative descriptors. For this reason, it is retained here. HCI continues to be in a permanent state of change. [1] As a result, no description of the field is excluded. HCI is interpreted inclusively and is considered to comprise ease of use/usability, applied psychology, engineering, human-centred design, cognitive engineering, interaction design, user experience (UX) design, technical art, graphic design and digital interaction, along with others.

Given the growth and diversity of new computing technology, however, HCI is understood as human–computing technology interaction, rather than just human–computer interaction. The latter term is more associated with personal computing. The term 'HCI', however, has been retained, as having greater currency in the HCI research literature at this time. This is in contrast to others, such as 'UX design' and 'digital interaction design', more favoured by the practitioner community.

1.2 State of HCI

Since its inception in the late 1970s, HCI has grown and diversified extensively and continues to do so. This growth and diversification constitutes a challenge for HCI research.

A roughly historical perspective suggests the following development of human, interaction and computing technology scopes. The human scope has increased to include more abilities, ages, social classes, communities, societies and cross-national communication groups. The interaction scope has increased to include keying, pointing/clicking, drawing, speaking, touching, gesturing, smelling, electro-mediated communicating, tasting, whole-body moving and electrode-conducted thinking. The computing technology scope has increased to include portability, distributed social media communicability, artificial intelligence, autonomous devices, implantability, interconnectivity, robots, wearability, mobile and ubiquitous digital technology. Together they constitute the increase in the scope and diversification[2] of HCI and the challenge for HCI research.

1.3 State of HCI Research

It is assumed here that HCI research of whatever kind acquires and validates HCI knowledge as design knowledge. Or at least as knowledge associated with, derived from or potentially applicable to design. Different assumptions would require different proposals to those made here. Some alternative and additional assumptions, however, are reflected in the differences between the specific frameworks proposed (see 4.3–9.3). However, while retaining these differences, the specific frameworks are all based on a common core framework. In this way, the general overall assumption is made compatible with different underlying assumptions. This compatibility is essential for researchers to build on and to validate each other's work. Such compatibility is almost entirely absent from current HCI research. It has been absent historically from its beginning. This is the case both for its frameworks (see 12.3) and for its theories (see 13.3).

HCI research has responded to the increase in the scope and diversification of HCI with growth and diversification of its own. Following the HCI literature, the latter can be considered to take two forms – fields and theories. This increase in growth and diversification of HCI research constitutes an ongoing challenge.

First is the growth and diversification of the fields of HCI. For example, Rogers (2012) distinguishes seven academic disciplines, five design practices and seven interdisciplinary overlapping fields. This constitutes 19 fields of HCI in all.[3]

Second is the growth and diversification of types of HCI theory. For example, Rogers (2012) distinguishes three classical, nine modern and five contemporary types of theory. This constitutes 17 types of HCI theory in all.

1.4 Challenges for HCI Research

The growth and diversification of HCI research has led, in the absence of consensus among researchers about either, to two outcomes: first, to a failure to build on and to validate each other's work and second, to a fragmentation of both HCI fields and theories. The challenge for HCI research, then, is to address the growth and diversification of HCI and of the associated research, while decreasing the fragmentation of fields and theories. The latter requires researchers to build on and to validate each other's work and so to increase consensus. The result would be to increase HCI discipline progress.

A number of authors, while celebrating the growth and diversification of HCI and its community, have analysed and documented the lack of HCI discipline progress (Long and Dowell, 1989; Newman, 1984; Rogers, 2012). For example, Newman claims that only 30 per cent of HCI research reports enhancements in modelling techniques, solutions and design tools. This is against 90 per cent for the discipline of engineering more generally. The remainder of HCI research describes radical solutions, not derived from incremental solutions of the same problem. Also included are experience and/or heuristics gained from studies of radical solutions. Radical solutions and experience and/or heuristics characterise the 'design-an-application-for -a-good-user-experience' line of HCI design practice research, identified earlier. Analysis of more recent research reported in the literature or presented at conferences, such as the ACM CHI Conference on Human Factors in Computing Systems series, indicates the situation as being unchanged since Newman's findings. If anything, the percentage of radical solutions and experience and/or heuristics continues to increase (Dix, 2010; Long, 2010).

1.5 Aims of Research Textbook

The aim of the research textbook is to propose a way of meeting the challenge to HCI research outlined in the previous section. The proposal consists of identifying and grouping common approaches to HCI research reported in the literature. On the basis of an existing HCI conception, a core framework for HCI, including HCI research, is proposed. The latter is particularised to create a specific framework for HCI research for each approach identified. The specific frameworks are then generalised to create a general framework for HCI research. The latter is assessed against other HCI frameworks and HCI theories.

The book illustrates and then shows researchers in some detail how their own approaches may be identified and new approaches created. The application of the frameworks to the approaches is intended to support the explicit specification of both. This application, in turn, better supports researchers building on and validating each other's work. The aim is to increase discipline progress, as required by Newman (1984) – see earlier. Progress here includes the acquisition of HCI discipline knowledge and the practices which it supports. Also included is the validation of both by research. Following Kuhn (1970), discipline progress is to be contrasted with community progress. The latter refers to the cultural/social activities of the researchers, such as attending workshops and conferences, informal communications and the formation of interest groups in the manner of the CHI and other conferences.

1.6 HCI Research Approaches and Frameworks

Here, approaches and frameworks are defined as having the same scope – that of HCI research. However, frameworks are more rigorously specified. They are more complete, coherent and fit for purpose with respect to HCI research than approaches. Included here are HCI research approaches classified as innovation, art, craft, applied, science and engineering. Each type of approach has an associated HCI research framework (see 4.3–9.3). Other types of HCI approach and framework could be created as required. The creation would follow the same process proposed here, as supported by the textbook's research practice assignments, presented at the end of each chapter (see 15.3).

The frameworks to be applied to the approaches have a common basis in a conception for HCI originally proposed respectively for the HCI discipline (Long and Dowell, 1989) and for the HCI design problem (Dowell and Long, 1989). Detailed reference to, and the importance of the relations between, this conception and the General Framework proposed here are made throughout the book.

Conclusion

This chapter introduces HCI and HCI research in general. It describes both their current states and challenges, as they relate to the textbook and its aims. The concepts of approach and framework are outlined, together with their relations.

The outline provides the necessary basis for the separate and respective address of approaches and frameworks in the following two chapters.

1.7 Research Practice Assignment

- Describe in writing the state of your research in terms of the state of HCI research, as presented in 1.3. If you have no research of your own at this time, select a suitable publication from the HCI literature.
- List the challenges to your (or others') research. How do they compare with the challenges presented in 1.4?
  - Evaluate how well your (or others') research meets your research challenges and those presented in 1.4.
  - Identify what changes to your (or others') research might better meet your research challenges.
- Do you think the concept of challenge is useful in this assignment? If so, give your reasons. If not, suggest and justify an alternative concept motivating your (or others') research.

Hints and Tips

Difficult to get started?
Try reading the chapter again, while at the same time thinking about how to describe your own research. Note similarities and differences between the two lines of thought as you go along.
Describe your research in its own terms, before attempting to apply those of 1.3.

Difficult to complete?
Familiarise yourself with the major challenges to HCI research identified in the HCI research literature before attempting to address those in 1.4.
Consider synonyms of the term 'challenge', before considering its utility and suggesting alternatives.

Test[4]

- Write down the titles of 1.1 to 1.4. Complete the sections very briefly from memory and in your own words.
- Propose a new and improved set of titles for 1.1 to 1.4.

- Complete the new 1.1 to 1.4 in your own words.
- Read and reflect on the chapter endnotes (see 1.8).
- Suggest additions to the chapter endnotes.

1.8 Notes

1. Extended descriptions of these changes in information technology, constituting the growth and diversity of new computing technology, can be found in Harper et al. (2008). As stated, the chapter introduces HCI and HCI research in general. It describes their current states and challenges within a roughly historical perspective, as they relate to the textbook and its aims. Other general descriptors of the field include 'cognitive ergonomics', 'software engineering' and 'interface design'. Other domain-specific descriptors include 'architectural informatics', 'medical applications', 'digital archives' and 'library information technology'. Cockton (2014) is a useful additional source for information on this point, together with Rogers (2012).
2. A more complete description of the scope and diversification of the state of HCI can be found in Harper et al. (2008) and Rogers, Sharp and Preece (2011).
3. Following Rogers (2012), these 19 fields comprise:

   - academic disciplines: ergonomics, psychology/cognitive science, design, informatics, engineering, computer science/software engineering and social sciences
   - design practices: graphic design, product design, artist design, industrial design and film industry
   - interdisciplinary overlapping fields: ubiquitous computing, human factors, cognitive engineering, human–computer interaction, cognitive ergonomics, computer-supported cooperative work and information systems.
4. The test encourages researchers to commit the approaches and frameworks to memory. Such internalisation facilitates their subsequent application.

2

Approaches to HCI Research

This chapter defines the concept of 'approach', along with its derivation and exemplification. A general definition of approach is proposed. The latter is then applied to HCI research in particular. The definition is both explicit and sufficiently well specified for the later application of frameworks to the approaches selected here: innovation, art, craft, applied, science and engineering.

2.1 Approach

The concept of approach is characterised generally as follows.

First, an approach is a way of addressing a topic or problem. Other ways of addressing the same topic or problem are also possible.

For example, traditional and modern approaches are both ways of addressing the topic or problem of how to educate young children, but are different ways.

Second, performing the actions of an approach, in addressing a topic or problem, constitutes a way to progress that approach.

For example, traditional and modern approaches to educating young children are both ways to progress child education.

Third, evaluating an approach is a way of assessing the success of the actions to progress that approach.

For example, traditional and modern approaches to educating young children are able to evaluate rote learning and play learning approaches respectively to establish which approach leads to better progress in the education of young children.

Fourth, an approach cumulates the successes of whether the topic or problem has been addressed or not.

For example, instances of the better education of young children in the form of educational good practice or an educational principle or some such constitute the cumulating of successes of traditional or modern education approaches.

Concerning their derivation, approaches are expressed informally in terms of everyday language. A number of representative information sources were selected, both online, for example Wikipedia, and offline, for example Webster's Dictionary. The definitions of 'approach' were compared and the main common aspects were identified, for example, approach as a way of addressing a topic or problem. Everyday language here might alternatively be termed 'lay language'. This is in contrast with technical language, as might be used by researchers to express their frameworks or their theories. Specific HCI research frameworks are later expressed in such technical language (see 4.3–9.3). Such technical language is also used in the research literature to express HCI frameworks (see 12.3) and HCI theories (see 13.3).

2.2 Approaches to HCI Research

The general concept of approach, outlined earlier, is now applied to HCI research in particular.

First, an HCI research approach requires the addressing of the topic or problem of human–computer interaction research. Other ways of addressing such research are also possible.

For example, innovation and science approaches both require the addressing of human–computer interaction research, but in different ways.

Second, an HCI research approach requires the performing of actions to progress the approach to the addressing of the topic or problem of human–computer interaction research.

For example, innovation and science approaches both require the performing of actions for research, respectively to create new types of interaction and to understand those interactions.

Third, an HCI research approach requires the evaluating of the success of the actions performed to progress an approach to the addressing of the topic or problem of human–computer interaction research.

For example, innovation and science approaches to research both require the evaluating of the success of actions for research to create new types of interaction and the understanding of interactions. The evaluation might be respectively by customer survey and by user experiments.

Fourth, an HCI research approach requires the cumulating of the successes of whether the topic or problem of human–computer interaction research has been addressed or not.

For example, innovation and science approaches both require the cumulating of the successes by research of new types of interaction and the understanding of interactions. The evaluation might be respectively by continued commercial success and by validated explanatory or predictive theory.

Concerning their derivation, approaches to HCI research are expressed informally in terms of everyday language. A number of representative information sources were selected, both online, for example Wikipedia, and offline, for example Webster's Dictionary. The definitions of 'approach' and 'HCI research' were each compared. The main common aspects for each were identified. For example, an approach to HCI research is a way of researching the topic or problem of human–computer interaction.

Some researchers might find the lay language definition informal, brief and high level. However, these aspects are critical to its function of encapsulating the different descriptions of approach to be found in the HCI literature. The aspects are also appropriate for the distinction between approach and framework for research proposed here. First, the definition is informal, because the approaches to be found in the HCI research literature are themselves described informally. Second, the definition is brief, because descriptions of approach in the HCI research literature lack detail. Third, the definition is necessarily very general to accommodate the wide range of approaches to be found in the HCI research literature.

In addition, the key concepts of approach (addressing of topic or problem, performing of actions, evaluating of success and cumulating of successes) are also reflected in the core framework underlying the specific frameworks proposed here (see 3.4 and 10.2.1). As will become clear, the approach concepts are both explicit and sufficiently well specified for the subsequent application of frameworks to them (see 4.3.5–9.3.5), and also to accommodate the descriptions reported in the literature as concerns HCI frameworks (see 12.3) and as concerns HCI theories (see 13.3).

This definition of HCI approach was then checked informally to validate its applicability against a range of papers published in HCI research journals that use the term 'approach' to describe HCI research.

2.3 Current Approaches to HCI Research

Approaches to HCI research were identified from the HCI research literature. Each research paper describing a particular approach was classified with other like papers, for example, as engineering or as science. The classification, then, is descriptive and empirical. This 'bottom-up' identification strategy does not necessarily lead to orthogonal outcomes with respect to the resulting classification categories. A given paper might be classified as belonging to more than one category, for example, to innovation and to craft. The paper might embody some or all aspects of both categories. The possibility of multiple classifications, however, does not constitute a problem for the application of the classification.

The critical decision to apply a particular approach, a particular framework or one of each to their research rests with the researcher planning the work. The limits to such possible application depend on compatibility, practicality and complexity, for example, as concerns compatibility, between science and applied approaches and frameworks. Applied approaches and frameworks cannot precede the acquisition of the to-be-applied knowledge by science. For example, as concerns practicality, an application would include the budget for, the duration of and the number of groups involved in a particular research project. Last, for example, as concerns complexity, an application would include the scope of the research, the nature of the acquisition or validation of the knowledge and the number of approaches and/or frameworks involved.

The commonly classified approaches identified in the HCI research literature, as described earlier, were then compared to a comprehensive listing of HCI fields by category, for example, academic disciplines (such as social sciences), interdisciplinary overlapping fields (such as human factors) and design practices (such as graphic design), following Rogers (2012).[1]

The HCI approaches were then generified as concerns their main aspect(s) or feature(s) against the HCI fields, both at the category and at the individual level. For example, the innovation approach is closely related to the category of design practices, including the specific design practice of graphic design. The applied approach is closely related to the category of academic disciplines, including the specific discipline of social science. The art approach is closely related to the category of design practices, including the specific practice of graphic design. Generification requires approaches classified as belonging to the same category to have at least one aspect or feature in common, as concerns that category. Other aspects may or may not be so shared. Hence, the categories are not true abstractions. This point is consistent with that made earlier concerning multiple classifications.

Approaches to HCI research were selected for the classification scheme if they exhibited a distinctive relationship with HCI fields both at the category and at the individual level. The approaches selected are innovation, art, craft, applied, science and engineering. Other approaches could, of course, be added, using the same process and criteria as those described here.

Conclusion

This chapter proposes a general definition of the concept of approach. The latter is applied to HCI research in particular. The definition of an HCI research approach is sufficiently well specified for the classification of HCI research approaches and the subsequent application of frameworks to the approaches. The following approaches are selected: innovation, art, craft, applied, science and engineering.

2.4 Research Practice Assignment

- Describe your approach to HCI research explicitly, for example in writing, in the general terms of selecting of topic or problem, performing of actions, evaluating of success and cumulating of successes, as presented in 2.2. If you have no research of your own at this time, select a suitable publication from the HCI literature.
  - Does your characterisation (of your own research or of the research of others) have anything in common with the approaches identified in 2.3, as you understand them in terms of your current knowledge? List the similarities and differences.

Hints and Tips

Difficult to get started?
Try reading the chapter again, while thinking about how to describe your (or others') approach to HCI research.
Describe your research (or that of others) in its own terms, before attempting to apply those of 2.2.
How might your approach (or that of others) best be further characterised?

Difficult to complete?
Familiarise yourself with other approaches in the HCI and other literature.
Note the similarities and differences between other approaches, as concerns their main concepts.

Test[2]

- Write down the titles of 2.1 to 2.3. Complete the sections briefly from memory and in your own words.
- Propose a new and improved set of titles for 2.1 to 2.3.
- Suggest additional chapter endnotes to the two provided.
- Suggest improvements to the chapter endnotes.

2.5 Notes

1. Following Rogers (2012), the complete listing of HCI fields comprises:

   - academic disciplines: ergonomics, psychology/cognitive science, design, informatics, engineering, computer science/software engineering and social sciences
   - design practices: graphic design, product design, artist design, industrial design and film industry
   - interdisciplinary overlapping fields: ubiquitous computing, human factors, cognitive engineering, human–computer interaction, cognitive ergonomics, computer-supported cooperative work and information systems.

2. The test encourages researchers to commit the approaches and frameworks to memory. Such internalisation facilitates their subsequent application.

3

Frameworks for HCI Research

This chapter proposes a general definition of the concept of 'framework', together with its derivation and exemplification. The definition and an existing conception are then applied to HCI research. The resulting core HCI research framework comprises discipline, general problem, particular scope, research, knowledge and practices. The core framework is sufficiently well specified for its application to approaches.

3.1 Framework

First, a framework is a basic supporting structure for thinking about and doing something.

For example, the application of social and infrastructural frameworks to urban development is such a supporting structure. The social framework supports consideration of domestic and work relations for urban development. The infrastructural framework supports implementation of transport and communications relations for urban development.

Second, a framework supports thinking about and doing something.

For example, social and infrastructural frameworks support the consideration of urban development and the creation of different types of integrated and modular forms of urban development.

Third, a framework's support for thinking about and doing something constitutes an application of the framework.

For example, social and infrastructural frameworks for urban development both propose concepts and actions, along with their associated relations, which are thought about and acted upon as part of the framework's application.

Fourth, a framework can be assessed for its appropriateness as a supporting structure for thinking about and doing something.

For example, social and infrastructural frameworks for urban development can be assessed for the appropriateness of their application in terms of completeness, coherence and fitness for purpose.

3.2 Framework for HCI

The general framework definition is now applied to HCI.

First, a framework for HCI is a basic supporting structure for thinking about and doing human–computer interaction.

For example, the cognitive and interaction frameworks, which support the design of human–computer interactions are such frameworks. The cognitive framework comprises mental functions, such as perception, memory and thought. The interaction framework comprises interactive functions, such as goal formation, planning and feedback.

Second, a framework for HCI supports thinking about and doing human–computer interaction.

For example, cognitive and interaction frameworks for HCI support thinking about and creating process-led and performance-led design of human–computer interactions respectively.

Third, an HCI framework's support for thinking about and doing human–computer interaction constitutes an application of that framework.

For example, cognitive and interaction frameworks both propose concepts and actions and their associated relations for human–computer interactions.

Fourth, a framework for HCI can be assessed for its appropriateness as a supporting structure for thinking about and doing human–computer interaction.

For example, cognitive and interaction frameworks for HCI can be assessed for their appropriateness as supporting structures for interaction design in terms of their completeness, coherence and fitness for purpose.

An illustration of a cognitive framework for HCI is to be found in Hill et al. (1993, 1995). They present a model of the planning and control of multiple tasks in the domain of medical reception. The framework contains two representations – knowledge of tasks, and plans. It contains in addition four processes – perceiving, planning, controlling and executing. A further illustration of a framework is to be found in Barnard (1991). He presents a cognitive task model, comprising goal formation and action. The latter are expressed in terms of process configuration, procedural knowledge, record contents and dynamic coordination/control. The expression also comprises cognitive models, such as interacting cognitive subsystems. For further examples of cognitive frameworks see 12.3.

An illustration of an interaction framework for HCI is to be found in Long and Timmer (2000, 2001). They present a model of a reconstructed air traffic management application. The framework contains working and long-term memory behaviours. It contains in addition four goal store behaviours – reactivate, suspend, pop and form. A further illustration is to be found in Carroll, Kellogg and Rosson (1991). They present an interaction task model, comprising the task artefact cycle as task, psychology of tasks, artefact in situation of use, and cycle. For further examples of interaction frameworks, see 12.3.

3.3 Framework for a Discipline

The general framework definition is now applied to a discipline.

First, a framework for a discipline is a basic supporting structure for thinking about and creating a discipline, which comprises a general problem and a particular scope.

For example, the general problem of understanding natural phenomena is the general problem for the discipline of science. Also, the particular scope of that general problem, for example, understanding human behaviour for psychology, is a sub-discipline of science.

Second, a framework for a discipline supports thinking about and creating a discipline.

For example, the general problem of science, as understanding natural phenomena, comprises the practices of explaining known phenomena and predicting unknown phenomena. For the discipline of science, the explanation together with the prediction of natural phenomena constitute an understanding of those phenomena.

Third, a framework for a discipline's thinking about and creating a discipline comprises practices and the knowledge required to support them.

For example, in science, theory is the knowledge supporting the practices of explanation and prediction and so understanding.

Fourth, a framework for a discipline can be assessed for its appropriateness as a supporting structure for thinking about and creating a discipline.

For example, a framework for a discipline can be assessed for its appropriateness as a supporting structure in terms of its completeness, coherence and fitness for purpose.

3.4 Core Framework for a Discipline of HCI Including HCI Research

A framework for a discipline of HCI is a basic supporting structure for thinking about and creating a discipline of HCI. The core framework proposed here is based on a conception respectively for the discipline of HCI (Long and Dowell, 1989) and for the design problem of HCI (Dowell and Long, 1989). Long and Dowell prefer the term 'conception' to 'framework' to describe their work, although both terms comprise a set of related concepts. The terms can be taken to mean the same for the purposes in hand. Consistent with their preference, however, 'conception' is used to refer to their work. 'Framework' is retained more generally for the proposals made here and the work of others (see 12.3). The distinction further serves to differentiate the conception from the General Framework (see 10.2.2). Their conception, then, comprising the HCI discipline and the HCI design problem, constitutes the basis for the core framework, having the same scope. The latter in turn forms the basis for the instantiations of the specific frameworks for the different approaches to HCI research selected here – innovation, art, craft, applied, science and engineering (see 2.3 and 4.3– 9.3). The specific frameworks in turn form the basis for their generalisation to the General Framework for HCI research (see 10.2.2).

The conception forming the basis of the core framework is itself based on earlier frameworks and conceptions. The origins of the latter are generally of an engineering nature. The Long and Dowell/Dowell and Long (1989) conception is for the HCI discipline and the HCI design problem, rather than for its research. However, the latter is also referenced. Further, the two papers do not identify the individual concepts comprising the conception. They can nevertheless be generally identified in terms of their criticality, frequency of reference and technical use. Some interpretation and judgement, however, is still required. For example, the design problem is a primary concept, because it relates knowledge to the design solution and so to performance. Likewise, HCI knowledge, HCI practices and their relations are referenced throughout the conception. Last, the terms 'work', 'worksystem' and 'domain' have technical meanings, which are defined. The shortcoming of incomplete concept identification was later made good by Dowell and Long (1998). The making good takes the form of a glossary for the conception of the cognitive engineering design problem, which identifies and defines the associated concepts individually.

The shortcoming of incomplete concept identification is also made good here by the explicit and complete identification and definition of framework concepts to support their application by researchers. The core framework uses a number, but not all, of the concepts of the Long and Dowell/Dowell and Long conception. Some concepts retain the same expression and meaning, for example, 'design problem'. Other concepts use a different descriptor, more suited to the present context of use, but with the same or very similar meaning, for example, 'application' instead of 'domain'. Last, some concepts may not be used at all, for example, 'structural costs'.[1]

The relationship between the conception and the core framework is obviously a complex one. However, the latter is clearly based on the former, as indicated above. Further, since the specific frameworks (see 4.3–9.3) and the General Framework (see 10.2) are for HCI research and their concepts are explicitly identified, defined and exemplified, they can be judged on their own terms.

In the following specification, the main core concepts are presented in **Boldface** at first mention for easy identification, reference and application, but hold throughout. Each main core concept is followed first by its definition in terms of other core framework concepts and then by its exemplification.

The core HCI framework comprises the following:

Discipline, as an academic field of study.

For example, a discipline can take many forms, science and engineering being two of the most general. Many disciplines have been associated with HCI, in particular applied psychology and interaction design. New disciplines or sub-disciplines continue to be so associated, for example, distributed cognition and user experience.

General Problem, as the design of human–computer interactions.

For example, the design of human–computer interactions can take many forms – simulation and implementation at their most general. More specific forms of design include storyboard, wire-frame model, prototype and initial system version.

Particular Scope, as the design of human–computer interactions to do something as desired.

For example, both users and computers can be characterised in various ways for the purposes of design. An instance of the design of human–computer interactions to do something as desired might be the initial prototype of a portable interactive online dating system.

Research, as the diagnosis of design problems and the prescription of design solutions, as they relate to performance, for the acquisition and for the validation of knowledge to support practices.

For example, research can take many forms – for example, observational study, laboratory experiment and model/method development. Knowledge acquisition may involve different criteria – for example, completeness, coherence and fitness for purpose. An instance of research might be the application of face recognition to the checking of traveller identity at national boundaries.

Knowledge, as acquired and validated, supporting practices.

For example, knowledge may be of different kinds – for example, design methods, design heuristics and design guidelines. Knowledge may be more or less formal – for example, design models and successful designs, respectively. Knowledge may also offer more or less strongly guaranteed support – for example, design principles and design heuristics, respectively. An instance of research might be the production of guidelines for the engendering of trust in online banking transactions.

Practices, as supported by knowledge acquired and validated by research.

For example, design practices include specifying and implementing human–computer interactions. Users of an interactive online shopping system might complain that they cannot manage their shopping budget well enough. They are unable to keep track of the cost of the goods in their shopping cart. Were this considered a problem, design practice might determine a solution in the form of a display of the running total of the cost of the goods in the users' cart. The solution might then be specified and implemented.

3.5 Lower-Level Framework for a Discipline of HCI Including HCI Research

The core framework for a discipline of HCI, including HCI research, is expressed in the previous section at the highest level of description. However, to conduct research to acquire and to validate HCI design knowledge, lower levels of description are required. Researchers might have their own preferred lower-level descriptions or subscribe to some more generally recognised levels.[2] Such descriptions are easily accommodated by the core framework, providing they are compatible with its higher-level description and are complete, coherent and fit for purpose.

3.6 HCI Discipline and HCI Research Illustration

The core HCI framework, as proposed in 3.4, comprises discipline, general problem, particular scope, research, knowledge and practices. Each is illustrated in turn. All are drawn from the same research, that of Hill (2010), such that the relations between key core framework concepts are also illustrated. Additional sources, however, are also referenced. Strictly speaking, Hill's research illustrated, at the time of its publication, the conception of Long and Dowell/Dowell and Long. However, since the conception serves as the basis for the core framework for HCI proposed here, including HCI research, Hill's research can also be used to illustrate the concepts common to both.

Hill's research concerns the UK system for the coordination of the emergency services in response to disasters (Emergency Management Combined Response System – EMCRS). It is a complex three-tier command and control system. It was set up in response to the need for better coordination between agencies such as police, ambulance and fire services when they respond together to disasters.

For the purposes of supporting HCI practice, Hill's research developed models of the EMCRS intended for use in the diagnosis of design problems as concern coordination between agencies. Data for the models were acquired from the observation and documentation of training exercises. Coordination problems were identified on the basis of behaviour conflicts between the agencies. For example, the fire service behaviours of setting up a cordon around the disaster site conflicted with the ambulance service behaviours of accessing the site for the treatment of casualties.

The EMCRS models proposed by the research constitute HCI knowledge, that is, knowledge that is both explicit and is intended to support design. Such knowledge supports design practice directly, as the diagnosis of design problems, and indirectly, as support for the proposed prescription of design solutions. An initial method for coordination design problem diagnosis by means of EMCRS models was also developed by Hill.

Illustrated concepts common to both the conception and to the core framework, as described earlier in 3.4, appear in **Boldface** at first mention for identification, reference and application, but hold throughout.

As concerns the HCI **Discipline**, Hill distinguishes long-term HCI knowledge, as principles supporting design, from short-term HCI knowledge, as methods and models. The latter, expressed as design-oriented frameworks, also support design. Her research constitutes an example of the latter. The discipline relationship is explicit and takes the form of engineering.[3]

As concerns the HCI **General Problem**, Hill develops models and a method intended to support the design of future interactive EMCRS computing systems. The associated coordination problems and solutions are identified on the basis of behaviour conflicts between the different emergency management agencies.[4]

As concerns the HCI **Particular Scope**, Hill's models and method are intended to support the design of future EMCRS interactive systems with the particular scope of EMCRS human–computer interactions.[5]

As concerns HCI **Research**, Hill acquires new knowledge in the form of a method for the direct diagnosis of design problems and for the indirect support of the prescription of design solutions. The latter are as they relate to performance, concerning the coordination of future EMCRS applications. The method is intended to support redesign of the latter and is a product of the research.[6]

As concerns HCI **Knowledge**, Hill proposes EMCRS models, constituting HCI design knowledge, which is both explicit and is intended to support design directly.[7]

As concerns HCI **Practices**, Hill proposes an initial method for diagnosing coordination problems by means of EMCRS models. The latter is intended to support HCI design practices directly.

This completes the Hill illustration of core framework concepts for HCI, including HCI research.

Conclusion

The chapter proposes a general definition of the concept of framework. The latter is applied to HCI research, in particular, to create the HCI research core framework. Concepts from the latter are exemplified. The core framework is sufficiently well specified to be applied later to each of the HCI research approaches retained here – innovation, art, craft, applied, science and engineering.

3.7 Research Practice Assignment

- Is your research conceived in terms of a discipline, as presented in 3.3? If you have no research of your own select a suitable paper from the HCI research literature.
  - In the affirmative, which discipline?
  - If not, how is it conceived at its most general?
- Characterise your research (or that of others) in writing in the context of an HCI discipline comprising discipline, general problem, particular scope, research, knowledge and practices, as presented in 3.4.
  - List your difficulties in creating such a characterisation.
  - Exemplify and evaluate the completeness of your characterisation with the illustration taken from Hill's research and presented in 3.6.

Hints and Tips

Difficult to get started?

Describe your research (or that of others) in its own terms, before attempting to
apply those of 3.4.

Try reading the chapter again, while at the same time thinking about
a discipline classification for your approach (or that of others) to
HCI research.

Difficult to complete?

Familiarise yourself with the concept of discipline as it is applied in the HCI
research and other literature.

Note the similarities and differences between the different concepts of disci
pline identified in the HCI research literature.

Test[8]

- Write down the titles of 3.1 to 3.4. Complete the sections briefly from
  memory and in your own words.
- Propose a new and improved set of titles for 3.1 to 3.4.
- Complete the new 3.1 to 3.4 in your own words.
- Read the chapter endnotes (see 3.8) and add appropriate notes and examples
  of your own.

3.8 Notes

1. Alternative assumptions concerning the concept identification and selection would
   require alternative proposals. Some alternative assumptions, for example, are
   reflected in the differences between the specific frameworks (see 4.3–9.3). The
   specific frameworks, however, derive from the common core framework (see 3.4). In
   this way, the overall assumption is made compatible with different underlying
   assumptions. This compatibility is essential for researchers to build on each other's
   work. Such compatibility is absent from current HCI research (see 12.3 and 13.3;
   also Rogers, 2012).
2. Such generally recognised lower-level framework descriptions might include some
   of the HCI comparison frameworks (see 12.3), for example, Card, Moran and Newell
   (1983) and Carroll et al. (1991), and also some of the HCI comparison theories (see
   13.3), for example, human values theory (Harper et al. 2008) and technology as
   experience theory (McCarthy and Wright, 2004). Alternatively and in addition,
   a lower-level framework description is presented in the associated chapter for each
   type of specific HCI framework, applied to each type of HCI approach (see 4.3.4–
   9.3.4).

3. See also Long and Dowell (1989); Cummaford and Long (1998); Dowell and Long (1998); Stork, Long and Lambie, 1999; Timmer (1999) and Lambie and Long (2002).
4. See also Stork and Long (1994); Dowell (1998); Dowell and Long (1998) and Long and Timmer (2001).
5. See also Stork and Long (1994); Dowell and Long (1998); Long and Monk (2002) and Timmer and Long (2002).
6. See also Cummaford and Long (1998); Cummaford (2000); Long and Brostoff (2002) and Long and Hill (2002).
7. See also Stork, Middlemass and Long (1995); Cummaford and Long (1999); Denley and Long (2001); Long (2002) and Timmer and Long (2002).
8. The test encourages researchers to commit the approaches and frameworks to memory. Such internalisation facilitates their subsequent application.

4

Innovation Approach and Framework for HCI Research

This chapter presents the specific innovation approach to HCI research, including an illustration from the literature. It then presents the specific innovation framework for HCI research. The latter is followed by the innovation design research exemplar and the lower-level innovation framework. Both the exemplar and the lower-level framework are applied to the same illustration of the innovation approach taken from the literature.

4.1 Innovation Approach to HCI Research

An innovation approach to HCI research is based on the general concept of approach (see 2.2). For a more general overview of the relationship between HCI and innovation, see Rauterberg (2006), Harper et al. (2008) and Cockton (2014). The general concept of approach is now applied to HCI research in particular.

First, an innovation approach to HCI research is a way of addressing the topic or problem of designing innovation human–computer interactions by introducing a new idea, a method or a device, the introduction of which constitutes a significant positive change, adding value.

For example, different innovation research approaches have resulted in novel forms of human–computer interactions. These include virtual reality, voice recognition, gesture sensing, force feedback, wearable interfaces, whole-body sensing, spatial interactions and transparent interfaces. Some of these novel forms of human–computer interaction are so far only at an invention stage of development, but have innovation potential, for example, wearable interfaces. Other forms are moving from the invention to the innovation stage of development, for example, medical simulation. Note that the added value of these innovations may accrue to their users, to their developers or to their producers or to any combination of the three.

Second, an innovation approach to HCI research requires the performing of actions to progress that approach to the topic or problem of human–computer interaction.

For example, the innovation of the graphical user interface (GUI) resulted from a range of different (and still disputed) patents, the latter emanating from Xerox, Apple and other research and development companies. The innovation also resulted from many different ideas and the experience afforded by the exchange of employees between such companies. For example, Apple engineers visited the Xerox Parc facilities, and Parc employees subsequently moved to Apple to work on the Lisa and the Macintosh. Patents, expert advice, experience and the design of other innovations supported both preliminary and final actions. The knowledge also supported how such actions dealt with the topic or problem of designing innovation human–computer interactions.

Third, an innovation approach to HCI research requires the evaluating of the success of the actions performed to progress that approach.

For example, the Apple Lisa, released in 1983, featured a high-resolution, stationery-based (document-centric) graphical user interface. However, the most significant, positive change, adding value, came later with the Apple Macintosh – the first commercially successful product to use a multi-panel user interface. The Macintosh used trial-and-error design, among others, to build on the experience acquired from the earlier design of the Lisa. The evaluation of patents, expert advice, experience and the design of other innovations also indicates the success of whether the topic or problem of designing human–computer interactions has been addressed or not.

Fourth, an innovation approach to HCI research requires the cumulating of the successes as a way of establishing whether the topic or problem of designing human–computer interactions has been addressed or not.

For example, the continuing commercial success of the Apple Lisa and the Apple Macintosh, such as they constitute innovations, exemplifies the cumulating of such successes. The latter indicates that the topic or problem of designing innovation human–computer interactions has been addressed.

4.2 Example of an Innovation Approach to HCI Research

As an example of an innovation approach to HCI research, Obrist, Tuch and Hornbaek (2014) suggest how novel, emerging smell technology might be applied to develop smell-enhanced human–computer interactions. They argue that technologies for capturing and generating smell are emerging, and also that the ability to engineer such technologies and use them in HCI is rapidly developing. In contrast, the understanding of how these technologies might match the experiences of smell that people have or want is limited.

Obrist et al. (2014) investigate the experience of smell and the emotions that accompany it. They collected stories from participants, who described personally memorable smell experiences in an online questionnaire. Based on these stories, Obrist et al. developed 10 categories of smell experience. They then explored the implications of the categories for smell-enhanced technology design. They prompted participants to envision technologies that matched their smell story. They also had HCI researchers brainstorm technologies, using the categories as design stimuli. Obrist et al. discuss how the findings can, in addition, benefit research on personal memories, momentary and first-time experiences, and well-being.

On what grounds might the Obrist et al. (2014) paper be classified as an innovation approach to HCI research?

First, an innovation approach to HCI research is a way of addressing the topic or problem of designing human–computer interactions by introducing a new idea, a method or a device that constitutes a significant positive change, adding value.

Obrist et al. claim to address the problems of engineering and understanding novel smell-enhanced human–computer interactions that apply new smell technologies to interactive systems. There is no doubting the novelty of smell-mediated interactions, even if their address is more invention than innovation at this time. Although the potential for a significant positive change is illustrated, with the promise of eventually adding value, that innovation potential remains to be realised and demonstrated. It is certainly a new idea, but not as yet a new method or a new device. Its innovation potential, however, is clear.

Second, an innovation approach to HCI research requires the performing of actions to progress that approach to the topic or problem of human–computer interaction.

Obrist et al. suggest that implications for the engineering of smell-enhanced human–computer interactions can be derived from their research data. The latter resulted from the application of envisioning and brainstorming techniques. Their research constitutes a starting point for such engineering, but the implications need to be further developed before they can be specified and implemented.

Third, an innovation approach to HCI research requires the evaluating of the success of the actions performed to progress that approach.

Obrist et al. do not attempt to assess explicitly how well the problems of understanding and engineering smell-enhanced human–computer interactions have been addressed by the research. At this stage, address of both could, at best, only be considered preliminary. Indeed, given the novelty and rudimentary nature of smell technology, even assessment might be considered premature.

Fourth, an innovation approach to HCI research requires the cumulating of the successes as a way of establishing whether the topic or problem of designing human–computer interactions has been addressed or not.

As Obrist et al. report no assessment, there can be no such cumulating of successes. The latter is not possible at the early stage of smell technology development reported by their research.

Conclusion: On balance, the Obrist et al. (2014) research can be classified as an innovation approach to HCI research, as it relates to smell-enhanced human–computer interactions. The approach is novel. Further, it comprises many of the aspects required by innovation, for example, a new idea. However, the approach is currently at an early stage of development, more akin to invention than innovation. There is nevertheless potential for development into the latter. As might be expected, neither conducting evaluations nor cumulating successes has been possible at this time.

This classification suggests that Obrist et al. could decide to support any of their future smell technology HCI research either on the basis of the innovation approach to HCI research, presented earlier (see 2.2 and 4.1), or on the basis of the specific innovation framework, which follows.

4.3 Innovation Framework for HCI Research

This section covers the core framework for HCI, including HCI research, the specific innovation framework for HCI research, the innovation design research exemplar and the lower-level innovation framework.

4.3.1 Core Framework for HCI Including HCI Research

The specific innovation framework for HCI research is based on the core framework for the discipline of HCI, including HCI research. The core framework comprises discipline, general problem, particular scope, research, knowledge and practices (see 3.4).

4.3.2 Specific Innovation Framework for HCI Research

The specific innovation framework for HCI research, such as to be applicable to an innovation approach to HCI, follows. It comprises the concepts and definitions of the core framework for the discipline of HCI, including HCI research (see 3.4), particularised for innovation. Conceptualisation to application constitutes a one-to-many mapping. Providing more than one descriptor for the same concept is a way of facilitating this mapping. To aid researchers to apply the specific innovation framework, an applications-supportive format follows. The specific innovation framework includes the main concepts, their definitional concepts and their extended definitional concepts, such as to be applicable to an innovation approach. The main concepts are presented in **Boldface** at first mention for easy identification, reference and application, but hold throughout. The definitional concepts appear in lower case. The extended definitional concepts appear in lower case and in (brackets). Each extended definition appears only once, but applies throughout, as appropriate.

The specific innovation HCI framework comprises the following:

Discipline, as an academic (that is, scholarly) field (that is, branch/subject area) of study (that is, investigation of knowledge as division of information/learning) and

Innovation, as novel (that is, a new idea/method/device constituting a significant positive change and adding value) and

Innovation General Problem, as the design (that is, specification) of innovation human–computer interactions and

Innovation Particular Scope, as the design of innovation human (that is, individual/group)–computer (that is, interactive/embedded) interactions (that is, active/passive) to do something (that is, action/task), as desired (that is, wanted/needed/experienced/felt/valued) and

Innovation Research, as the diagnosis of innovation design problems (that is, not as desired) and the prescription of innovation design solutions (that is, as desired), as they relate to performance (that is, desired) for the acquisition (that is, creation) and for the validation (that is, confirmation) of knowledge to support practices and

Innovation Knowledge, as patents/expert advice/experience/examples (that is, as acquired and validated by innovation research) and supports (that is, as facilitates/makes possible) innovation practices and

Innovation Practices, as trial and error/specify, implement and test (that is, supported by innovation knowledge acquired and validated by innovation research).

4.3.3 Innovation Design Research Exemplar

The specific innovation framework for HCI research is considered to be more complete, coherent and fit for purpose than the earlier description afforded by the innovation approach to HCI research (see 4.1). Hence, the innovation framework is more rigorously specified than the innovation approach and so more effectively supports thinking about and doing innovation HCI research. As the framework is more rigorous, it offers firmer support to researchers attempting to apply it. Once applied and shared, it enables researchers to build on each other's work. Innovation researchers share and build on each other's work in many ways, but perhaps primarily by means of the innovative artefacts they create, for example, the Apple Lisa. However, exactly what is shared often remains implicit. In addition, these researchers also report on their work explicitly, both internally to their companies/communities and externally at conferences, for example, the ACM CHI Conference on Human Factors in Computing Systems series. The innovation framework might be expected to support further these explicit types of exchanges and so the sharing of and building on each other's work.

The latter is further supported here by a summary re-expression of the innovation framework as a design research exemplar. The use of the term 'exemplar' originates with Kuhn (1970). He conceives a scientific discipline as comprising a paradigm, a disciplinary matrix and shared exemplars. Building on the work of Long and Dowell (1989), Salter (2010) develops the concept of exemplar further and applies it to the engineering of economic systems. Here, the application is to HCI research in general and to specific HCI research frameworks in particular. The innovation design research exemplar represents the complete innovation design research cycle. Once performed, the cycle constitutes a case study of innovation HCI research. The exemplar is intended to support researchers in the application of the innovation framework. It does so by setting out in detail what is involved in the acquisition of different kinds of innovation knowledge to support different kinds of innovation practices. The exemplar is presented in Figure 4.1. The empty boxes are not required for the innovation exemplar. They are required elsewhere for other specific design research exemplars, and have been included here for completeness. They facilitate comparison between the different exemplars. Design research concepts are Capitalised at first mention for easy identification, reference and application, but apply throughout.

The four first-level boxes represent the innovation design cycle. The cycle starts on the outer left with User Requirements (Unsatisfied) and terminates on the outer right with an Interactive System (assumed to satisfy the user requirements). The design cycle details are not included here. First, much of innovation design is implicit or indirect and so cannot be represented explicitly or directly. Second, the function of the figure is to represent design research and not design per se. The design cycle, however, following the practices of the specific innovation framework for HCI research (see 4.3.2) and for present

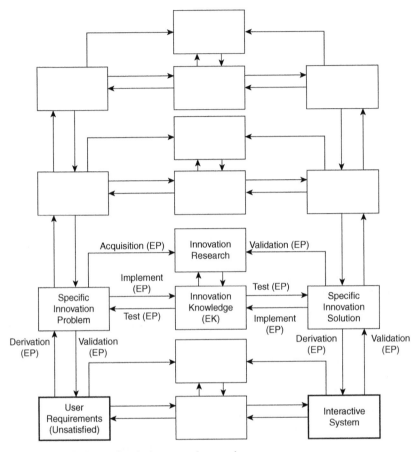

Figure 4.1 Innovation design research exemplar
Key: Innovation Knowledge: patents, expert advice, experience and examples
EP: Empirical Practice
EK: Empirical Knowledge

purposes, might be assumed to include a design process (the two central boxes). The latter might be further assumed to comprise some combination of specification and implementation, interspersed with iterative trial-and-error cycles.

The Obrist et al. smell technology research (see 4.2) is reused as an illustration of a possible innovation design research cycle. The latter might comprise specifying and implementing a graphical user interface (GUI), including smell-based technology, text, images and video. The application might be for the e-shopping reordering of perfumes already known to the customer. The smell-based GUI is intended to be innovative, as are the accompanying text/image/

video interactions. The latter are intended successfully to support the perfume experience and the reordering of perfumes by the customer. Reusing the Obrist et al. smell technology research example for the innovation design research exemplar is intended better to support researchers attempting to apply the specific innovation framework.

The four second-level boxes represent the innovation design research cycle. The latter starts on the left with the Specific Innovation Problem (of design) and terminates on the right with the Specific Innovation Solution (for design), which solves the specific innovation problem.

In terms of the Obrist et al. smell technology research illustration, the specific innovation problem might be some aspect of the ordering of perfumes. These aspects are assumed not to be known to the customer and not well supported by the current interface. The lack of support might be reflected in the number of returned perfume purchases. The specific innovation solution might be an innovative smell-based technology GUI interface. The latter would successfully support innovation interactions for the e-shopping ordering of perfumes not previously known to the customer. To continue the innovation design research exemplar, the Derivation of the specific innovation problem is from, and its Validation is against, the user requirements. The specific innovation problem is human–computer interactions not doing something as desired.

In terms of the smell technology research illustration, the user requirement might be to order successfully any perfume goods not previously known to the customer. The user requirement might be an actual requirement; but it might also be a possible and plausible requirement. Note that the difference between problems and user requirements is that the latter may or may not be satisfiable in practice. The former are formulated so as to be soluble, at least in principle. Following this reasoning, a smell technology researcher might formulate the specific problem as not being able to order at least two perfumes not previously known to the customer. The limitation of the specific innovation problem, relative to the possible and plausible user requirements, might be justified by the early stage of smell technology and the associated research. Such an early stage is demonstrated in the work of Obrist et al.

The Acquisition of an expression of the specific innovation problem is made by Innovation Research; for example, a customer not being able to order at least two perfumes not previously known to them. The latter also effects the validation of the specific innovation solution against the expression of the specific design problem acquired by innovation research. The specific innovation problem is also Implemented. That is expressed as the Innovation Knowledge needing to be Tested, that is, checked against the specific innovation solution. The latter is implemented, that is, expressed as innovation knowledge. The latter is tested, that is, checked against the specific innovation problem. Note that all the innovation research processes are empirical, as is the resulting innovation knowledge.

In terms of the Obrist et al. (2014) illustration, the innovation knowledge might take the form of smell technology patents/expert advice/experience/ examples. Such innovation knowledge could be recruited to future smell technology research, but would remain empirical, that is, applicable neither analytically nor without test nor with guarantee.

Finally, the derivation of the specific innovation solution is expressed for application to an interactive system, satisfying the user requirements. The validation of the inclusion of the specific design solution in the interactive system is effected. In terms of the smell technology illustration, the inter- active system inclusion would be a smell interface, such as to support a customer in ordering successfully two perfumes not previously known to them.

4.3.4 Lower-Level Innovation Framework

The specific innovation framework has so far been expressed only at the highest level of description. That level is of the core HCI framework for research. However, to conduct and to report innovation design research and to acquire/validate innovation knowledge a lower-level description is required. The latter is consistent with the design research exemplar.

Researchers might have their own innovation lower-level descriptions or subscribe to some more generally recognised levels (for examples of such levels, see 12.3). Such descriptions are compatible with the specific innovation framework if they are complete, coherent and fit for purpose with respect to the higher-level core framework. Alternatively, and in addition, a lower-level framework description is presented in the associated chapter, along with the design research exemplar for each type of specific HCI research framework (see 4–9.3.4).

These higher and lower levels of description need to go respectively, for example, from the general human to the specific web manager and from the general computer to the specific smartphone with face recognition function- ality. The lowest level must also reference the innovation itself, in terms of the application. For example, for an innovation business voice recognition system, the application might be for a salesperson and a laptop-based electronic messaging system.

Following the innovation design research exemplar, researchers need to identify the specific innovation problem (as it relates to user requirements), innovation research, innovation knowledge and specific innovation solution (as it relates to the interactive system).

These levels of description need also to include the innovation application, the innovation interactive system and the innovation interactive system performance. Innovation design requires the interactive system to do something (the application) as desired (performance). Innovation research acquires and validates innovation knowledge to support innovation design practice. Hence, the following lower-level innovation framework includes application, interactive system and performance.

The key lower-level concepts are shown in **Boldface** at first mention for easy identification, reference and application, but hold throughout.

4.3.4.1 Innovation Application

An innovation application can be described in many different ways for the purposes of HCI research. Here, following Dowell and Long (1989), the application is represented as objects, attributes and states. This is a standard way of representing applications and domains (Dinu and Nadkarni, 2007). Researchers are welcome to use alternative types of representation, providing the application specification is different from that of the interactive human–computer technology system. This difference is to support design by allowing either to be varied independently of the other. Whatever the approach or the framework providing structural support, design as specification and implementation inevitably involves the selection between alternative possible interactive design options. The latter are intended to achieve the same performance goals. To avoid confounding the means – the interactive system – with the ends – performance – it is important for the two to be described independently. This independence allows the means and the ends to be co-varied separately and independently. As stated, it is for this reason that researchers are welcome to use alternative types of representation to those proposed here. However, the lower-level description must be compatible with the higher-level core HCI research framework and be complete, coherent and fit for purpose.

An **Application** is described in terms of objects.

Innovation Objects The innovation application (what the interactive system does) can be described in terms of **Objects**. The latter comprise both **Physical Objects** and **Abstract Objects**. They are characterised by their attributes. Physical attributes are those of matter and energy. Abstract attributes are those of knowledge and information.

For example, an innovation smell-enhanced graphical user interface (GUI) e-shopping application for buying perfumes can be represented, for HCI research purposes, in terms of objects. The abstract attributes of the latter support the sending and receiving of perfume orders. Their physical attributes support the smell-enhanced GUI visual/verbal representation. Innovation smell technology, following the research of Obrist et al. (see 4.2), is used here to exemplify the application of the lower-level framework. This provides continuity in the support for researchers attempting to apply the specific innovation approach and framework.

Although representable at different levels of description, the user must at least be described for HCI research purposes at a level that relates to the transformation of innovation objects.

For example, a user described as a regular e-shopper who orders only known perfumes would constitute such a description.

Innovation Attributes The **Attributes** of an innovation application object are represented at different levels of description.

For example, letters and their ordering on a GUI page and perfume smell are physical attributes of the e-shopping object perfume order, expressed at one level. The content of the perfume order and the meaning of the smell to the customer are abstract meaning attributes, expressed at a higher level of description.

Innovation Attribute States The attributes of innovation application objects can be represented in terms of **States**, which may change.

For example, the content and letters (attributes) of a smell-enhanced GUI e-shopping order (object) may change state – the content as concerns meaning, its letters as concern size and font, and likewise, the smell attributes of the order with respect to the content as meaning and as concerns the strength or weakness of the smells.

4.3.4.2 Innovation Interactive System

Users have aims and the associated behaviours are considered to be goal-oriented/intentional.

For example, the behaviours of an office worker and GUI electronic email application for processing perfume orders are such behaviours. Their goal is to manage the associated correspondence. Innovation interactive systems change objects by producing transformations in their physical and abstract attributes. The office worker and GUI email application together transform the object perfume order correspondence. They do so by changing its meaning attributes and those of its layout. Behaviour is what the user does. What is done is expressed as the attribute state changes of application objects.

Users The **Behaviours** of an innovation **Interactive System** are both abstract and physical. Interactive system **Abstract Behaviours** include the acquisition, storage and transformation of information. They represent and process information concerning application objects. Also represented are their attributes, relations and states. Further, they represent the transformations required by user goals/intentions. Interactive system **Physical Behaviours** are associated with, and express, abstract behaviours.

The user, then, is represented as a system of mental (that is, abstract) and physical (that is, overt) behaviours. User **Mental Behaviours** transform abstract application objects. The latter are represented by cognition or express, through user **Physical Behaviours**, plans for transforming application objects.

For example, a perfume company promotions manager has the goal of setting up and maintaining the circulation of an e-newsletter. The latter is intended to inform actual and potential customers of perfume special offers. The manager interacts with the computer by means of the innovative smell-enhanced GUI interface. The latter's behaviours include the transmission of information provided by the e-newsletter. The manager acquires an understanding of the latter's present circulation by integrating the information displayed by the GUI. The manager evaluates it with respect to the goals of the various promotional special offers. The promotions manager's acquisition, collection, evaluation and circulation of the e-newsletter are all mental behaviours. These can be described in terms of representing and processing information. The manager plans the attribute state changes necessary to produce and circulate the e-newsletter, as desired. That plan is expressed in the instructions issued to the interactive computer through physical behaviour. The latter might include, for example, selecting GUI menu options, including the smells associated with particular perfumes on special offer. The selection and the menu options are both objects of the design process and so potentially of innovation HCI research. Both mental and physical user behaviours contribute to doing something, as desired, that is, as wanted/needed/experienced/felt/valued.

Interactions Interaction of **User Behaviours** and **Computer Behaviours** is the basic unit of innovation HCI research. The concern here is with the interactive system, rather than with the individual behaviours of its parts.

For example, the behaviours of a perfume promotions manager interact with the behaviours of a smell-enhanced innovative GUI e-shopping application. The promotions manager's behaviours interact with the behaviours of the e-shopping system – selection of the look-up dictionary function. The behaviours of the interactive e-shopping system interact with the selection behaviours of the promotions manager – proposing correct spellings. The design of their interaction – the manager's selection of the look-up dictionary function, the system's proposing of spelling corrections – constitutes the behaviours of the interactive system. The latter consists of the promotions manager and the interactive e-shopping system behaviours in their management of perfume special offers. The interaction is the object of innovation HCI research. Hence, the importance of the assignment of task goals either to the manager or to the interactive smell-enhanced GUI e-shopping system.

For example, replacing an incorrectly spelled word describing a special perfume offer is a goal, which can be expressed as a task goal of attribute state changes. The correctly spelled perfume offer requires an attribute state change in the text spacing of the perfume order. That state change may be a task goal assigned to the promotions manager. This was the case with early text editors. Or it may be a task goal assigned to the interactive system. This might be the case with the innovation GUI wrap-round behaviours.

4.3.4.3 Innovation Interactive System Performance

To do something (see 4.3.2 – specific innovation framework) derives from the relationship of an interactive system with its application. It assimilates both how well the application is performed by the interactive system – as desired – and the costs incurred by it in performing that well. They are expressed together as performance. Costs can be further differentiated, as in the case of innovation research, for example, as wanted/needed/experienced/felt/valued. Performance may be absolute or relative, in terms of a comparison to be improved upon or to be equalled. Human Performance, as expressed in the literature as time and errors, relates to performance, as proposed here. Errors are behaviours that increase user costs or reduce how well the application is performed or both. The time taken by user behaviours may loosely be associated with increased behavioural user costs.

For example, an innovation smell-enhanced GUI perfume e-shopping application might be expected to improve performance. This improvement might be in terms of reduced behavioural costs of perfume re-ordering, relative to an earlier non-smell-enhanced application.

User Costs Doing something as desired by means of an interactive system incurs costs for the human. Costs associated with the user are termed **User Behavioural Costs**.

For example, the behavioural costs for a promotions manager clicking on or attending to unfamiliar menu options of a perfume order may be experienced over time as tiredness, irritation or impatience.

User behavioural costs comprise both **Physical Costs** and **Mental Costs**.

For example, the costs of clicking on or of attending to GUI menu options or alternative perfume smells constitute such costs. User behavioural physical costs may be expressed for innovation HCI research purposes as **Physical Workload**.

User behavioural mental costs are associated with knowing, thinking and deciding. User behavioural mental costs may be expressed for HCI research purposes as **Mental Workload**. Physical and mental costs are often closely associated.

For example, the physical and mental behavioural costs of a promotions manager may be associated with GUI e-shopping menu option selection or the assessment of perfume smell strength.

4.3.5 Example Application of an Innovation Framework to an Innovation Approach to HCI Research

The research of Obrist et al. (2014) can be considered to constitute an actual or potential innovation approach to HCI research (see 4.2). Their paper suggests how novel, emerging smell technology might be applied to develop smell-enhanced human–computer interactions. What potential does the Obrist et al. approach to innovation research offer the specific innovation framework presented here?

First, the specific innovation framework is for a discipline, as an academic field of study.

Potential: Obrist et al.'s approach mentions engineering, design and understanding, but all only in passing. The concepts are not related to any particular discipline or field of knowledge, for example, science for the problem of understanding, in terms of explanation and prediction, or engineering for the codification of knowledge to support design. Obrist et al.'s approach makes no attempt to develop or instantiate these terms or the relations between them. There is no mention of discipline as it might relate to innovation.

Second, the specific innovation framework is for innovation, as novel.

Potential: Obrist et al.'s approach recognises the novelty of smell technology and the possibilities it offers HCI, once developed and applied. Their research is intended to contribute to that development. However, they make no specific allusion to innovation.

Third, the specific innovation framework is for the general problem as the design of innovation human–computer interactions.

Potential: Obrist et al.'s approach clearly views smell-enhanced technology itself to be a new and inventive technology and to require new and inventive forms of interaction. However, no reference is made to innovation per se or to how their research might contribute to such innovation potential.

Fourth, the specific innovation framework is for the particular scope of innovation human–computer interactions to do something as desired.

Potential: Obrist et al.'s approach is intended to support the design of human–computer smell interactions in the longer term. They report no design conducted by their research. However, they claim that their stories and associated data can be used by designers. They do not say how.

Fifth, the specific innovation framework is for innovation research as the diagnosis of innovation design problems and the prescription of innovation design solutions, as they relate to performance for the acquisition and for the validation of knowledge to support practices.

Potential: Obrist et al.'s approach supports the acquisition of knowledge, which they claim will support interaction design. They do not say or show how. The knowledge includes smell stories, a smell classification and smell technology envisioning.

Sixth, the specific innovation framework is for innovation knowledge, acquired and validated, as patents/expert advice/experience/examples supporting innovation practices.

Potential: Obrist et al.'s approach makes no mention of patents/expert advice/experience/examples. This is not surprising, since the research itself does not undertake any design. However, the smell data are offered in support of the future smell design of others.

Seventh, the specific innovation framework is for innovation practices, acquired and validated by research, as trial and error/implement and test.

Potential: Obrist et al.'s approach does not include design practice, although their smell data are intended to support the work of designers in the longer term.

Conclusion: Obrist et al.'s approach to innovation design is an interesting and valuable addition to the research literature, as concerns smell technology. Also, the research identifies its potential for application to human–computer interactions. Smell interaction research and design, however, are at a very early stage, as demonstrated in their research. The approach needs to be further developed with respect to the discipline relations of the two general problems of understanding and design, both of which they reference. The level of discipline description needs to be lower. The inclusion of novelty as innovation needs to be explicit. Last, the validation of its claims concerning the proposed contribution of the reported data to innovation design needs to be addressed.

The innovation framework proposed here is considered to have potential for contributing to such developments.

Conclusion

This concludes the presentation of the specific innovation approach and the specific innovation framework for HCI research and their exemplification. Also presented are the innovation design research exemplar and the lower-level innovation framework.

4.4 Research Practice Assignment

The assignment comprises two sections: General and Research Design Scenarios.

4.4.1 General

- Using the innovation criteria presented in 4.3, select a recent paper from the HCI research literature that suggests itself to be potentially classifiable as innovation research, as concluded for the paper of Obrist et al. (2014) (see 4.2).
  - o Analyse and record the potential innovation research example, in the manner of 4.1 and 4.2.
  - o In the light of your analysis, decide whether the research example can be classified as innovation research or not. If so classifiable, continue with the assignment. If not so classifiable, return to the beginning of the assignment and start again. Continue until a classifiable example of innovation research is identified.
- Apply the specific innovation framework for HCI research, presented in 4.3.2, to the research example you have classified as innovation. Try to classify as many of the research example's concepts in terms of those of the specific innovation framework.
- Create a design research exemplar, following 4.3.3 and Figure 4.1, for the research example to which you have applied the innovation framework.
- Re-express the research example to which you have applied the specific innovation framework, at the lower level of innovation framework description, presented in 4.3.4. Try to use all the key concepts.

Hints and Tips

Difficult to get started?

Try reading the chapter again, while at the same time thinking explicitly about
   innovation in all its forms, whether in the arts or the sciences, in the
   development of information technology or indeed your own professional
   or social life.

Describe your research (or that of others) in terms of novelty (of any type)
   before attempting to apply those of 4.1 and 4.2.

Difficult to complete?

Familiarise yourself with the concept of innovation as it is applied in the HCI
   research (and other) literature.

Note the similarities and differences between the different concepts of innova
   tion identified in the HCI research literature.

Test

- Write down the titles of 4.1 and 4.3. Complete the sections in your own
  words.
- Propose a new and improved set of titles for 4.1 and 4.3.
- Complete the new 4.1 and 4.3 in your own words.

4.4.2 Research Design Scenarios

All the research design scenarios in 4.4.2–9.4.2 require you to characterise your
own work or that of others. The same characterisation, however, can be used for
all the scenarios. This is because they each involve the application of a different
specific approach or framework. The requirement, however, is repeated in each
scenario to support researchers who may be completing the research practice
assignments out of order. They may not have produced a characterisation at that
particular point in the book. It is also repeated for those researchers wishing to
work with a range of different characterisations. They are encouraged and
supported to create such multiple characterisations.

Research Design Scenario 4.1: Characterising Your Own or Another's
Approach to HCI Research

Characterise your own HCI research approach by answering the following
questions in writing. The latter are intended to support you in creating such

a characterisation. You should also call on any other relevant aspects of the assignment as required. The characterisation should preferably be of your own current project. If you are not working on a project at this time, base the characterisation on a past project. Failing that, base the characterisation on a project of your supervisor or of a colleague. In the last resort, choose a research project published in the HCI literature. The most important function of the research design scenario is the support and practice it gives researchers in planning their research. Additional hints and tips follow each question in the form of notes.

The selection of the topic or problem per se by the research is not directly supported by the assignment or more generally by the textbook. What is supported, however, is the manner (of innovation approach or of innovation framework) by which the topic or problem is addressed, once selected. However, the former needs to be identified to carry out the latter. Further, the selection of the approach or the framework supports the researcher in under-standing the possibilities and implications for the selection of the research topic or problem. The latter is generally some combination of the following: funding available for the project, researcher's curiosity or interest, supervisor's interests and previous work, and gaps in the HCI research literature. The latter may be identified by the researcher, the supervisor or the sponsor.

1. What topic or problem of designing human–computer interactions is addressed by the research and how is that topic or problem addressed?

Note: 'topic or problem' here should be understood widely to include any and all research activities considered to be relevant and important.

2. Which actions are performed by the research as a way of addressing the topic or problem of designing human–computer interactions?

Note: 'actions' here should be understood widely to include any and all research activities considered to be relevant and important.

3. Which ways of evaluating the success or not of the actions are performed by the research to address the topic or problem of designing human–computer interactions?

Note: 'evaluating success' here should be understood widely. The particular forms of evaluation will depend on the approach taken by the research.

4. How does the research cumulate its successes in addressing the topic or problem of designing human–computer interactions?

Note: 'cumulating successes' here should be understood widely. The particular forms of cumulating will depend on the approach taken by the research.

Research Design Scenario 4.2: Applying the Innovation Approach
to Your Own or to Another's Approach to HCI Research

Suppose that you decide to change your current approach to HCI research in your next project to that of innovation. Or if your present approach is already one of innovation, suppose that you decide to apply the specific innovation approach proposed here. In both cases, apply the innovation approach to the earlier characterisation of your own or another's HCI research approach (see 4.4.1) by answering the following questions. They are intended to support you in making such an application. Any other relevant aspects of the assignment should also be called upon as required. Additional hints and tips follow each question in the form of notes.

The selection of the topic or problem per se by the innovation research is not directly supported by the assignment or more generally by the book. What is supported is the manner (of innovation approach) by which the topic or problem is addressed, once selected. However, a topic or problem needs to be identified to apply an innovation approach. Further, the latter supports the researcher in understanding the possibilities and implications for the innovation research of selecting the former. Innovation research topic selection is generally some combination of the following: funding available for the project, researcher's curiosity or interest, supervisor's interests and previous work, and gaps in the HCI research literature. The latter may be identified by the researcher, the supervisor or the sponsor.

1. What topic or problem of designing innovation human–computer interactions by introducing a new idea, a method or a device constituting a significant positive change and adding value is to be addressed by the research, and how will that topic or problem be addressed?
Note: 'topic or problem' here should be understood widely to include any and all innovation research activities considered to be relevant and important.

2. Which actions are to be performed by the research as a way of addressing the topic or problem of designing innovation human–computer interactions by introducing a new idea, a method or a device constituting a significant positive change and adding value?
Note: 'actions' here should be understood widely to include any and all innovation research activities considered to be relevant and important.

3. What are the ways of evaluating the success or not of the actions performed by the research to address the topic or problem of designing innovation human–computer interactions by introducing a new idea,

a method or a device constituting a significant positive change and adding value?

Note: 'evaluating success' here should be understood widely. The particular forms of evaluation will depend on the innovation approach taken by the research.

4. How will the research cumulate its successes in addressing the topic or problem of designing innovation human–computer interactions by introducing a new idea, a method or a device constituting a significant positive change and adding value?

Note: 'cumulating successes' here should be understood widely. The particular forms of cumulating will depend on the innovation approach taken by the research.

Research Design Scenario 4.3: Applying the Innovation Framework to Your Own or to Another's Approach to HCI Research

Suppose that you decide to change your current planned innovation approach to HCI research, as you set out earlier (see 4.4.2), to research, supported by the specific innovation framework proposed here. The reason might be for increased rigour. In this research design scenario, apply the innovation framework to your proposed innovation approach by answering the following questions. You should also call upon any other relevant aspects of the research practice assignment as required. Additional hints and tips follow each question in the form of notes.

The selection of the topic or problem per se by the innovation research is not directly supported by the assignment or more generally by the textbook. What is supported is the manner (of innovation framework) by which the topic or problem is addressed, once selected. However, a topic or problem needs to be identified to apply an innovation framework. Further, the latter supports the researcher in understanding the possibilities and implications for the innovation research of selecting the former. Innovation research topic selection is generally some combination of the following: funding available for the project, researcher's curiosity or interest, supervisor's interests and previous work, and gaps in the HCI research literature. The latter may be identified by the researcher, the supervisor or the sponsor.

1. Which discipline, as an academic field of study, will be espoused by the conduct of the research, as supported by the innovation framework?

Note: additional discipline aspects should be referenced as appropriate, such as scholarliness, branch/subject area, knowledge and information/learning.

2. How will novel human–computer interactions be addressed by the conduct of the research, as supported by the innovation framework?
Note: additional novel aspects should be referenced as appropriate, such as new idea, method/device and significant positive change, adding value.

3. What general problem of innovation design of human–computer interaction will be addressed by the conduct of the research, as supported by the innovation framework?
Note: additional general problem aspects should be referenced as appropriate, such as specification.

4. What particular scope of the general problem of innovation design of human–computer interaction to do something as desired will be addressed by the conduct of the research, as supported by the innovation framework?
Note: additional particular scope aspects of the general problem of innovation design should be referenced as appropriate, such as individual/group human interactions and interactive/embedded computer interactions, and also aspects such as to do something – actions/task – as desired – wanted/needed/experienced/felt/valued.

5. What research, as the diagnosis of design problems and the prescription of design solutions, as they relate to performance for the acquisition and for the validation of knowledge to support practices, will be addressed by the conduct of the research, as supported by the innovation framework?
Note: additional research aspects should be referenced as appropriate, such as the desired state or not of design problems/solutions, performance as doing something as desired, acquisition as creation, and validation as confirmation.

6. What knowledge, such as patents/expert advice/experience/examples, supporting innovation practices will result from the conduct of the research, as supported by the innovation framework?
Note: additional knowledge aspects should be referenced as appropriate, such as innovation knowledge acquisition, validation and support for practice.

7. What practices, as trial and error/specify, implement and test will be involved in the conduct of the research, as supported by the innovation framework?
Note: additional practice aspects should be referenced as appropriate, such as innovation knowledge support, acquisition and validation.

5

Art Approach and Framework for HCI Research

This chapter presents the specific art approach to HCI research, including an illustration from the literature. It then presents the specific art framework for HCI research. The latter is followed by the art design research exemplar and the lower-level art framework. Both the exemplar and the lower-level framework are applied to the same illustration of the art approach taken from the literature.

5.1 Art Approach to HCI Research

An art approach to HCI research is based on the general concept of approach (see 2.2). For a more general overview of the relationship between HCI and art, see Edmonds (2018).

First, an art approach to HCI research is a way of addressing the topic or problem of designing art human–computer interactions to produce a creative, technical and imaginative expression of the relationship between people and the world, to be experienced interactively by the user.

For example, different art research approaches have produced artistic forms of human–computer interactions. The latter include interactive robots, multimedia websites, digital paintings, contingent novels, as in interactive fiction, and plays and video games. More artistic forms continue to be developed, such as digital theatricals and interactive art artefacts. These art expressions are intended to correspond to some ideal or criterion, such as beauty or aesthetic form more generally. Art includes visual and literary arts, fine and craft arts, performing arts, as well as combinations of these.

Second, an art approach to HCI research requires the performing of actions to progress that approach to the topic or problem of art human–computer interaction.

For example, currently, the aesthetics of the emotional and social interactions of humans and robots are at best rudimentary. They are poorly understood and not well expressed. However, the artistic potential of such artefacts has been demonstrated and continues to be realised.

Third, an art approach to HCI research requires the evaluating of the success of the actions performed to progress that approach.

For example, interactive robots, digital paintings and multimedia videos have been exhibited in museums and galleries. The success of the artefacts is attested by manifestos, artistic biographies/reflections and art criticism.

Fourth, an art approach to HCI research requires the cumulating of the successes as a way of establishing whether the topic or problem of designing art human–computer interactions has been addressed or not.

For example, current versus initial implementations of both interactive robots and digital paintings, such as they constitute art, exemplify the cumulating of such successes. The latter indicates that the topic of art human–computer interactions has been addressed.

5.2 Example of an Art Approach to HCI Research

As an example of an art approach to HCI research, Salisbury (2014) claims that empirical investigations of video-game play and video-game engagement are often delimited along demographic or genre lines. He attempts to generate a theory of video-game play and engagement. The theory is not restricted to types of players or types of games. To construct this theory, a version of classic grounded theory was employed.

The results are expressed at a high level as indicating that players engage with games if they can find a sense of net personal cultural value. The engagement is associated with both the selecting and playing of games, as well as players reflecting on their play experiences. Salisbury presents and explains the theory, along with the contributing hypotheses. He also makes suggestions as to the possible utility of the theory in the fields of game design and video-game research. Further work is suggested, which Salisbury hopes will clarify and modify the theory. The modifications would aim to increase its perceived fit, relevance and utility both to game design and to video-game research.

On what grounds might the Salisbury research be classified as an art approach to HCI research?

First, an art approach to HCI research is a way of addressing the topic or problem of designing art human–computer interactions by using them to produce a creative, technical and imaginative expression of the relationship between people and the world to be experienced interactively by the user.

Salisbury's art (as video games and so performing art) approach to HCI research assumes the seeking of cultural value to be a phenomenon to be understood. He considers that such understanding may have utility for the field of game design. However, this notion is not addressed explicitly by the research or developed further. The game designer is assumed to produce a creative, technical and imaginative expression of the cultural relationship between game players and the world. No ideal or other criteria are offered for such an expression. Video games include text, images (both static and animated) and combinations of both.

Second, an art approach to HCI research requires the performing of actions to progress that approach to the topic or problem of art human–computer interactions.

Salisbury suggests that his theory of understanding video-game engagement as a process of seeking cultural value might be of utility in the field of game design. However, there is no suggestion as to how this might be effected.

Third, an art approach to HCI research requires the evaluating of the success of the actions performed to progress that approach to the topic or problem of art human–computer interactions.

Salisbury does not attempt to assess explicitly how well the topic of understanding has been addressed by the research, nor how he has dealt with the problem of designing human–computer interactions. Address of both might, at best, be considered preliminary and cursory at this stage of the research.

Fourth, an art approach to HCI research requires the cumulating of the successes as a way of establishing whether the topic or problem of designing art human–computer interactions has been addressed or not.

Salisbury reports no assessment, so no such cumulating of successes.

Conclusion: On balance, Salisbury's research can be classified as an art approach to HCI research. This assumes that video games are considered to be art, for example, as a kind of performance art. Either way, engagement with art can be characterised in terms of a process seeking cultural value, as in the title of his research. However, as an art approach, it is at a very early stage of development, although it does exhibit some potential for such development.

This classification suggests that Salisbury could decide to support any of his future video-game HCI research either on the basis of the art approach to HCI research, presented earlier (see 2.2 and 5.1), or on the basis of the specific art framework, which follows.

5.3 Art Framework for HCI Research

This section covers the core framework for HCI, including HCI research, the specific art framework for HCI research, the art design research exemplar and the lower-level art framework.

5.3.1 Core Framework for HCI, Including HCI Research

The specific art framework for HCI research is based on the core framework for the discipline of HCI, including HCI research. The core framework comprises discipline, general problem, particular scope, research, knowledge and practices (see 3.4).

5.3.2 Specific Art Framework for HCI Research

The specific art framework for HCI research, such as to be applicable to an art approach to HCI, follows. It comprises the concepts and definitions of the core framework for the discipline of HCI, including HCI research (see 3.4), particularised for art. Conceptualisation to application constitutes a one-to-many mapping. Providing more than one descriptor for the same concept is one way of facilitating this mapping. To aid researchers to apply the specific art framework, an applications-supportive format follows. The specific art framework includes the main concepts, their definitional concepts and their extended definitional concepts, such as to be applicable to an art approach. The main concepts are presented in **Boldface** at first mention for easy identification, reference and application, but hold throughout. The definitional concepts appear in lower case. The extended definitional concepts appear in lower case and in (brackets). Each extended definition appears only once, but applies throughout, as appropriate.

The specific art HCI framework comprises the following:

Discipline, as an academic (that is, scholarly) field (that is, branch/subject area) of study (that is, investigation of knowledge as division of information/learning) and

Art, as a creative, technical and imaginative expression (that is, of the relationship between people and the world to be experienced interactively by the user) and

Art General Problem, as the design (that is, specification) of art human–computer interactions and

Art Particular Scope, as the design of art human (that is, individual/group)–computer (that is, interactive/embedded) interactions (that is, active/passive) to do something (that is, action/task) as desired (that is, wanted/needed/experienced/felt/valued) and

Art Research, as the diagnosis of art design problems (that is, not as desired) and the prescription of art design solutions (that is, as desired) as they relate to performance (that is, desired) for the acquisition (that is, creation) and for the validation (that is, confirmation) of knowledge to support practices and

Art Knowledge, as experience/expert advice/other artefacts (that is, as acquired and validated by art research) and supports (that is, as facilitates/makes possible) art practices and

Art Practices, as trial and error/specify, implement and test (that is, as supported by art knowledge acquired and validated by art research).

5.3.3 Art Design Research Exemplar

The specific art framework for HCI research is considered to be more complete, coherent and fit for purpose than the earlier description afforded by the art approach to HCI research (see 5.1). Hence, the art framework is more rigorously specified than the art approach and more effectively supports thinking about and doing art HCI research. As the framework is more rigorous, it offers firmer support to researchers attempting to apply it. Once applied and shared, it enables researchers to build on each other's work. Art researchers share and build on each other's work by means of the art artefacts they create, for example, successive paint applications, such as Artset. However, exactly what is shared often remains implicit. These researchers also report on their work both internally to their companies/communities and externally at conferences, for example, the ACM CHI Conference on Human Factors in Computing Systems series. The art framework might be expected to support further these explicit types of exchanges and so the sharing of and building on each other's work.

The latter is further supported here by a summary re-expression of the art framework as a design research exemplar. The use of the term 'exemplar' originates with Kuhn (1970). He conceives a scientific discipline as comprising a paradigm, a disciplinary matrix and shared exemplars. Building on the work of Long and Dowell (1989), Salter (2010) develops the concept of exemplar further and applies it to the engineering of economic systems. Here, the application is to HCI research in general and to specific HCI research frameworks in particular. The art design research exemplar represents the complete art design research cycle. Once performed, the cycle constitutes a case study of art HCI research. The exemplar is intended to support researchers in the application of the art framework. It does so by setting out in detail what is involved in the acquisition of different kinds of art knowledge to support different kinds of art practices. The exemplar is presented in Figure 5.1. The empty boxes are not required for the art exemplar. However, they are required elsewhere for other specific design research exemplars. The empty boxes have been included here for completeness. They facilitate comparison between the different exemplars. Design research concepts are Capitalised at first mention for easy identification, application and reference, but apply throughout.

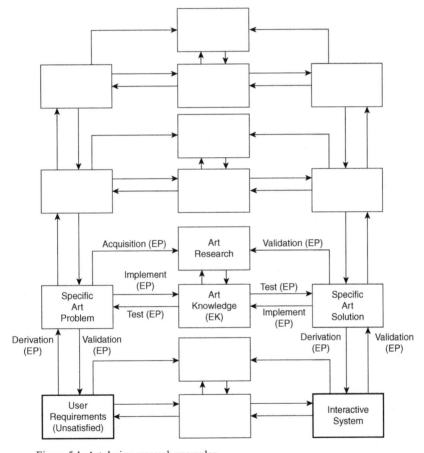

Figure 5.1 Art design research exemplar
Key: Art Knowledge: experience, expert advice, other artefacts
EP: Empirical Practice
EK: Empirical Knowledge

The four first-level boxes represent the art design cycle, starting on the outer left with User Requirements (Unsatisfied) and terminating on the outer right with an Interactive System (assumed to satisfy the user requirements). The design cycle details have not been included here. First, much of art design is implicit or indirect and so cannot be represented explicitly or directly. Second, the function of the figure is to represent design research and not design per se. The design cycle, however, following the practices of the specific art framework for HCI research (see 5.3.2), and for present purposes, might be assumed to include a design process (the two central boxes). The latter might be further assumed to comprise some combination of specification and implementation, interspersed with iterative trial-and-error cycles.

The Salisbury video-games research (see 5.2) is reused as illustration of a possible art design cycle. The latter might comprise specifying and implementing a new video-game interface intended to increase the desire to play and engage, compared with the current interface. Reusing the Salisbury video-game research example for the art design research exemplar is intended better to support researchers attempting to apply the specific art framework.

The four second-level boxes represent the art design research cycle, starting on the left with the Specific Art Problem (of design) and terminating on the right with the Specific Art Solution (of design), which solves the specific art problem.

In terms of the Salisbury video-game research illustration, the specific art problem might be the failure of the demographic/generic expression of the current interface to achieve desired performance. The reason might be the failure of the avatars to stimulate a strong enough engagement to play. The evidence might take the form of negative player feedback. The specific art solution might involve avatars expressing the player's net personal values of engaging in play, so achieving desired performance. The avatars might support more engaging art interactions, such that player feedback becomes positive. To continue the art design research exemplar, the Derivation of the specific art problem is from, and its Validation is against, the user requirements. The specific art problem is art human–computer interactions not doing something as desired.

In terms of the video-game research illustration, the user requirement might be to stimulate a stronger engagement to play: that is, stronger than that afforded by the demographic/generic expression of the current interface, as supported by the associated avatars. The user requirement might be an actual requirement, but could also be a possible and plausible requirement. Note that the difference between problems and user requirements is that the latter may or may not be satisfiable in practice. The former are formulated so as to be soluble, at least in principle. Following this reasoning, a video-game researcher might formulate the specific problem as relative to current video-game performance. The limitation of the specific art problem, relative to the possible and plausible user requirements, might be justified by the early stage of net personal, cultural value research, as demonstrated in the work of Salisbury.

The Acquisition of an expression of the specific art problem is made by Art research, for example, players not showing a strong enough engagement to play. Art research also effects the validation of the specific art solution against an expression of the specific art problem acquired by art research. The specific art problem is also Implemented, that is, expressed as the Art Knowledge needed to be Tested, that is, checked against the specific art solution. The latter is implemented, that is, expressed as art knowledge, which is tested, that is, checked against the specific art problem. Note that all the art research processes are empirical, as is the resulting art knowledge.

In terms of the Salisbury illustration, the art knowledge might take the form of experience, expert advice and artefacts. Such art knowledge could be recruited to future video-game research, but would remain empirical, that is, applicable neither analytically nor without test nor with guarantee.

Finally, the derivation of the specific art solution is expressed for application to an interactive system that satisfies the user requirements. The validation of the inclusion of the specific design solution in the interactive system is effected.

In terms of the video-game illustration, the interactive system inclusion would be such as successfully to support players engaging more strongly in interactions, such that feedback becomes positive.

5.3.4 Lower-Level Art Framework

The specific art framework has so far been expressed only at the highest level of description. That level is of the core HCI framework for research. However, to conduct and to report art design research and to acquire/validate art knowledge, as suggested by the design research exemplar, a lower-level description is required. The latter is consistent with the design research exemplar.

Researchers might have their own art lower-level descriptions or subscribe to some more generally recognised levels (for examples of such levels, see 12.3). Such descriptions are compatible with the specific art framework, as long as they are complete, coherent and fit for purpose, as concerns the higher-level core framework. Alternatively, and in addition, a lower-level framework description is presented in the associated chapter, along with the design research exemplar for each type of specific HCI research framework (see 4.3.4–9.3.4).

These higher and lower levels of description need to go respectively, for example, from the general human to the specific digital painter and from the general computer to the specific tablet with sketching functionality. The lowest level must reference the art itself, in terms of the application, for example, for an art sketching interactive system, digital painter and tablet-based electronic digital painting facility.

Following the art design research exemplar, researchers need to identify the specific art problem (as it relates to user requirements), art research, art knowledge and specific art solution (as it relates to the interactive system).

These specifications need also to include the art application, the art interactive system and the art interactive system performance. Art design requires the interactive system to do something (the application) as desired (performance). Art research acquires and validates art knowledge to support art design practice. Hence, the following lower-level art framework includes application, interactive system and performance.

The key lower-level concepts are shown in **Boldface** at first mention for easy identification, reference and application, but hold throughout

5.3.4.1 Art Application

An art application can be described in many different ways for the purposes of HCI research. Here, following Dowell and Long (1989), the application is represented as objects, attributes and states. This is a standard way of representing applications and domains (Dinu and Nadkarni, 2007). Researchers are welcome to use alternative types of representation, providing the application specification is different from that of the interactive human–computer technology system. This difference is to support design by allowing either to be varied independently of the other. Whatever the approach or the framework providing structural support, design as specification and implementation inevitably involves the selection between alternative possible interactive design options. The latter are intended to achieve the same performance goals. To avoid confounding the means – the interactive system – with the ends – performance – it is important for the two to be described independently. This independence allows the means and the ends to be co-varied separately and independently. As stated, it is for this reason that researchers are welcome to use alternative types of representation to those proposed here. However, the lower-level description must be compatible with the higher-level core HCI research framework and be complete, coherent and fit for purpose.

An **Application** is described in terms of objects.

Art Objects Art applications (what the interactive system does) can be described in terms of **Objects**. The latter comprise both **Physical Objects**

and **Abstract Objects**. They are characterised by their attributes. Physical attributes are those of matter and energy. Abstract attributes are those of knowledge and information.

For example, an art digitised video-game application (such as includes avatars) can be represented for HCI research purposes in terms of objects. The abstract attributes of the latter support the creation of the content of a video-game avatar. Their physical attributes support the representation of its structure. Video-game technology, following the research of Salisbury (see 5.2), is used here to exemplify the application of the lower-level framework. This provides continuity in the support for researchers attempting to apply the specific art approach and framework.

Although representable at different levels of description, the user must at least be described for HCI research purposes at a level that relates to the transformation of art objects.

For example, a user described as an experienced video-game player, whose engagement includes a range of avatars would be just such a level.

Art Attributes The **Attributes** of an art application object are represented at different levels of description.

For example, shapes and colours are physical attributes of the art object avatar, expressed at one level, that of appearance. The meaning of the avatar, for example, its emotion, is an abstract attribute, expressed at a higher level of description.

Art Attribute States The attributes of art application objects can be represented in terms of **States**, which may change.

For example, the content and appearance (attributes) of an enhanced video-game avatar may change state. The content change may concern meaning, for example, emotion. The appearance change may concern the size and colour of its paint strokes.

5.3.4.2 Art Interactive System

Users have aims and their associated behaviours are said to be goal-oriented or intentional.

For example, the behaviours of an artist and painting application would express such an aim in the production of a more engaging demographic and generic interface by changing the associated avatars. Interactive systems transform objects by producing state changes in the abstract and physical attributes of those objects. The artist and painting application may transform the object avatar by changing both the attributes of its physical expression and the attributes of its structure and content, as used to express emotion. Behaviour is what the user does. What is done is expressed as the attribute state changes of application objects.

Users The **Behaviours** of an art **Interactive System** are both abstract and physical. Interactive system **Abstract Behaviours** include the acquisition, storage and transformation of information. They represent and process information concerning application objects, and also their attributes, relations and states. Further, they represent the transformations required by user goals. Interactive system **Physical Behaviours** are associated with, and express, abstract behaviours.

The user, then, is represented as a system of mental (that is, abstract) and physical (that is, overt) behaviours. User **Mental Behaviours** transform abstract application objects, represented by cognition, or express, through user **Physical Behaviours**, plans for transforming application objects.

For example, a video-game artist has the aim to create the image of an avatar that increases game-player engagement. The artist interacts with the computer by means of the art application interface (whose behaviours include the transmission of information about the avatar image). Hence, the artist acquires a representation of the initial version of the avatar image by evaluating source information displayed by the computer, and also by assessing the information with respect to their goals. The artist plans the attribute state changes necessary to produce the avatar image as desired. That plan is expressed in the instructions issued to the interactive computer system through physical behaviour – selecting relevant menu options, such as shape and colour. The selection and the menu options are both objects of the design process and so potentially of art HCI research.

Both mental and physical user behaviours contribute to doing something, as desired as wanted/needed/experienced/felt/valued.

Interactions Interaction of the **User Behaviours** and **Computer Behaviours** is the basic unit of art HCI research. The concern here is with the interactive system, rather than with the individual behaviours of its parts.

For example, the behaviours of an artist interact with the behaviours of a painting application used to create the image of an avatar. The latter is intended to increase the engagement of players of a video game. The artist's behaviours influence the behaviours of the interactive computer system (access the colour function). The behaviours of the interactive computer system influence the selection behaviour of the artist (display the range of colours). The design of their interaction – the artist's selection of the colour function, the computer's presentation of possible colours – determines the interactive system. The latter comprises the artist and interactive computer behaviours in their planning and control of avatar image creation. The interaction is the object of art HCI research. Hence, the importance of the assignment of task goals either to the user or to the interactive computer system.

For example, changing the shape of an avatar image is a goal, which can be expressed as attribute state changes. In particular, selecting the field for the changed shape, as demanded by an attribute state change for the avatar's appearance. Specifying that state change may be a task goal assigned to the artist, as in interaction with the behaviours of early art applications. Or it may be a goal assigned to the interactive computer, as in interaction with the fill-in behaviours of more recent art applications.

5.3.4.3 Art Interactive System Performance

To do something as desired (see 5.3.2 – specific art framework) derives from the relationship of an interactive system with its application. It assimilates both how well the application is performed by the interactive system and the costs incurred by it in performing that well. They are expressed together as performance. Costs can be further differentiated, for example, as wanted/needed/experienced/felt/valued. Performance may be absolute or relative in terms of a comparison to be improved upon or to be equalled. Human Performance, as expressed in the literature as time and errors, relates to performance, as proposed here. Errors are behaviours that increase user costs or reduce how well the application is performed, or both. The time taken by user behaviours may loosely be associated with increased behavioural user costs.

For example, a video-game artist may make errors such as inserting the wrong image into a scenario or linking inappropriate text and images.

User Costs Doing something as desired by means of an interactive system incurs costs for the human. Costs associated with the user are termed **User Behavioural Costs**.

For example, the behavioural costs for a video-game player selecting or attending to unfamiliar menu options may be experienced over time as tiredness, irritation or impatience.

User behavioural costs comprise both **Physical Costs** and **Mental Costs**.

For example, the costs of selecting or of attending to the paint colour menu options constitute such costs. User behavioural physical costs may be expressed for art design purposes as **Physical Workload**.

User behavioural mental costs are associated with knowing, thinking and deciding. User behavioural mental costs may be expressed for HCI research purposes as **Mental Workload**. Physical and mental costs are often associated.

For example, the physical and mental behavioural costs of a video-game player may be associated with colour or shape menu option selection.

5.3.5 Example Application of an Art Framework to an Art Approach to HCI Research

The research of Salisbury (2014) can be considered to constitute an art approach to HCI research (see 5.2). The work attempts to generate a theory of video-game play and engagement unrestricted to types of players or games. Salisbury interprets his results as showing that players engage with games if they can find a sense of net personal cultural value. The latter is associated with the selecting and playing of games, and also players reflecting on their play experiences. Suggestions are made as to how these findings might support video-game design. What potential does the Salisbury approach to HCI art offer the art framework proposed here?

First, the specific art framework is for a discipline, as an academic field of study.

Potential: Salisbury's approach to video games, as performing art, assumes the seeking of net personal, cultural value to be a matter of understanding the related phenomena. He considers that such understanding may have utility for the field of game design. Salisbury associates neither understanding nor design with any particular discipline.

Second, the specific art framework is for art as a creative, technical and imaginative expression.

Potential: Salisbury's approach implies the game designer produces a creative, technical and imaginative expression of the cultural relationship between game players and the world. No explicit ideal or other criteria are offered for such an expression. Neither performance art nor art per se is referenced.

Third, the specific art framework is for the general problem of the design of art human–computer interactions.

Potential: Salisbury's art approach references both design and understanding, but neither is developed as part of a general problem.

Fourth, the specific art framework is for the particular scope of art human–computer interactions to do something as desired.

Potential: The particular scope of the art framework, including human–computer interactions with video games, is referenced by Salisbury. The reference is in terms of the interactions themselves and the experience and engagement which may result. No explicit reference, however, is made to art or to performance art, or to doing something as desired, other than may be implied by engagement.

Fifth, the specific art framework is for art research as the diagnosis of art design problems and the prescription of art design solutions, as they relate to performance for the acquisition and for the validation of knowledge to support practices.

Potential: Salisbury's proposed art theory constitutes acquired knowledge, as derived from study. There is no reference to validation of the theory proposed, either in terms of understanding or of design.

Sixth, the specific art framework is for art knowledge as experience/expert advice/other artefacts, and supports art practices.

Potential: Salisbury's proposed art theory makes no explicit mention of experience/expert advice/other artefacts.

Seventh, the specific art framework is for art practices as trial and error/ implement and test.

Potential: Salisbury's art approach is not applied to design, as implement and test or to any other design practice, although evaluation is implicitly referenced.

Conclusion: Salisbury's approach to art design can be considered as preliminary, but having potential as an approach. Further development is required concerning discipline relations of the two general problems referenced (understanding and design). Also, the high level of description needs to be lower and its links to the lower-level descriptions, as they relate to design, made explicit. More details concerning the aesthetics of art and the validation of its proposals are also required.

The art framework proposed here is considered to have potential for contributing to such developments.

Conclusion

This concludes the presentation of the specific art approach and the specific art framework for HCI research and their exemplification. Also presented are the art design research exemplar and the lower-level art framework.

5.4 Research Practice Assignment

The assignment comprises two sections: General and Research Design Scenarios.

5.4.1 General

- Using the art criteria presented in 5.3, select a recent paper from the HCI research literature that suggests itself to be potentially classifiable as art research, as concluded for Salisbury (2014) (see 5.2).

- Analyse the potential art research example, in the manner of 5.1 and 5.2.
- In the light of your analysis, decide whether the research example can be classified as art research or not. If so classifiable, continue with the assignment. If not so classifiable, return to the beginning of the assignment and start again. Continue until a classifiable example of art research is identified.
- Apply the specific art framework for HCI research, presented in 5.3.2, to the research example you have classified as art. Try to classify as many of the research example's concepts in terms of those of the specific art framework.
- Create a design research exemplar, following 5.3.3 and Figure 5.1, for the research example to which you have applied the art framework.
- Re-express the research example to which you have applied the art framework, at the lower level of art framework description, presented in 5.3.4. Try to use all the key concepts.

Hints and Tips

Difficult to get started?

Try reading the chapter again, while at the same time thinking explicitly about art in all its forms, whether in the arts or in commerce.

Describe your research (or that of others, if more appropriate) in terms of art (of any type) before attempting to apply those of 5.1 and 5.2.

Difficult to complete?

Familiarise yourself with the concept of art as it is applied in the HCI research (and other) literature.

Note the similarities and differences between the different concepts of art identified in the HCI research literature.

Test

- List the titles of 5.1 and 5.3. Complete the sections in your own words.
- Propose a new and improved set of titles for 5.1 and 5.3.
- Complete the new 5.1 and 5.3 in your own words.

5.4.2 Research Design Scenarios

All the research design scenarios in 4.4.2–9.4.2 require you to characterise your own work or that of others. The same characterisation can be used for all the scenarios. This is because they each involve the application of a different specific approach or framework. The requirement, however, is repeated in each scenario to support researchers who may be completing the research practice assignments out of order. They may not have produced a characterisation at that particular point in the book. It is also repeated for those researchers wishing to work with a range of different characterisations. They are encouraged and supported in creating such multiple characterisations.

Research Design Scenario 5.1: Characterising Your Own or Another's Approach to HCI Research

Characterise your own HCI research approach by answering the following questions, which are intended to support you in creating such a characterisation. You should also call upon any other relevant aspects of the assignment as required. The characterisation should preferably be of your own current project. If you are not working on a project at this time, base the characterisation on a past project. Failing that, base the characterisation on a project of your supervisor or of a colleague. In the last resort, choose a research project published in the HCI literature. The most important part of the research design scenario is the support and practice it gives researchers in planning their research. Additional hints and tips follow each question in the form of notes.

The selection of the topic or problem per se by the research is not directly supported by the assignment or more generally by the textbook. What is supported, however, is the manner (of art approach or of art framework) by which the topic or problem is addressed, once selected. However, the former needs to be identified to carry out the latter. Further, the selection of the approach or framework supports the researcher in understanding the possibilities and implications for the selection of the research topic or problem. The latter is generally some combination of the following: funding available for the project, researcher's curiosity or interest, supervisor's interests, and previous work and gaps in the HCI research literature. The latter may be identified by the researcher, the supervisor or the sponsor.

1. What topic or problem of designing human–computer interactions is addressed by the research and how is that topic or problem addressed?
Note: 'topic or problem' here should be understood widely, to include any and all research activities considered to be sufficiently relevant and important.

2. Which actions are performed by the research as a way of addressing the topic or problem of designing human–computer interactions?

Note: 'actions' here should be understood widely, to include any and all research activities considered to be sufficiently relevant and important.

3. What are the ways of evaluating the success or not of the actions performed by the research to address the topic or problem of designing human–computer interactions?

Note: 'evaluating success' here should be understood widely. The particular forms of evaluation will depend on the approach taken by the research.

4. How does the research cumulate its successes in addressing the topic or problem of designing human–computer interactions?

Note: 'cumulating successes' here should be understood widely. The particular forms of cumulating will depend on the approach taken by the research.

Research Design Scenario 5.2: Applying the Art Approach to Your Own or to Another's Approach to HCI Research

Suppose that you decide to change your current approach to HCI research in your next project to that of art. Or, if your present approach is already one of art, suppose that you decide to apply the specific art approach proposed here. In both cases, apply the art approach to the earlier characterisation of your own or another's HCI research approach by answering the following questions. They are intended to support you in making such an application. Any other relevant aspects of the assignment should also be called upon as required. Additional hints and tips follow each question in the form of notes.

The selection of the topic or problem per se by the art research is not directly supported by the assignment or more generally by the book. What is supported is the manner (of art approach) by which the topic or problem is addressed, once selected. However, a topic or problem needs to be identified to apply an art approach. Further, the latter supports the researcher in understanding the possibilities and implications for the art research of selecting the former. Art research topic selection is generally some combination of the following: funding available for the project, researcher's curiosity or interest, supervisor's interests and previous work, and gaps in the HCI research literature. The latter may be identified by the researcher, the supervisor or the sponsor.

1. What topic or problem of designing art human–computer interactions by producing a creative, technical and imaginative expression of the relationship between people and the world, to be experienced interactively by the

user, is addressed by the research and how will that topic or problem be addressed?

Note: 'topic or problem' here should be understood widely to include any and all art research activities considered to be sufficiently relevant and important.

2. Which actions are to be performed by the research as a way of addressing the topic or problem of designing art human–computer interactions by producing a creative, technical and imaginative expression of the relationship between people and the world to be experienced interactively by the user?

Note: 'actions' here should be understood widely to include any and all art research activities considered to be sufficiently relevant and important.

3. Which ways of evaluating the success or not of the actions performed by the research will be employed to address the topic or problem of designing art human–computer interactions by producing a creative, technical and imaginative expression of the relationship between people and the world to be experienced interactively by the user?

Note: 'evaluating success' here should be understood widely. The particular forms of evaluation will depend on the art approach taken by the research.

4. How will the research cumulate its successes in addressing the topic or problem of producing a creative, technical and imaginative expression of the relationship between people and the world to be experienced interactively by the user?

Note: 'cumulating successes' here should be understood widely. The particular forms of cumulating will depend on the art approach taken by the research.

Research Design Scenario 5.3: Applying the Art Framework to Your Own or to Another's Approach to HCI Research

Suppose that you decide to change your current planned art approach to HCI research, as you set out earlier, in Research Design Scenario 5.1 (see also 5.4.2), to research supported by the art framework proposed here. The reason might be, for example, for increased rigour. In this research design scenario, apply the art framework to your proposed art approach by answering the following questions. You should also call upon any other relevant aspects of the assignment as required. Additional hints and tips follow each question in the form of notes.

The selection of the topic or problem per se by the art research is not directly supported by the assignment or more generally by the book. What is supported is the manner (of art framework) by which the topic or problem is addressed, once selected. However, a topic or problem needs to be identified to apply an art framework. Further, the latter supports the researcher in understanding the possibilities and implications for the art research of selecting the former. Art research topic selection is generally some combination of the following: funding available for the project, researcher's curiosity or interest, supervisor's interests, and previous work and gaps in the HCI research literature. The latter may be identified by the researcher, the supervisor or the sponsor.

1. Which discipline, as an academic field of study, will be espoused by the conduct of the research, as supported by the art framework?
Note: additional discipline aspects should be referenced as appropriate, such as scholarliness, branch/subject area, knowledge and information/ learning.

2. How will art human–computer interactions be addressed by the conduct of the research, as supported by the art framework?
Note: additional art aspects should be referenced as appropriate, such as a creative, technical and imaginative expression of the relationship between people and the world to be experienced interactively by the user.

3. What general problem of art design of human–computer interaction will be addressed by the conduct of the research, as supported by the art framework?
Note: additional general problem aspects should be referenced as appropriate, such as specification.

4. What particular scope of the general problem of art design of human–computer interaction to do something as desired will be addressed by the conduct of the research, supported by the art framework?
Note: additional particular scope aspects of the general problem of art design should be referenced as appropriate, such as individual/group human interactions and interactive/embedded computer interactions, and also aspects such as to do something – actions/task – as desired – wanted, needed, experienced, felt and/or valued.

5. What research, as the diagnosis of design problems and the prescription of design solutions as they relate to performance for the acquisition and for the validation of knowledge to support practices, will be addressed by the conduct of the research, as supported by the art framework?
Note: additional research aspects should be referenced as appropriate, such as the desired state or not of design problems/solutions, performance as doing something as desired, acquisition as creation, and validation as confirmation.

6. What knowledge, such as experience/expert advice/other artefacts, supporting art practices will result from the conduct of the research as supported by the art framework?

Note: additional knowledge aspects should be referenced as appropriate, such as art knowledge acquisition, validation and support for practice.

7. What practices, as trial and error/specify, implement and test, will be involved in the conduct of the research, as supported by the art framework?

Note: additional practice aspects should be referenced as appropriate, such as art knowledge support, acquisition and validation.

6

Craft Approach and Framework for HCI Research

This chapter presents the specific craft approach to HCI research, including an illustration from the literature. It then presents the specific craft framework for HCI research. The latter is followed by the craft design research exemplar and the lower-level craft framework. Both the exemplar and the lower-level framework are applied to the same illustration of the craft approach taken from the literature.

6.1 Craft Approach to HCI Research

A craft approach to HCI research is based on the general concept of approach (see 2.2). For a more general overview of the relationship between HCI and craft, see Long and Dowell (1989), Carroll et al. (1991) and Carroll (2010).

First, a craft approach to HCI research is a way of addressing the topic or problem of the craft design of human–computer interactions by developing best practice design to satisfy user requirements in the form of an interactive system.

For example, best practice craft design of different kinds has informed the specification and implementation of interactive systems. The latter include aspects of email, internet banking, online government services and electronic shopping.

Second, a craft approach to HCI research requires the performing of actions to progress that approach to the topic or problem of craft human–computer interactions.

For example, best practice craft design research has supported the evolution of interface specifications from sketches to wire-frame models. Further, the associated evaluation has evolved from verbal ratings of alternative designs to online real-time assessment of user performance and experience. The scope of best practice craft design has evolved from usability to fun, to emotion and to experience. Best practice craft research has produced heuristics, methods, expert advice, successful designs and case studies. Such best practice craft research can now be found on HCI courses, in textbooks and in practitioner case-study reports.

Third, a craft approach to HCI research requires the evaluating of the success of the actions performed to progress that approach.

For example, the design and evaluation of successive versions of interactive systems such as email and internet banking can be assessed in terms of their success. The latter may be reflected in user satisfaction and experience, uptake of the ideas by other designers and professional awards. The extent to which this success is supported by heuristics, methods, expert advice, other designs and case studies in satisfying or not user requirements, in the form of an interactive system, can also be assessed. Current email systems meet many (if not all) of these different design criteria.

Fourth, a craft approach to HCI research requires the cumulating of successes, as a way of establishing whether the topic or problem of the craft design of human–computer interactions has been addressed or not.

For example, current versus initial implementations of email, internet banking and online shopping, such as they constitute craft, exemplify the cumulating of such successes. They indicate that the topic or problem of the craft design of human–computer interactions has been addressed.

6.2 Example of a Craft Approach to HCI Research

As an example of a craft approach to HCI research, Balaam et al. (2015) note that breastfeeding is positively encouraged in many countries as a matter of public health. The World Health Organization (WHO) recommends breastfeeding exclusively for the first six months of an infant's life. However, it may be difficult for women to meet this criterion for reasons of technique and of social acceptance. Balaam et al. report four phases of a design and research project. The phases comprise sensitising user engagement, applying user-centred design, developing/deploying an application and in-the-wild evaluation. The application is called FeedFinder, a location-mapping mobile application for breastfeeding women.

Balaam et al. discuss how mobile technologies can be designed to achieve public health goals. They suggest that related technologies may be better aimed at communities and societies, rather than at individuals, as currently.

On what grounds can Balaam et al. (2015) be classified as a craft approach to HCI research?

First, a craft approach to HCI research is a way of addressing the topic or problem of designing human–computer interactions by developing best practice design to satisfy user requirements in the form of an interactive system.

Balaam et al. report a research and design project that addresses the topic or problem of designing human–computer interactions. The result is FeedFinder, a location-mapping mobile application for breastfeeding women. The application of user-engagement sensitisation and user-centred design techniques, along with Balaam et al.'s own design experience, constitute the best practice.

Second, a craft approach to HCI research requires the performing of actions to progress that approach to the topic or problem of human–computer interactions.

Balaam et al. report two ways forward for their approach to research and design: first, the particular form of the research they conducted and second, how in addition, notions of consumers, communities and citizens might inform the basis for the design of humans interacting with computers. Their research reports both design and evaluation activities.

Third, a craft approach to HCI research requires the evaluating of the success of the actions performed to progress that approach.

Balaam et al. identify a number of user requirements for women who want to breastfeed their babies in public. The extent to which these requirements have been met by the FeedFinder application is evaluated in-the-wild and reported.

Fourth, a craft approach to HCI research requires the cumulating of the successes as a way of establishing whether the topic or problem of the craft design of human–computer interactions has been addressed or not.

Balaam et al. report no such cumulating of successes or any indication that such a grouping is possible.

Conclusion: On balance, Balaam et al.'s research and design project can be classified as a craft approach to HCI research. It applies a best-practice generic user-centred design method and techniques. The validation of the latter is not declared as an aim of the project. The best practice, as well as being in part generic, almost certainly derives from the researcher/designers' previous research and design experience. The latter will contribute to future (even better) such practice.

This classification suggests that Balaam et al. could decide to support any of their future HCI research either on the basis of the craft approach to HCI research, presented earlier (see 2.2 and 6.1), or on the basis of the specific craft framework, which follows.

6.3 Craft Framework for HCI Research

This section covers the core framework for HCI, including HCI research, the specific craft framework for HCI research, the craft design research exemplar and the lower-level craft framework.

6.3.1 Core Framework for HCI, Including HCI Research

The specific craft framework for HCI research is based on the core framework for the discipline of HCI, including HCI research. The core framework comprises discipline, general problem, particular scope, research, knowledge and practices (see 3.4).

6.3.2 Specific Craft Framework for HCI Research

The specific craft framework for HCI research, such as to be applicable to a craft approach to HCI, follows. It comprises the concepts and definitions of the core framework for the discipline of HCI, including HCI research (see 3.4), particularised for craft. Conceptualisation to application constitutes a one-to-many mapping. Providing more than one descriptor for the same concept is a way of facilitating this mapping. To aid researchers to apply the specific craft framework, an applications-supportive format follows. The specific craft framework includes the main concepts, their definitional concepts and their extended definitional concepts, such as to be applicable to a craft approach. The main concepts are presented in **Boldface** at first mention for easy identification, reference and application, but hold throughout. The definitional concepts appear in lower case. The extended definitional concepts appear in lower case and in (brackets). Each extended definition appears only once, but applies throughout, as appropriate.

The specific craft HCI framework comprises the following:

- **Discipline**, as an academic (that is, scholarly) field (that is, branch/subject area) of study (that is, investigation of knowledge as division of information/learning) and
- **Craft**, as best practice, satisfying user requirements (that is, in the form of an interactive system) and
- **Craft General Problem**, as the design (that is, specification) of craft human–computer interactions and
- **Craft Particular Scope**, as the design of craft human (that is, individual/group)–computer (that is, interactive/embedded) interactions (that is, active/

passive) to do something (that is, action/task) as desired (that is, wanted/needed/experienced/felt/valued) and

- **Craft Research**, as the diagnosis of craft user requirements (that is, not as desired) and the prescription of a craft interactive system (that is, as desired) as they relate to performance (that is, desired) for the acquisition (that is, creation) and for the validation (that is, confirmation) of knowledge to support practices and
- **Craft Knowledge**, as heuristics/methods/expert advice/successful designs/case studies (that is, as acquired and validated by craft research) and supports (that is, as facilitates/makes possible) craft practices and
- **Craft Practices**, as trial and error/specify, implement and test (that is, as supported by craft knowledge acquired and validated by craft research).

6.3.3 Craft Design Research Exemplar

The specific craft framework for HCI research is considered to be more complete, coherent and fit for purpose than the earlier description afforded by the craft approach to HCI (see 6.1). Hence, the craft framework is more rigorously specified than the craft approach and so more effectively supports thinking about and doing craft HCI research. As the framework is more rigorous, it offers firmer support to researchers attempting to apply it. Once applied and shared, it enables researchers to build on each other's work. Craft researchers share and build on each other's work by means of the craft artefacts they create, for example, the craft contribution to internet banking. However, exactly what is shared remains largely implicit. These researchers also report on their work both internally to their companies/communities and externally at conferences, for example, the ACM CHI Conference on Human Factors in Computing Systems series. The craft framework might be expected to support further these explicit types of exchanges and so the sharing of and building on each other's work.

The latter is further supported here by a summary re-expression of the craft framework as a design research exemplar. The use of the term 'exemplar' originates with Kuhn (1970). He conceives a scientific discipline as comprising a paradigm, a disciplinary matrix and shared exemplars. Building on the work of Long and Dowell (1989), Salter (2010) develops the concept of exemplar further and applies it to the engineering of economic systems. Here, the application is to HCI research in general and to specific HCI research frameworks in particular. The craft exemplar represents the complete design research cycle. Once performed, the cycle constitutes a case study of craft HCI research.

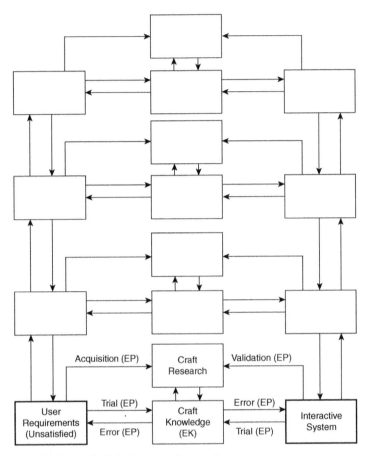

Figure 6.1 Craft design research exemplar
Key: Craft Knowledge: heuristics, methods, expert advice, successful designs, case studies
EP: Empirical Practice
EK: Empirical Knowledge

The exemplar is intended to support researchers in the application of the craft framework; it is presented in Figure 6.1. The empty boxes are not required for the craft exemplar. However, they are required elsewhere for other specific design research exemplars. The empty boxes have been included here for completeness. They facilitate comparison between the different exemplars. Design research concepts are Capitalised at first mention for easy identification, application and reference, but apply throughout.

The four first-level boxes represent the craft research and design cycle. The cycle starts on the outer left with User Requirements (Unsatisfied) and terminates on the outer right with an Interactive System (assumed to satisfy the user requirements). The design cycle details are not included here. First, much of craft design is implicit or indirect and so cannot be represented explicitly or indirectly. Second, the function of the figure is to represent design research and not design per se. The design cycle, however, following the practices of the specific craft framework for HCI research (see 6.3.2) and for present purposes, might be assumed to include a design process (the two central boxes). The latter might be further assumed to comprise some combination of specification and implementation, interspersed with iterative trial-and-error cycles.

The Balaam et al. research (see 6.2) is reused as illustration of a possible craft design research cycle.

Following the craft design research exemplar, the Acquisition of user requirements (as unsatisfied) is effected empirically by Craft Research. The Validation of the specification of the interactive system is empirically effected by craft research against the user requirements. In the Balaam et al. illustration, craft research involves craft knowledge, including researcher design experience and best practice design methods. The user requirements include finding locations that meet technique-friendly and social-acceptance-friendly conditions for breastfeeding women. The interactive system is a location-mapping mobile application for such women.

A Trial of user requirements is empirically effected against Craft Knowledge, having the potential to transform the user requirements into an interactive system. The craft knowledge is then empirically checked for Error against a specification of the interactive system. In the Balaam et al. illustration, user requirements include finding locations that meet technique-friendly and social-acceptance-friendly conditions. The craft knowledge includes design experience of the researcher/designers and best practice methods for sensitising user engagement, for applying user-centred design, for deploying and for the in-the-wild evaluation. Last, the specification of the interactive system is of a location-mapping mobile application for breastfeeding women.

A trial of the interactive system specification is empirically effected against craft knowledge used in its specification. The craft knowledge is then empirically checked for error against user requirements. In the Balaam et al. illustration, the trial is of the specification of the location-mapping application against design experience of the researcher/designers and best practice methods for sensitising user engagement, for user-centred design/deployment and for the in-the-wild evaluation. This craft knowledge is then checked for error against expression of the technique- and socially acceptance-friendly user requirements of breastfeeding women.

6.3.4 Lower-Level Craft Framework

The specific craft framework has so far been expressed at the highest level of description. That level is of the core framework. However, to conduct and to report craft design research and to acquire/validate craft knowledge, as suggested by the design research exemplar, a lower level of description is required. The latter is consistent with the design research exemplar.

Researchers might have their own craft lower-level descriptions or subscribe to some more generally recognised levels (for examples of such levels, see 12.3). Such descriptions are compatible with the specific craft framework as long as they are complete, coherent and fit for purpose as concerns the higher-level core framework. Alternatively, and in addition, a lower-level framework description is presented in the associated chapter, along with the design research exemplar for each type of specific HCI research framework (see 4.3.4–9.3.4).

These higher and lower levels of description need to go respectively, for example, from the general human to the specific breastfeeding women and from the general computer to the specific smartphone. The lowest level must reference the craft design itself in terms of the application, for example, for a location-mapping interactive system and mobile facility.

Following the craft design research exemplar, researchers need to specify user requirements (unsatisfied), craft research, craft knowledge and interactive system (satisfying user requirements).

These specifications need also to include the application, the interactive system and performance, relating the former to the latter. Craft design requires the interactive system to do something (the application) as desired (performance). Craft research acquires and validates craft knowledge to support craft design practice. Hence, the following lower-level craft framework includes application, interactive system and performance.

The key lower-level concepts are shown in **Boldface** at first mention for easy identification, reference and application, but hold throughout.

6.3.4.1 Craft Application

A craft application can be described in many different ways for the purposes of HCI research. Here, following Dowell and Long (1989), the application is represented as objects, attributes and states. This is a standard way of representing applications and domains (Dinu and Nadkarni, 2007). Researchers are welcome to use alternative types of representation, providing the application specification is different from that of the interactive human–computer technology system. This difference is to support design by allowing either to be varied independently of the other. Whatever the approach or the framework providing structural support, design as specification and implementation inevitably involves the selection between alternative possible interactive design options. The latter are intended to achieve the same performance goals. To avoid confounding the means – the interactive system – with the ends – performance – it is important for the two to be described independently. This independence allows the means and the ends to be co-varied separately and independently. As stated, it is for this reason that researchers are welcome to use alternative types of representation to those proposed here. However, the lower-level description must be compatible with the higher-level core HCI research framework and be complete, coherent and fit for purpose.

An **Application** is described in terms of objects.

Craft Objects The Craft application (what the interactive system does) can be described as **Objects**. The latter comprise both **Physical Objects** and **Abstract Objects**. They are characterised by their attributes. Physical attributes are those of matter and energy. Abstract attributes are those of knowledge and information.

For example, the application of a location-mapping mobile application can be described, for design research purposes, in terms of objects. The abstract attributes of the latter support the communication of messages, including their physical attributes. The latter support the visual/verbal representation of displayed information by means of language. Craft mobile technology, following the research of Balaam et al. (see 6.2), is used here to exemplify the application of the lower-level framework. This provides continuity in the support for researchers attempting to apply the specific craft approach and framework.

Although representable at many levels of description, the user must at least be described for HCI research purposes at a level that relates to the transformation of craft application objects.

For example, a user described as a breastfeeding mother seeking a public location in which to feed her child would constitute such a level.

Craft Attributes The **Attributes** of a craft application object are expressed at different levels of description.

For example, characters and their configuration on a mobile display are physical attributes of the object location message, expressed at one level. The content of the location message is an abstract attribute, expressed at a higher-level of description.

Craft Attribute States The attributes of craft application objects can be represented as **States**, which may change.

For example, the content and characters (attributes) of a location message (object) may change state – the content with respect to meaning and grammar, its characters with respect to size and font.

6.3.4.2 Craft Interactive System

Users have aims and the associated behaviours are considered to be goal-oriented/intentional.

For example, the behaviours of a woman and location-mapping mobile application would express the aim of identifying socially acceptable locations for breastfeeding. Interactive systems transform objects by producing state changes in the abstract and physical attributes of those objects. The breastfeeding woman and the location-mapping mobile application may transform the object by changing both the attributes of its meaning and the attributes of its layout. Behaviour is what the user does. What is done is expressed as the attribute state changes of application objects.

Users The **Behaviours** of a craft **Interactive System** are both abstract and physical. Interactive system **Abstract Behaviours** include the acquisition, storage and transformation of information. They represent and process information concerning application objects, and also their attributes, relations and states. Further, they represent the transformations required by user goals. Interactive system **Physical Behaviours** are associated with and express abstract behaviours.

The user, then, is represented as a system of mental (that is, abstract) and physical (that is, overt) behaviours. User **Mental Behaviours** transform abstract application objects. The latter are represented by cognition or express, through user **Physical Behaviours**, plans for transforming application objects.

For example, a breastfeeding woman, out shopping with her baby, has the aim of identifying a near and socially acceptable location for feeding the baby. The woman interacts with her mobile phone by means of the display. The latter's behaviours include the transmission of information about breastfeeding locations. The woman acquires a representation of the current list of local, suitable locations by synthesising the information presented on the display. She also assesses it against her goals. The woman plans the attribute state changes necessary to achieve her goals of identifying a location as desired. That plan is expressed in the instructions given to the interactive mobile system through physical behaviour, such as selecting menu options. The selection and the menu options are part of the design and so potentially part of craft HCI research. Both mental and physical user behaviours contribute to doing something, as desired as wanted/needed/experienced/felt/valued.

Interactions Interaction of **User Behaviours** and **Computer Behaviours** is the basic unit of craft HCI research. The concern here is with the interactive system, rather than with the individual behaviours of the parts.

For example, the behaviours of a breastfeeding woman interact with the behaviours of a location-mapping mobile application. The woman's behaviours influence the behaviours of the mobile phone (access the image function). The behaviours of the mobile phone influence the selection behaviour of the woman (among possible image types). The design of their interaction – the woman's selection of the image function, the phone's presentation of possible image types – determines the interactive system. The latter comprises the woman and interactive phone's behaviours in their planning and control of display creation. The interaction is the object of craft HCI research. Hence the importance of the assignment of task goals to either the woman or to the mobile phone.

For example, replacing an inappropriate location image is a goal, which can be expressed as a task goal of attribute state changes, in particular, the field for the appropriate image on a display as an attribute state change in the spacing of the display. Specifying that state change may be a task goal assigned to the woman, as in interaction with the behaviours of early image editor designs. Or it may be a task goal assigned to the mobile phone, as in interaction with more recent fill-in behaviours.

6.3.4.3 Craft Interactive System Performance

To do something (see 6.3.2 – specific craft framework) derives from the relationship of an interactive system with its application. It assimilates both how well the application is performed by the interactive system – as desired – and the costs incurred by it in performing that well. They are expressed together as performance. Costs can be further differentiated, for example, as wanted/needed/experienced/felt/valued. Performance may be absolute or relative, in terms of a comparison to be improved upon or to be equalled. Human Performance, as expressed in the literature as time and errors, relates to performance, as proposed here. Errors are behaviours that increase user costs or that reduce how well the application is performed or both. The time taken by user behaviours may loosely be associated with increased behavioural user costs.

For example, a craft location-mapping mobile application might be expected to improve performance in terms of reduced behavioural costs of identifying socially acceptable breastfeeding locations, relative to an earlier non-mobile application.

User Costs Doing something as desired by means of an interactive system incurs costs for the human. Costs associated with the user are termed **User Behavioural Costs**.

For example, the behavioural costs for a woman keying or attending to difficult or overcomplicated colour and image menu options, representing socially acceptable locations for breastfeeding, may be experienced over time as tiredness, irritation or impatience.

User behavioural costs comprise both **Physical Costs** and **Mental Costs**.

Such costs are associated, for example, with the keying or attending to location menu options. User behavioural physical costs may be expressed for craft HCI research purposes as **Physical Workload**.

User behavioural mental costs are associated with knowing, thinking and deciding. User behavioural mental costs may be expressed for HCI research purposes as **Mental Workload**. Physical and mental costs are often closely associated.

For example, the physical and mental behavioural costs of a breastfeeding woman may be associated with mobile menu option selection or text input keying.

6.3.5 Example Application of a Craft Framework to a Craft Approach to HCI Research

The research of Balaam et al. (2015) can be considered to constitute a craft approach to HCI research (see 6.2). The paper reports the design of a location-mapping mobile application for breastfeeding women. The research comprises user-engagement sensitisation, user-centred design, development/deployment and in-the-wild evaluation. Balaam et al. discuss how mobile technologies can be designed to achieve public health goals. What potential does the Balaam et al. approach to craft research offer the craft framework presented here?

First, the specific craft framework is for a discipline, as an academic field of study.

Potential: Balaam et al.'s approach is concerned with designing a specific application. There is no explicit commitment to a superordinate discipline or field of study/branch of knowledge, for example, science as it relates to understanding, or engineering as it relates to codified design.

Second, the specific craft framework is for craft as best practice to satisfy user requirements.

Potential: Balaam et al.'s approach includes user requirements and an interactive system designed to satisfy them, and also how notions of consumers, communities and citizens might inform such design. The concepts of craft and best practice are not explicitly identified or addressed as such, although the latter is clearly implied.

Third, the specific craft framework is for the general problem of the design of craft human–computer interactions.

Potential: Balaam et al. address the particular breastfeeding problem as the design of an application. Their approach, however, does not explicitly refer to a general design problem.

Fourth, the specific craft framework is for the particular scope of craft human–computer interactions to do something as desired.

Potential: Balaam et al. address the particular breastfeeding application problem as something desired, based on user requirements and user engagement sensitisation.

Fifth, the specific craft framework is for craft research as the diagnosis of craft user requirements and the prescription of a craft interactive system for the acquisition and validation of knowledge to support practices.

Potential: Balaam et al.'s approach applies a generic user-centred design method, whose validation is not declared as an aim of the research. In addition, the application of the method is almost certainly informed by the authors' implicit previous research and design experience. The application of the method would also be expected to improve such experience, consistent with craft assumptions. No emphasis is accorded the acquisition of explicit design knowledge in its own right.

Sixth, the specific craft framework is for craft knowledge, as heuristics/ methods/expert advice/successful designs/case studies.

Balaam et al.'s approach includes sensitising user engagement, user-centred design, development/deployment and in-the-wild evaluation of a mobile phone location-mapping mobile application for breastfeeding women. The design is evaluated as being successful and is presented as a case study. No explicit heuristics or methods are reported as being acquired.

Seventh, the specific craft framework is for craft practices, as trial and error/ implement and test.

Balaam et al.'s approach to craft design appears to support design practices of trial and error and implement and test. Such practices, however, are not the object of this particular research, nor is the validation of the knowledge that supported those practices.

Conclusion: Balaam et al.'s approach to craft design could be further developed with respect to the associated discipline/field of study of design; its level of description needs to be higher and to link with the lower-level descriptions referenced. In addition, there is a need to express whether its components are implicit or explicit and what constitutes its concept of design knowledge acquisition and validation. However, it is a successful design practice research application on its own terms.

The craft framework proposed here is considered to have potential for contributing to such developments.

Conclusion

This concludes the presentation of the specific craft approach and the specific craft framework for HCI research and their exemplification. Also presented are the craft design research exemplar and the lower-level craft framework.

6.4 Research Practice Assignment

The assignment comprises two sections: General and Research Design Scenarios.

6.4.1 General

- Using the craft criteria presented in 6.3, select a recent paper from the HCI research literature that suggests itself to be potentially classifiable as craft research, as concluded for Balaam et al. (2015) (see 6.2).
  - Analyse and record the potential craft research example, in the manner of 6.1 and 6.2.
  - In the light of your analysis, decide whether the research example can be classified as craft research or not. If so classifiable, continue with the research practice assignment. If not so classifiable, return to the beginning of the assignment and start again. Continue until a classifiable example of craft research is identified.
- Apply the craft framework for HCI research, presented in 6.3.2, to the research example you have classified as craft.
- Create a research design exemplar, following 6.3.3 and Figure 6.1, for the research example to which you have applied the craft framework.
- Re-express the research example to which you have applied the craft framework at the lower level of craft framework description, presented in 6.3.4. Try to use all the key concepts.

Hints and Tips

Difficult to get started?
Try reading the chapter again, while at the same time thinking explicitly about craft in all its forms, whether in the arts or in commerce.
Describe your research (or that of others, if more appropriate) in terms of craft (of any type) before attempting to apply those of 6.1 and 6.2.

Difficult to complete?

Familiarise yourself with the concept of craft as it is applied in the HCI
   research (and other) literature.

Note the similarities and differences between the different concepts of craft
   identified in the HCI research literature.

Test

- Write down the titles of 6.1 and 6.3. Complete the sections in your own
  words.
- Propose a new and improved set of titles for 6.1 and 6.3.
- Complete the new 6.1 and 6.3 in your own words.

6.4.2 Research Design Scenarios

All the research design scenarios in 4.4.2–9.4.2 require you to characterise your
own work or that of others. The same characterisation, however, can be used for
all the scenarios. The requirement, however, is repeated in each scenario to
support researchers who may be completing the research practice assignments
out of order. They may not have produced a characterisation at that point in the
book. It is also repeated for those researchers wishing to work with a range of
different characterisations. They are encouraged and supported in creating such
multiple characterisations.

Research Design Scenario 6.1: Characterising Your Own or Another's
Approach to HCI Research

Characterise your own HCI research approach by answering the following questions, which are intended to support you in creating such a characterisation. You
should call on any other relevant aspects of the assignment as required. The
characterisation should preferably be of your own current project. If you are not
working on a project at this time, base the characterisation on a past project.
Failing that, base the characterisation on a project of your supervisor or of
a colleague. In the last resort, choose a research project published in the HCI
literature. The most important part of the research design scenario is the support
and practice it gives researchers in planning their research. Additional hints and
tips follow each question in the form of notes.

   The selection of the topic or problem per se by the research is not directly
supported by the assignment or more generally by the book. What is supported,
however, is the manner (of craft approach or of craft framework) by which the

topic or problem is addressed, once selected. However, the former needs to be identified to carry out the latter. Further, the selection of the approach or the framework supports the researcher in understanding the possibilities and implications for the research topic or problem. The latter is generally some combination of the following: funding available for the project, researcher's curiosity or interest, supervisor's interests and previous work, and gaps in the HCI research literature. The latter may be identified by the researcher, the supervisor or the sponsor.

1. What topic or problem of designing human–computer interactions is addressed by the research and how is that topic or problem addressed?
Note: 'topic or problem' here should be understood widely to include any and all research activities considered to be relevant and important.

2. Which actions are performed by the research as a way of addressing the topic or problem of designing human–computer interactions?
Note: 'actions' here should be understood widely to include any and all research activities considered to be sufficiently relevant and important.

3. What are the ways of evaluating the success or not of the actions performed by the research to address the topic or problem of designing human–computer interactions?
Note: 'evaluating success' here should be understood widely. The particular forms of evaluation will depend on the approach taken by the research.

4. How does the research cumulate its successes in addressing the topic or problem of designing human–computer interactions?
Note: 'cumulating successes' here should be understood widely. The particular forms of cumulating will depend on the approach taken by the research.

Research Design Scenario 6.2: Applying the Craft Approach to Your Own or to Another's Approach to HCI Research

Suppose that you decide to change your current approach to HCI research in your next project to that of craft. Or if your present approach is already one of craft, suppose that you decide to apply the specific craft approach proposed here. In both cases, apply the craft approach to the earlier characterisation of your own or another's HCI research approach by answering the following questions. They are intended to support you in making such an application. Any other relevant aspects of the assignment should also be called upon as required. Additional hints and tips follow each question in the form of notes.

The selection of the topic or problem per se by the craft research is not directly supported by the assignment or more generally by the book. What is supported, however, is the manner (of craft approach) by which the topic or problem is addressed, once selected. However, a topic or problem needs to be identified to apply a craft approach. Further, the latter supports the researcher in understanding the possibilities and implications for the craft research of selecting the former. Craft research topic selection is generally some combination of the following: funding available for the project, researcher's curiosity or interest, supervisor's interests and previous work, and gaps in the HCI research literature. The latter may be identified by the researcher, the supervisor or the sponsor.

1. What topic or problem of designing craft human–computer interactions by developing best practice design to satisfy user requirements in the form of an interactive system is to be addressed by the research and how will that topic or problem be addressed?
   Note: 'topic or problem' here should be understood widely to include any and all craft research activities considered to be relevant and important.

2. Which actions are to be performed by the research as a way of addressing the topic or problem of designing craft human–computer interactions by developing best practice design to satisfy user requirements in the form of an interactive system?
   Note: 'actions' here should be understood widely to include any and all craft research activities considered to be sufficiently relevant and important.

3. Which ways of evaluating the success or not of the actions performed by the research will be employed to address the topic or problem of designing craft human–computer interactions by developing best practice design to satisfy user requirements in the form of an interactive system?
   Note: 'evaluating success' here should be understood widely. The particular forms of evaluation will depend on the craft approach taken by the research.

4. How will the research cumulate its successes in addressing the topic or problem of designing craft human–computer interactions by developing best practice design to satisfy user requirements in the form of an interactive system?
   Note: 'cumulating successes' here should be understood widely. The particular forms of cumulating will depend on the craft approach taken by the research.

Research Design Scenario 6.3: Applying the Craft Framework to Your Own or to Another's Approach to HCI Research

Suppose that you decide to change your current planned craft approach to HCI research, as you set out earlier (see 6.4.2), to research, supported by the craft framework proposed here. The reason might be for increased rigour. In this research design scenario, apply the craft framework to your proposed craft approach by answering the following questions. You should also call upon any other relevant aspects of the research practice assignment as required. Additional hints and tips follow each question in the form of notes.

The selection of the topic or problem per se by the craft research is not directly supported by the assignment or more generally by the book. What is supported is the manner (here of craft framework) by which the topic or problem is addressed, once selected. However, a topic or problem needs to be identified to apply a craft framework. Further, the latter supports the researcher in understanding the possibilities and implications for the craft research of selecting the former. Craft research topic selection is generally some combination of the following: funding available for the project, researcher's curiosity or interest, supervisor's interests and previous work, and gaps in the HCI research literature. The latter may be identified by the researcher, the supervisor or the sponsor.

1. Which discipline, as an academic field of study, will be espoused by the conduct of the research, as supported by the craft framework?
Note: additional discipline aspects should be referenced as appropriate, such as scholarliness, branch/subject area, knowledge and information/learning.

2. How will craft as best practice human–computer interaction satisfying user requirements be addressed by the conduct of the research, as supported by the craft framework?
Note: additional best practice aspects should be referenced as appropriate, such as the interactive system.

3. What general problem of craft design of human–computer interactions will be addressed by the conduct of the research, as supported by the craft framework?
Note: additional general problem aspects should be referenced as appropriate, such as specification.

4. What particular scope of the general problem of craft design of human–computer interaction to do something as desired will be addressed by the conduct of the research, as supported by the craft framework?
Note: additional particular scope aspects of the general problem of craft design should be referenced as appropriate, such as individual/group human interactions and interactive/embedded computer interactions, and also aspects such as to do something – actions/task – and as desired – as wanted/needed/experienced/felt/valued.

5. What research as the diagnosis of craft user requirements and the prescription of a craft interactive system for the acquisition and for the validation of knowledge to support practices will be addressed by the conduct of the research, as supported by the craft framework?

Note: additional research aspects should be referenced as appropriate, such as the desired state or not of user requirements/interactive system, acquisition as creation and validation as confirmation.

6. What knowledge, such as experience/expert advice/other artefacts, supporting craft practices will result from the conduct of the research, as supported by the craft framework?

Note: additional knowledge aspects should be referenced as appropriate, such as craft knowledge acquisition, validation and support for practice.

7. What practices, as trial and error/specify, implement and test, will be involved in the conduct of the research, as supported by the craft framework?

Note: additional practice aspects should be referenced as appropriate, such as craft knowledge support, acquisition and validation.

7

Applied Approach and Framework for HCI Research

This chapter presents the specific applied approach to HCI research, including an illustration from the literature. It then presents the specific applied framework for HCI research. The latter is followed by the applied design research exemplar and by the lower-level applied framework. Both the exemplar and the lower-level framework are applied to the same illustration of the applied approach taken from the literature.

7.1 Applied Approach to HCI Research

An applied approach to HCI research is based on the general concept of approach (see 2.2). For a more general overview of the relationship between HCI and applied, see Card et al. (1983), Long (1987), Long and Dowell (1989), Barnard (1991), Rauterberg (2006) and Carroll (2010).

First, an applied approach to HCI research is a way of addressing the topic or problem of designing applied human–computer interactions by using knowledge of other disciplines to support that design.

For example, disciplines such as psychology, sociology, ethnomethodology, linguistics and artificial intelligence have all been applied in different ways to support the design of human–computer interactions.

Second, an applied approach to HCI research requires the performing of actions to progress that approach to the topic or problem of applied human–computer interactions.

For example, relevant knowledge of other disciplines continues to be identified as being supportive of HCI design. Such knowledge is almost always descriptive, as in scientific knowledge, for example, psychology's finding that under many conditions recognition memory is more effective than recall memory. This knowledge needs to be rendered prescriptive for the purposes of applied design, for example, 'use recognition rather than recall memory for menu option selection, wherever possible'. Such prescription may take the form of guidelines, heuristics, methods, expert advice, other designs and case studies.

Third, an applied approach to HCI research requires the evaluating of the success of the actions performed to progress that approach.

For example, interactive systems whose design has been informed by applying knowledge of other disciplines can be assessed in terms of their success. The latter may be reflected in user satisfaction, workload, experience and design uptake. The extent to which this success has resulted from the application of guidelines, heuristics, methods, expert advice and other design case studies derived from other disciplines can also be assessed. In the absence of success, however, it is unclear (without further research) whether the original description of the knowledge of other disciplines or the derived HCI applied design prescription (or indeed both) is responsible.

Fourth, an applied approach to HCI research requires the cumulating of the successes as a way of establishing whether the topic or problem of applied HCI interactions has been addressed or not.

For example, current icon-based versus command-language-based implementations of email, internet banking and online shopping, such as the application of knowledge of other disciplines supported their design, exemplify the cumulating of such successes. This indicates that the topic or problem of applied human–computer interactions has been addressed.

7.2 Example of an Applied Approach to HCI Research

As an example of an applied approach to HCI research, Mancini et al. (2012) explore interspecies sense-making. The latter is in the context of dog-tracking and in the light of multi-species ethnography.

Mancini et al. claim that the domestic use of tracking technology with pets, although increasing, remains under-researched. They report an investigation of how tracking practices reconfigure human–dog relationships, changing both human and dog behaviours. They question the sense-making mechanisms by which both humans and dogs engage in context-based, meaningful exchanges via interactive technology's mediation. Mancini et al. claim to show how an indexical semiotic perspective, derived from anthrozoology, can be applied to inform the development of interspecies technology. Finally, they discuss the methodological issues raised by doing research with animals and propose an interspecies semiotics. The latter integrates both animal companions' and animal researchers' accounts into a common ethnographic observation.

On what grounds might Mancini et al. (2012) be classified as an applied approach to HCI research?

First, an applied approach to HCI research is a way of addressing the topic or problem of designing human–computer interactions by applying knowledge of other disciplines to support that design.

Mancini et al. claim that indexical semiotics can be applied to inform the development of interspecies interactive technology.

Second, an applied approach to HCI research requires the performing of actions to progress that approach to the topic or problem of designing human–computer interactions.

Mancini et al. investigate how tracking practices reconfigure human–dog relations, using an ethnographic approach. The investigation takes an anthrozoological perspective.

Third, an applied approach to HCI research requires the evaluating of the success of the actions performed to progress that approach.

Mancini et al. suggest that their account could be evaluated in relation to the semiotic work of animal behavioural researchers. They propose an integrative interspecies semiotic approach to studying the relation between humans, animals and technology.

Fourth, an applied approach to HCI research requires the cumulating of the successes as a way of establishing whether the topic or problem of applied HCI interactions has been addressed or not.

Mancini et al. report no such cumulating of successes. The latter is clearly not possible at this early stage of dog-tracking technology development demonstrated in their work.

Conclusion: On balance, Mancini et al.'s work can be classified as an applied approach to HCI research. The latter applies an ethnographic approach to the investigations reported. They interpret the findings within an anthrozoological perspective. However, there is little or no application of the knowledge to design at this time. This classification suggests that Mancini et al. could decide to support any of their future HCI research either on the basis of the applied approach, presented earlier (see 2.2 and 7.1), or on the basis of the specific applied framework, which follows.

7.3 Applied Framework for HCI Research

This section covers the core framework for HCI, including HCI research, the specific applied framework for HCI research, the applied design research exemplar and the lower-level applied framework.

7.3.1 Core Framework for HCI, Including HCI Research

The specific applied framework for HCI research is based on the core framework for the discipline of HCI, including HCI research. The core framework comprises discipline, general problem, particular scope, research, knowledge and practices (see 3.4).

7.3.2 Specific Applied Framework for HCI Research

The specific applied framework for HCI research, such as to be applicable to an applied approach to HCI, follows. It comprises the concepts and definitions of the core framework for the discipline of HCI, including HCI research (see 3.4), particularised for applied. Conceptualisation to application constitutes a one-to -many mapping. Providing more than one descriptor for the same concept is a way of facilitating this mapping. To aid researchers to apply the specific applied framework, an applications-supportive format follows. The specific applied framework includes the main concepts, their definitional concepts and their extended definitional concepts, such as to be applicable to an applied approach. The main concepts are presented in **Boldface** at first mention for easy identification, reference and application, but hold throughout. The definitional concepts appear in lower case. The extended definitional concepts appear in lower case and in (brackets). Each extended definition appears only once, but applies throughout, as appropriate.

The specific applied HCI framework comprises the following:

Discipline, as an academic (that is, scholarly) field (that is, branch/subject area) of study (that is, investigation of knowledge as division of information/learning) and

Applied, as applying knowledge of other disciplines (that is, to support design) and

Applied General Problem, as the design (that is, specification) of applied human–computer interactions and

Applied Particular Scope, as the design of applied human (that is, individual/group)–computer (that is, interactive/embedded) interaction (that is, active/passive) to do something (that is, action/task) as desired (that is, wanted/needed/experienced/felt/valued) and

Applied Research, as the diagnosis of applied design problems (that is, not as desired) and the prescription of applied design solutions (that is, as desired) as they relate to performance (that is, desired) for the acquisition (that is, creation) and for the validation (that is, confirmation) of knowledge to support practices and

Applied Knowledge, as heuristics/methods/expert advice/successful designs/ case studies (that is, as acquired and validated by applied research) and supports (that is, as facilitates/makes possible) applied practices and

Applied Practices, as trial and error/specify, implement and test (that is, as supported by applied knowledge, acquired and validated by applied research).

7.3.3 Applied Design Research Exemplar

The specific framework for HCI research, as applied, is considered to be more complete, coherent and fit for purpose than the earlier description afforded by the applied approach to HCI research (see 7.1). Hence, the applied framework is more rigorously specified than the applied approach and so more effectively supports thinking about and doing applied HCI research. As the framework is more rigorous, it offers firmer support to researchers attempting to apply it. Once applied and shared, it enables researchers to build on each other's work. Applied researchers share and build on each other's work by means of the applied artefacts they create, for example, aspects of internet banking, supported by applied design. However, exactly what is shared may remain implicit. These researchers also report on their work both internally to their academic institutions/communities and externally at conferences, for example, the ACM CHI Conference on Human Factors in Computing Systems series. The applied framework might be expected to support further these explicit types of exchanges and so the sharing of and building on each other's work.

The latter is further supported by a summary re-expression of the applied framework as an HCI design research exemplar. The use of the term 'exemplar' originates with Kuhn (1970). He conceives a scientific discipline as comprising a paradigm, a disciplinary matrix and shared exemplars. Building on the work of Long and Dowell (1989), Salter (2010) develops the concept of exemplar further and applies it to the engineering of economic systems. Here, the application is to HCI research in general and to specific HCI research frameworks in particular. The applied exemplar represents the complete design research cycle, which, once performed, constitutes a case study of applied HCI research. The exemplar is intended to support researchers in the application of the applied framework and is presented in Figure 7.1. The empty boxes are not required for the applied exemplar. However, they are required elsewhere for other specific design research exemplars. The empty boxes have been included here for completeness and to facilitate comparison between exemplars.

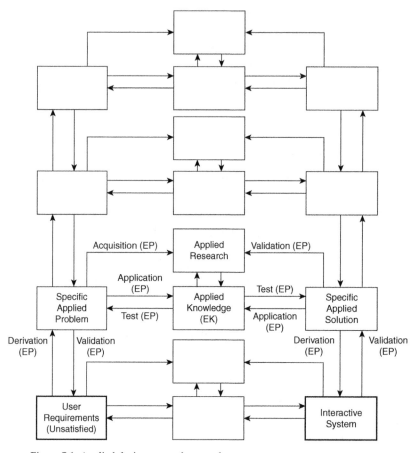

Figure 7.1 Applied design research exemplar
Key: Applied Knowledge: guidelines, heuristics, methods, expert advice, successful designs, case studies
EP: Empirical Practice
EK: Empirical Knowledge

The four first-level boxes represent the applied design cycle, starting on the outer left with User Requirements (Unsatisfied) and terminating on the outer right with an Interactive System (assumed to satisfy the user requirements). The design cycle details have not been included here. First, much of applied design is implicit or indirect and so cannot be represented explicitly or directly. Second, the function of the figure is to represent design research and not design per se. The design cycle, however, following the practices of the specific applied framework for HCI research (see 7.3.2) and for present purposes, might be assumed to include a design process (the two central boxes). The latter might be further assumed to comprise some combination of specification and implementation, interspersed with iterative trial-and-error cycles.

The Mancini et al. dog-tracking research (see 7.2) is reused as an illustration of a possible applied design research cycle. The latter might comprise specifying and implementing a domestic dog-tracking interactive system. The design of the latter is assumed to have been informed by an indexical semiotic perspective derived from anthrozoology. Reusing the Mancini et al. research example for the applied design research exemplar is intended better to support researchers attempting to apply the specific applied framework.

The four second-level boxes represent the applied design research cycle. The latter starts on the left with the Specific Applied Problem (of design) and terminates on the right with the Specific Applied Solution (of design), which solves the specific applied problem. In terms of the dog-tracking technology research illustration, the specific applied problem might be the failure of dogs to react appropriately to some of the signals sent by their owners to ensure their dogs' safety. The specific applied solution might be provided by a more recognisable and so appropriate set of signals, informed by indexical semiotics.

Following the applied design research exemplar, the Derivation of the specific applied problem is from, and its Validation is against, the user requirements. The specific applied problem is applied human–computer interactions not doing something as desired. In terms of the dog-tracking technology illustration, the user requirement might be to track pets more generally, and in particular as concerns safety. The user requirement might be an actual requirement, but could also be a possible and plausible requirement. Note that the difference between problems and user requirements is that the latter may or may not be satisfiable in practice. In contrast, the former are formulated so as to be soluble, at least in principle. Following this reasoning, a dog-tracking technology researcher might formulate the specific problem as the failure of dogs to react appropriately to some of the signals sent by their owners. The dogs' safety is jeopardised as a result. The limitation of the specific applied problem, relative to the possible and plausible user requirements, might be justified by the early stage of dog-tracking technology. This is exemplified by the research of Mancini et al.

The Acquisition of an expression of the specific applied problem, for example, the failure of dogs to react appropriately to some of the signals sent by their owners, is made by Applied Research. The latter also effects the validation, that is, confirms the specific applied solution against that expression, following the latter's initial formulation. The Application of the specific applied problem is expressed as the Applied Knowledge, needed for Test, that is, checked against the specific applied solution. The application of the latter is expressed as applied knowledge. The test of the latter is effected, that is, checked against the specific applied problem. Note that all the applied research processes are empirical, as is the resulting applied knowledge. In terms of the illustration, the applied knowledge might take the form of dog-tracking technology heuristics, methods, expert advice, successful designs and case studies. Such applied knowledge could be recruited to future dog-tracking technology research. However, the knowledge would remain empirical, that is, applicable neither analytically nor without test nor with guarantee.

Finally, the derivation of the specific applied solution is expressed for application to an interactive system (satisfying) the user requirements. The validation of the interactive system is effected against the specific design solution. In terms of the dog-tracking technology illustration, such a specific design solution might be as follows. The interactive system includes commands, which would be such as to support more appropriate reactions of dogs to signals. The latter might be sent by their owners to ensure the former's safety.

7.3.4 Lower-Level Applied Framework

The specific applied framework is here expressed at the highest level of description. That level is of the core HCI framework for research. However, to conduct and to report applied design research and to acquire/validate applied knowledge, a lower level of description is required. The latter is consistent with the design research exemplar.

Researchers might have their own applied lower-level descriptions or subscribe to some more generally recognised levels (for examples of such levels, see 12.3). Such descriptions are compatible with the specific applied framework as long as they are complete, coherent and fit for purpose, as concerns the higher-level core framework. Alternatively, and in addition, a lower-level framework description is presented in the associated chapter and design research exemplar for each type of specific HCI research framework (see 4.3.4–9.3.4).

These higher and lower levels of description go, for example, from the general human to the specific dog owner and from the general computer to the specific dog-tracking device. The lowest level must also reference the applied design itself, in terms of the application, for example, for an interactive system, dog owner and dog-tracking facility.

Following the applied design research exemplar, researchers need to specify specific applied problem (as it relates to user requirements), applied research, applied knowledge and specific applied solution (as it relates to interactive systems).

These specifications require the applied framework to include the application, interactive system and performance, relating the former to the latter. Applied design requires the interactive system to do something (the application) as desired (performance). Applied research acquires and validates applied knowledge to support applied design practices. Hence the following lower-level applied framework includes application, interactive system and performance.

The key lower-level concepts are shown in **Boldface** at first mention for easy identification, reference and application, but hold throughout.

7.3.4.1 Applied Application

An applied application can be described in many different ways for the purposes of HCI research. Here, following Dowell and Long (1989), the application is represented as objects, attributes and states. This is a standard way of representing applications and domains (Dinu and Nadkarni, 2007). Researchers are welcome to use alternative types of representation, providing the application specification is different from that of the interactive human–computer technology system. This difference is to support design by allowing either to be varied independently of the other. Whatever the approach or the framework providing structural support, design as specification and implementation inevitably involves the selection between alternative possible interactive design options. The latter are intended to achieve the same performance goals. To avoid confounding the means – the interactive system – with the ends – performance – it is important for the two to be described independently. This independence allows the means and the ends to be co-varied separately and independently. As stated, it is for this reason that researchers are welcome to use alternative types of representation to those proposed here. However, the lower-level description must be compatible with the higher-level core HCI research framework and be complete, coherent and fit for purpose.

An **Application** is described in terms of objects.

Applied Objects The applied application (what the interactive system does) can be described in terms of **Objects**. The latter comprise both **Physical Objects** and **Abstract Objects**. They are characterised by their attributes. Physical attributes are those of matter and energy. Abstract attributes are those of knowledge and information.

For example, an applied dog-tracking application favouring the recognition of meaningful owner-associated sounds over meaningless artificial sounds can be represented for design research purposes in terms of objects. Their abstract attributes support the communication of messages and their physical attributes support the audible representation of information by means of sounds. Dog-tracking technology following the research of Mancini et al. (see 7.2) is used here to exemplify the application of the lower-level framework. This provides continuity in the support for researchers attempting to apply the specific applied approach and framework.

Although representable at different levels of description, the user must at least be described for HCI research purposes at a level that relates to the transformation of applied objects.

For example, such a description might be a user as an experienced dog owner, who uses a dog-tracking application to allow their dog to self-exercise.

Applied Attributes The **Attributes** of an applied application object are represented at different levels of description.

For example, sounds and their ordering, transmitted by a dog-tracking application, are physical attributes of the object sound, expressed at one level. The dog-tracking message is an abstract attribute, expressed at a higher-level of description.

Applied Attribute States The attributes of an applied application object can be represented in terms of **States**, which may change.

For example, the content and sounds (attributes) of a dog-tracking application message (object) may change state, the content with respect to meaning and order, and its sounds with respect to volume and tone.

7.3.4.2 Applied Interactive System

Users have aims and the associated behaviours are considered to be goal-oriented/intentional.

For example, the behaviours of a dog owner and a tracking application whose goal is to track and to maintain the safety of dogs constitute an interactive system. Applied interactive systems change objects by producing transformations in their abstract and physical attributes. The dog owner and tracking application may transform the object message by changing both the attributes of its meaning and the attributes of its sound ordering. The changes may be brought about by means of owner-associated, as opposed to artificial, command instructions, the former being easier to use than the latter. This is a well-known psychology research finding for humans concerning the superior recall of meaningful material over non-meaningful material. Behaviour is what the user does. What is done is expressed as the attribute state changes of application objects.

Users The **Behaviours** of an applied **Interactive System** are both abstract and physical. Interactive system **Abstract Behaviours** include the acquisition, storage and transformation of information. They represent and process information concerning application objects, and also their attributes, relations and states. Further, they represent the transformations required by user goals. Interactive system **Physical Behaviours** are associated with and express abstract behaviours.

The user, then, is represented as a system of mental (that is, abstract) and physical (that is, overt) behaviours. **Mental behaviours** transform abstract application objects, represented by cognition, or express, through **physical behaviour**, plans for transforming application objects.

For example, an owner has the goal of maintaining the safety of their dog when the latter is self-exercising. The owner interacts with the tracking device by means of a digital sound-based interface. The latter's behaviours include the owner-associated sounds that embody their commands. Hence, the dog acquires a representation of the current message by listening to the information expressed by means of those sounds. The dog owner plans the attribute state changes necessary to maintain the dog's safety as desired. That decision is expressed in the instructions issued to the interactive tracking device through the overt behaviour of selecting menu options. The latter are meaningful owner-associated sounds, rather than artificial, non-meaningful ones.

Interactions Interaction of **User Behaviours** and **Computer Behaviours** is the basic unit of applied HCI research. The concern here is with the interactive system, rather than with the individual behaviours of its parts.

For example, the behaviours of an owner interact with the behaviours of a dog-tracking application. The owner's behaviours influence the behaviours of the interactive device, for example, accessing the command function. The behaviours of the interactive device influence the selection behaviour of the dog owner, for example, among possible commands. The design of their interaction – the owner's selection of the command function, the tracking device's suggestion of possible commands – constitutes the interactive system. The latter consists of the owner and interactive tracking device behaviours in their planning and control of the dog's safety. The interaction is the object of applied HCI research, favouring meaningful over artificial, non-meaningful sound commands. Hence the importance of the assignment of task goals to either the user or to the interactive computer.

For example, replacement of a misspoken command required by a message is a user goal, which can be expressed as a task goal of attribute state changes. The correctly spoken command requires an attribute state change in the sound ordering of the message. That state change may be a task goal assigned to the user by recalled command instructions, as in interaction with the behaviours of early text editor designs. Or it may be a task goal assigned to the interactive computer, as in interaction with the applied easily recognised GUI 'wrap-round' behaviours.

7.3.4.3 Applied Interactive System Performance

To do something (see 7.3.2 – specific applied framework) derives from the relationship of an interactive system with its application. It assimilates both how well the application is performed by the interactive system – as desired – and the costs incurred by it, in performing that well. They are expressed together as performance. They can be further differentiated, for example, as wanted/needed/experienced/felt/valued. Performance may be absolute or relative, in terms of a comparison to be improved upon or equalled. Human Performance, as expressed in the literature as time and errors, relates to performance, as proposed here. Errors are behaviours that increase user costs or reduce how well the application is performed or both. The time taken by user behaviours may loosely be associated with increased behavioural user costs.

For example, a new version of an applied dog-tracking application might be expected to improve dog/owner performance, relative to an earlier one.

User Costs Doing something as desired by means of an interactive system incurs costs for the human. Costs associated with the user are termed **User Behavioural Costs**.

For example, the behavioural costs of a dog owner selecting or attending to menu options of a tracking device may be experienced over time as tiredness, irritation or impatience.

User behavioural costs comprise both **Physical Costs** and **Mental Costs**.

For example, such costs might be of keying or of attending to sound command menu options. User behavioural physical costs may be expressed for applied design purposes as **Physical Workload**.

User behavioural mental costs are associated with knowing, reasoning and deciding. User behavioural mental costs may be expressed for HCI research purposes as **Mental Workload**. Recognition behavioural costs of meaningful material for humans, for example, have been shown by psychology to be lower than those of non-meaningful material. Physical and mental costs are often closely associated.

For example, the physical and mental behavioural costs of a dog owner may be associated with sound command menu option selection of a tracking device.

7.3.5 Example Application of an Applied Framework to an Applied Approach to HCI Research

The research of Mancini et al. (2012) can be considered to constitute an applied approach to HCI research (see 4.2). Their paper explores interspecies sense-making in the context of dog-tracking. The research investigates how tracking practices reconfigure human–dog relationships. The paper claims that an indexical semiotic perspective, derived from anthrozoology, can be applied to the development of interspecies technology. What potential does the Mancini approach to applied research offer the applied framework presented here?

First, the specific applied framework is for a discipline, as an academic field of study.

Potential: Mancini et al.'s approach adopts a semiotic perspective, which derives from the discipline of anthrozoology. Ethnographic observation constitutes the basis for their integration of the animal companions' and animal researchers' accounts. The concept of understanding, as in science, however, is not further developed, for example, in terms of explanation or prescription.

Second, the specific applied framework is for the application of knowledge of other disciplines.

Potential: Mancini et al. suggest additional functionality for dog-tracking technology on the basis of a semiotic perspective, derived from anthrozoology. The suggestions are informal. No further indexical semiotic prescriptions are proposed for the development of such interspecies technology.

Third, the specific applied framework is for the general problem as the design of applied human–computer interactions.

Potential: Mancini et al.'s approach associates their dog-tracking technology with interactions as desired and with the development of interspecies technology. However, the notion of the general problem of design, as it might relate to dog-tracking technology, is not developed further.

Fourth, the specific applied framework is for the particular scope of applied human–computer interactions to do something as desired.

Potential: Mancini et al.'s approach is intended to support the design of dog-tracking technology in the longer term. Their research reports no design, as such.

Fifth, the specific applied framework is for applied research as the diagnosis of applied design problems and the prescription of applied design solutions. The latter are as they relate to performance, for the acquisition and validation of knowledge to support practices.

Potential: Mancini et al.'s approach makes no reference as to how the acquisition and validation of indexical semiotic knowledge might be carried out, nor how that knowledge might be made prescriptive to support design and performance. Such references, however, at this stage of the research, might be considered premature.

Sixth, the specific applied framework is for applied knowledge, as heuristics/methods/expert advice/successful designs/case studies.

Potential: Mancini et al.'s approach offers an interesting, but general indexical semiotic perspective on human-interspecies interactions. No suggestions are made, however, in detail as to how that perspective can be made prescriptive such as to support applied design.

Seventh, the specific applied framework is for applied practices, as trial and error/implement and test.

Potential: Mancini et al.'s approach does not include design practice, although their indexical semiotic perspective is intended to support the work of designers in the longer term.

Conclusion: Mancini et al.'s approach to applied design could be further developed with respect to discipline details and in particular to the relations between the two general problems of understanding and design. Its level of description needs to be lower for design purposes. The explicit inclusion of applied design is also needed, along with the validation of its claims.

The applied framework proposed here is considered to have potential for contributing to such developments.

Conclusion

This concludes the presentation of the specific applied approach and the specific applied framework for HCI research and their exemplification. Also presented are the applied design research exemplar and the lower-level applied framework.

7.4 Research Practice Assignment

The assignment comprises two sections: General and Research Design Scenarios.

7.4.1 General

- Using the applied criteria presented in 7.3, select a recent paper from the HCI research literature that suggests itself to be potentially classifiable as applied research, as concluded for the paper of Mancini et al. (7.2).
  - Analyse and record the potential applied research example, in the manner of 7.1 and 7.2.
  - In the light of your analysis, decide whether on balance the research example can be classified as applied research or not. If so classifiable, continue with the research practice assignment. If not so classifiable, return to the beginning of the assignment and start again. Continue until a classifiable example of applied research is identified.

- Apply the specific applied framework for HCI research, presented in 7.3.2, to the research example you have classified as applied.
- Create a research design exemplar, following 7.3.3 and Figure 7.1, for the research example to which you have applied the applied framework.
- Re-express the research example to which you have applied the applied framework at the lower levels of applied framework description, presented in 7.3.4. Try to use all the key concepts.

Hints and Tips

Difficult to get started?

Try reading the chapter again, while at the same time thinking explicitly about applied in all its forms across a range of disciplines.

Describe your research (or that of others, if more appropriate) in terms of applied (of any type) before attempting to apply those of 7.1 and 7.2.

Difficult to complete?

Familiarise yourself with the concept of applied as it is described in the HCI research (and other) literature.

Note the similarities and differences between the different concepts of applied identified in the HCI research literature.

Test

- Write down the titles of 7.1 and 7.3. Complete the sections in your own words.
- Propose a new and improved set of titles for 7.1 and 7.3.
- Complete the new 7.1 and 7.3 in your own words.

7.4.2 Research Design Scenarios

All the research design scenarios in 4.4.2–9.4.2 require you to characterise your own work or that of others. The same characterisation can be used for all the scenarios. The requirement, however, is repeated in each scenario to support researchers who may be completing the research practice assignments out of order. They may not have produced a characterisation at that point in the book. It is also repeated for those researchers wishing to work with a range of different characterisations. They are encouraged and supported in creating multiple characterisations.

Research Design Scenario 7.1: Characterising Your Own or Another's Approach to HCI Research

Characterise your own HCI research approach by answering the following questions, which are intended to support you in creating such a characterisation. You should also call upon any other relevant aspects of the assignment as required. The characterisation should preferably be of your own current project. If you are not working on a project at this time, base the characterisation on a past project. Failing that, base the characterisation on a project of your supervisor or of a colleague. In the last resort, choose a research project published in the HCI literature. The most important part of the research design scenario is the support and practice it gives researchers in planning their research. Additional hints and tips follow each question in the form of notes.

The selection of the topic or problem per se by the research is not directly supported by the assignment or more generally by the book. What is supported, however, is the manner (of applied approach or of applied framework) by which the topic or problem is addressed, once selected. However, the former needs to be identified to carry out the latter. Further, the selection of the approach or framework supports the researcher in understanding the possibilities and implications for the selection of the research topic or problem. Research topic selection is generally some combination of the following: funding available for the project, researcher's curiosity or interest, supervisor's interests and previous work, and gaps in the HCI research literature. The latter may be identified by the researcher, the supervisor or the sponsor.

1. What topic or problem of designing human–computer interactions is addressed by the research and how is that topic or problem addressed?
Note: 'topic or problem' here should be understood widely to include any and all research activities considered to be relevant and important.

2. Which actions are performed by the research as a way of addressing the topic or problem of designing human–computer interactions?
Note: 'actions' here should be understood widely to include any and all research activities considered to be sufficiently relevant and important.

3. What are the ways of evaluating the success or not of the actions performed by the research to address the topic or problem of designing human–computer interactions?
Note: 'evaluating success' here should be understood widely. The particular forms of evaluation will depend on the approach taken by the research.

4. How does the research cumulate its successes in addressing the topic or problem of designing human–computer interactions?

Note: 'cumulating successes' here should be understood widely. The particular forms of cumulating will depend on the approach taken by the research.

Research Design Scenario 7.2: Applying the Applied Approach to Your Own or to Another's Approach to HCI Research

Suppose that you decide to change your current approach to HCI research in your next project to that of applied. Or if your present approach is already one of applied, suppose that you decide to apply the specific applied approach proposed here. In both cases, apply the applied approach to the earlier characterisation of your own or another's HCI research approach (see 7.4.1) by answering the following questions. They are intended to support you in making such an application. You should also call upon any other relevant aspects of the assignment as required. Additional hints and tips follow each question in the form of notes.

The selection of the topic or problem per se by the applied research is not directly supported by the assignment or more generally by the book. What is supported is the manner (of applied approach) by which the topic or problem is addressed, once selected. However, a topic or problem needs to be identified to apply an applied approach. Further, the latter supports the researcher in understanding the possibilities and implications for the applied research of selecting the former. Applied research topic selection is generally some combination of the following: funding available for the project, researcher's curiosity or interest, supervisor's interests and previous work, and gaps in the HCI research literature. The latter may be identified by the researcher, the supervisor or the sponsor.

1. What topic or problem of designing applied human–computer interactions by applying knowledge of other disciplines to support that design is to be addressed by the research and how will that topic or problem be addressed?

Note: 'topic or problem' here should be understood widely to include any and all research activities considered to be relevant and important.

2. Which actions are to be performed by the research as a way of addressing the topic or problem of designing applied human–computer interactions? How do these actions apply knowledge of other disciplines to support the design to be addressed by the research?

Note: 'actions' here should be understood widely to include any and all applied research activities considered to be sufficiently relevant and important.

3. Which ways of evaluating the success or not of the actions performed by the research will be employed to address the topic or problem of designing applied human–computer interactions by applying knowledge of other disciplines to support that design?

Note: 'evaluating success' here should be understood widely. The particular forms of evaluation will depend on the applied approach taken by the research.

4. How will the research cumulate its successes in addressing the topic or problem of designing applied human–computer interactions by applying knowledge of other disciplines to support that design?

Note: 'cumulating successes' here should be understood widely. The particular forms of cumulating will depend on the applied approach taken by the research.

Research Design Scenario 7.3: Applying the Applied Framework to Your Own or to Another's Approach to HCI Research

Suppose that you decide to change your current planned applied approach to HCI research, as you set out above, to research supported by the applied framework proposed here. The reason might be for increased rigour. In this research design scenario, apply the applied framework to your proposed applied approach by answering the following questions. Any other relevant aspects of the research practice assignment should also be called upon as required. Additional hints and tips follow each question in the form of notes.

The selection of the topic or problem per se by the applied research is not directly supported by the assignment or more generally by the book. What is supported is the manner (of applied framework) by which the topic or problem is addressed, once selected. However, a topic or problem needs to be identified to apply an applied framework. Further, the latter supports the researcher in understanding the possibilities and implications for the applied research of selecting the former. Applied research topic selection is generally some combination of the following: funding available for the project, researcher's curiosity or interest, supervisor's interests and previous work, and gaps in the HCI research literature. The latter may be identified by the researcher, the supervisor or the sponsor.

1. Which discipline, as an academic field of study, will be espoused by the conduct of the research, as supported by the applied framework?

Note: additional discipline aspects should be referenced as appropriate, such as scholarliness, branch/subject area, knowledge and information/learning.

2. How will applied as application of knowledge of other disciplines be conducted by the research, as supported by the applied framework?
Note: additional applied aspects should be referenced as appropriate, such as support for design.

3. What general problem of applied design of human–computer interaction will be addressed by the conduct of the research, as supported by the applied framework?
Note: additional general problem aspects should be referenced as appropriate, such as specification.

4. What particular scope of the general problem of applied design of human–computer interactions to do something as desired will be addressed by the conduct of the research, as supported by the applied framework?
Note: additional particular scope aspects of the general problem of applied design should be referenced as appropriate, such as individual/group human interactions and interactive/embedded computer interactions, and also aspects such as to do something – actions/task – as desired – wanted, needed, experienced, felt and/or valued.

5. What research, as the diagnosis of design problems and the prescription of design solutions, as they relate to performance for the acquisition and for the validation of knowledge to support practices, will be addressed by the conduct of the research, as supported by the applied framework?
Note: additional research aspects should be referenced as appropriate, such as the desired state or not of design problems/solutions, performance as doing something as desired, acquisition as creation, and validation as confirmation.

6. What knowledge, such as heuristics/methods/expert advice/successful designs/case studies, supporting applied practices will result from the conduct of the research as supported by the applied framework?
Note: additional knowledge aspects should be referenced as appropriate, such as applied knowledge acquisition, validation and support for practice.

7. What practices, as trial and error/specify, implement and test, will be involved in the conduct of the research, as supported by the applied framework?
Note: additional practice aspects should be referenced as appropriate, such as applied knowledge support, acquisition and validation.

8

Science Approach and Framework
for HCI Research

This chapter presents the science approach to HCI research, including an illustration from the literature. It then presents the specific science framework for HCI research. The latter is followed by the science design research exemplar and the lower-level science framework. Both the exemplar and the lower-level framework are applied to the same illustration of the science approach taken from the literature.

8.1 Science Approach to HCI Research

A science approach to HCI research is based on the general concept of approach (see 2.2). For a more general overview of the relationship between HCI and science, see Barnard (1991), Rauterberg (2006) and Carroll (2010).

First, a science approach to HCI research is a way of addressing the topic or problem of designing human–computer interactions by understanding such interactions in terms of explanation and prediction.

For example, scientific disciplines such as psychology, sociology, ethnomethodology, linguistics and artificial intelligence all seek to understand, in their different ways, human mental and physical behavioural phenomena. Human–computer interactions are an example of the latter.

Second, a science approach to HCI research requires the performing of actions to progress that approach to the topic or problem of human–computer interaction.

For example, the understanding offered by science can be indirectly applied to HCI design. It can be applied implicitly by trained psychologists. It can also be applied explicitly by the formulation of prescriptive design guidelines, as part of an applied approach to HCI (see 7.1).

Third, a science approach to HCI research requires the evaluating of the success of the actions performed to progress that approach.

For example, understanding human–computer interactions comprises the explanation of known HCI behavioural phenomena and the prediction of unknown phenomena, both by theory. Taken together, explanation and prediction constitute the validation of theory and so an understanding of the phenomena. The knowledge, however, can only be applied to HCI design indirectly by means of an applied approach to HCI (see 7.1) or somesuch.

Fourth, a science approach to HCI research requires the cumulating of the successes as a way of establishing whether the topic or problem of designing human–computer interactions has been addressed or not.

For example, incremental better understanding of icon-based versus text-based interactions in the form of a theory, such as it constitutes science, exemplifies the cumulating of such successes, the latter indicating that the topic or problem of designing science-based human–computer interactions has been addressed.

8.2 Example of a Science Approach to HCI Research

As an example of a science approach to HCI research, Barnard et al. (2000) argue that early HCI research was guided by a vision – that of using theory from psychology and cognitive science to develop engineering tools for HCI design. Given the extensive advances in computing technology, they present the case for developing new forms of deep theory, based on generic systems of inter-actors. Such an overlapping, layered structure of macro- and micro-theories could then serve an explanatory function, of human behaviour generally and human–computer interaction behaviour specifically. The resultant psychology-theory-based understanding would serve as the basis for developing engineering tools to support the design of interactive behaviours for using interactive computer systems.

On what grounds might Barnard et al.'s work be classified as a science approach to HCI research?

First, a science approach to HCI research is a way of addressing the topic or problem of designing human–computer interactions by understanding such interactions as explanation and prediction.

Barnard et al. argue that the new psychology theories, such as they propose, are candidate contributors to understanding the phenomena of humans inter-acting with computers. The theories can serve as the basis for developing engineering tools to support the design of such interactions.

Second, a science approach to HCI research requires the performing of actions to progress that approach to the topic or problem of human–computer interaction.

Barnard et al. argue that the understanding offered by new macro-theories in psychology, such as interacting cognitive subsystems, constitute the products of HCI research. The latter can inform the design of human–computer interactions indirectly by means of engineering tools derived from such theories.

Third, a science approach to HCI research requires the evaluating of the success of the actions performed to progress that approach.

Barnard et al.'s science approach to HCI research, for example, can be evaluated in terms of their psychology theories' success in understanding, that is, explaining and predicting, the phenomena of human–computer interactions. Their science approach can also be evaluated with respect to its support for HCI design by means of associated engineering tools.

Fourth, a science approach to HCI research requires the cumulating of the successes as a way of establishing whether the topic or problem of designing human–computer interactions has been addressed or not.

Barnard et al. report no assessment and so no such cumulating of successes. This is not surprising, given the early stage of the research into macro-theories, as demonstrated in their work.

Conclusion: On balance, Barnard et al.'s research can be classified as a science approach to HCI research. It satisfies most of the criteria. It assumes the ability of new theories of psychology, such as they propose, to contribute albeit indirectly to the design of human–computer interactions. The contribution takes the form of the understanding of the latter and by the engineering tools derived from that understanding. This classification suggests that Barnard et al. could decide to support any of their future HCI macro-theory research either on the basis of the science approach, presented earlier (see 8.1), or on the basis of the science framework, which follows.

8.3 Science Framework for HCI Research

This section covers the core framework for HCI, including HCI research, the specific science framework for HCI research, the science design research exemplar and the lower-level science framework.

8.3.1 Core Framework for HCI, Including HCI Research

The specific science framework for HCI research is based on the core framework for the discipline of HCI, including HCI research. The core framework comprises discipline, general problem, particular scope, research, knowledge and practices (see 3.4).

8.3.2 Specific Science Framework for HCI Research

The specific science framework for HCI research, such as to be applicable to a science approach to HCI, follows. It comprises the concepts and definitions of the core framework for the discipline of HCI, including HCI research (see 3.4), particularised for science. Conceptualisation to application constitutes a one-to-many mapping. Providing more than one descriptor for the same concept is a way of facilitating this mapping. To aid researchers to apply the specific science framework, an applications-supportive format follows. The specific science framework includes the main concepts, their definitional concepts and their extended definitional concepts, such as to be applicable to a science approach. The main concepts are presented in **Boldface** at first mention for easy identification, reference and application, but hold throughout. The definitional concepts appear in lower case. The extended definitional concepts appear in lower case and in (brackets). Each extended definition appears only once, but applies throughout, as appropriate.

The specific science HCI framework comprises the following:

Discipline, as an academic (that is, scholarly) field (that is, branch/subject area) of study (that is, investigation of knowledge as division of information/learning) and

Science, as understanding (that is, explanation and prediction) and

Science General Problem, as the design (that is, specification) of human–computer interactions on the basis of science understanding and

Science Particular Scope, as the design, on the basis of science understanding, of human (that is, individual/group)–computer (that is, interactive/embedded) interaction (that is, active/passive) to do something (that is, action/task) as desired (that is, wanted/needed/experienced/felt/valued) and

Science Research, as the diagnosis of science design problems (that is, not as desired) and the prescription of science design solutions (that is, as desired) as they relate to performance (that is, desired) for the acquisition (that is, creation) and for the validation (that is, confirmation) of knowledge to support practices and

Science Knowledge, as theories, models, laws, data, hypotheses, analytical and empirical methods and tools (that is, as acquired and validated by

science research) and supports (that is, as facilitates/makes possible)
science practices and

Science Practices, as understanding (that is, explanation and prescription)
to support trial and error/specify, implement and test (that is, acquired
and validated by science research).

8.3.3 Science Design Research Exemplar

The specific science framework for HCI research is considered to be more
complete, coherent and fit for purpose than the earlier description afforded
by the science approach to HCI research (see 8.1). Hence, the science
framework is more rigorously specified than the science approach and so
more effectively supports thinking about and doing science HCI research.
As the framework is rigorous, it offers firmer support to researchers
attempting to apply it. Once applied and shared, it enables researchers to
build on each other's work. Science researchers share and build on each
other's work by means of the theories they create. What is shared, then, is
explicit. However, many of these researchers also claim that their research
can be applied to the design of human–computer interactions by trained
psychologists, albeit indirectly. Thus, they also report on their work at
conferences both to HCI practitioners and to applied researchers, for example, the ACM CHI Conference on Human Factors in Computing Systems
series. The science framework might be expected to support further these
explicit types of exchanges and so the sharing of and building on each
other's work.

The latter is further supported by a summary re-expression of the science
framework as an HCI design research exemplar. The use of the term 'exemplar'
originates with Kuhn (1970). He conceives of a scientific discipline as comprising a paradigm, a disciplinary matrix and shared exemplars. Building on the
work of Long and Dowell (1989), Salter (2010) develops the concept of
exemplar further and applies it to the engineering of economic systems. Here,
the application is to HCI research in general and to specific HCI research
frameworks in particular. The science exemplar represents the complete design
research cycle, which, once performed, constitutes a case study of science HCI
research. The exemplar is intended to support researchers in the application of
the science framework and is presented in Figure 8.1. The empty boxes are not
required for the science exemplar. However, they are required elsewhere for
other specific design research exemplars. The empty boxes have been included
here for completeness. They facilitate comparison between exemplars. Design

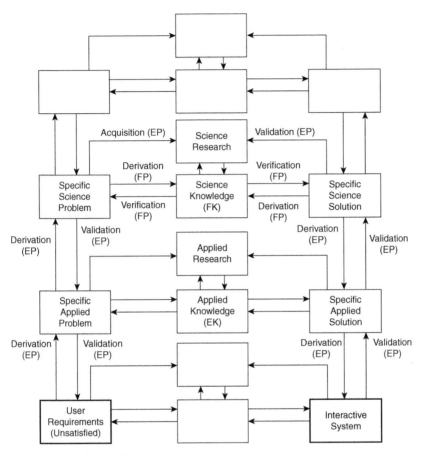

Figure 8.1 Science design research exemplar
Key: Science Knowledge: theories, models, laws, data, hypotheses, analytical and empirical
methods, tools
EP: Empirical Practice
EK: Empirical Knowledge
FP: Formal Practice
FK: Formal Knowledge

research concepts are Capitalised at first mention for easy identification, reference and application, but apply throughout.

The four first-level boxes represent the science design cycle, starting on the outer left with User Requirements (Unsatisfied) and terminating on the outer right with an Interactive System (assumed to satisfy the user requirements). The design cycle details have not been included here. First, much of science-based design is implicit or indirect and so cannot be represented explicitly or directly. Second, the function of the figure is to represent design research and not design per se. The design cycle, however, following the practices of the specific science framework for HCI research (see 8.3.2) and for present purposes, might be assumed to include a design process (the two central boxes) as some combination of specification and implementation, interspersed with iterative trial-and-error cycles.

The Barnard et al. deep theory research (see 8.2) is reused as an illustration of a possible science-based design research cycle. The latter might comprise specifying and implementing a system of additional interactors-informed video-communications channels to an interactive teleconferencing system. The addition of the latter might be in response to user requirements for improved video communication. Re-using the Barnard et al. research example for the science design research exemplar is intended better to support researchers attempting to apply the specific science framework.

The four second-level boxes represent the applied design research cycle, starting on the left with the Specific Applied Problem (of design) and terminating on the right with the Specific Applied Solution (of design), which solves the specific applied problem. In terms of the deep theory research illustration, the specific applied problem might be insufficient communication channels for an interactive teleconferencing system. The specific applied solution might be an interactive system with added video-communications channels. The design of the latter would be supported, for example, by an engineering tool conforming to interactors-informed guidelines.

Following the science design research exemplar, the Derivation of the specific applied problem is from, and its Validation is against, the user requirements. The specific applied problem is human–computer interactions not doing something as desired. In terms of the deep theory research illustration, the user requirement might be improved teleconferencing video communications, as desired. The user requirement might be an actual requirement, but could also be a possible and plausible requirement. Note that the difference between problems and user requirements is that the latter may or may not be satisfiable in practice. The former are formulated so as to be soluble, at least in principle. Following this reasoning, deep theory research might formulate the specific applied problem as insufficient communication channels for an interactive teleconferencing system. The limitation of the specific applied problem, relative to the possible and plausible user requirements, might be justified by the early stage of deep theory and the associated research, as exemplified by that of Barnard et al.

No further details are provided here concerning the research required to create a specific applied solution to a specific applied problem by use of a science-understanding-based tool. The design research exemplar is for science and not for applied science as such. Details concerning the latter, however, are presented for applied research elsewhere (see 7.3.3 and Figure 7.1). The specific applied solution supports the derivation of the interactive system, which in turn supports its validation by the specific applied solution.

The four third-level boxes represent the science design research cycle, starting on the left with the Specific Science Problem and terminating on the right with the Specific Science Solution, which solves the specific science problem. In terms of the deep theory research illustration, the specific science problem might be understanding the attentional integration of an additional video-communications channel for interactive teleconferencing systems. The specific science solution might be a deep, interactors-based theory, embodying the understanding of that attentional integration of an additional video-communications channel. The limitation of the specific science problem, relative to the possible and plausible specific applied problem, might be justified by the early stage of deep theory and the associated research, as exemplified by that of Barnard et al.

Following the science design research exemplar, the derivation of the specific science problem is from, and its validation is against, that of the specific applied problem. The processes are empirical. The specific applied problem is human–computer interactions not doing something as desired. In terms of the deep theory research illustration, the specific science problem might be formulated as the need to understand the attentional integration of an additional video-communications channel for interactive teleconferencing systems.

Also, following the design research exemplar, the derivation of the specific applied solution is from, and its validation is against, the specific science solution. The processes are empirical. The specific applied solution is prescriptive for human–computer interactions doing something as desired. In terms of the deep theory research illustration, the specific applied solution might take the form of an engineering tool, based on theory. The latter would embody the understanding of the attentional integration of an additional video-communications channel for interactive teleconferencing systems.

The Acquisition by Science Research comprises an expression of the specific science problem, for example, understanding the attentional integration of an additional video-communications channel for interactive teleconferencing systems. The validation of the specific science solution is effected by science research against an expression of the specific science problem. The derivation of the Science Knowledge is from the specific science problem and its Verification is against the specific science solution. In turn, the derivation of the science knowledge is from the specific science solution and its verification against the specific science problem. Note that the derivation of the science knowledge and its verification processes are formal only once the associated knowledge has been validated, that is, conceptualised, operationalised, tested and generalised (see 11.4). In terms of the deep theory illustration, the science knowledge might take the form of an interactors-based theory, embodying the understanding of the attentional integration of an additional video-communications channel for interactive teleconferencing systems.

Although not included here, a General Science Problem to General Science Solution level could be added to the exemplar in the empty boxes. The general science problem would be derived from and validated against the specific science problem. The general science solution would be derived from and validated against the specific science solution. The remaining components of the specific science problem/solution level would remain the same, but as applicable to the general science problem/general science solution level.

8.3.4 Lower-Level Science Framework

The specific science framework has so far been expressed only at the highest level of description. That level is of the core framework for research. However, to conduct and to report science design research and to acquire/validate science knowledge, a lower-level description is required. The latter is consistent with the design research exemplar.

Researchers might have their own science lower-level descriptions or subscribe to some more generally recognised levels (for examples of such levels, see 12.3). Such descriptions are compatible with the specific science framework, as long as they are complete, coherent and fit for purpose, as concerns the higher-level core framework. Alternatively, and in addition, a lower-level framework description is presented in the associated chapter, along with the design research exemplar for each type of specific HCI research framework (see 4.3.4–9.3.4).

These higher and lower levels of description need to go respectively, for example, from the general human to the specific teleconferencing participant and from the general computer to the specific multiple communications channels receiver. The lowest level must reference the science itself, in terms of the application, for example, the science phenomena to be understood, as concerns a teleconferencing interactive system involving participants and an electronic communications facility.

Following the science design research exemplar, researchers need to specify the specific science problem (as it relates to user requirements), science research, science knowledge and specific science solution (as it relates to interactive systems).

These specifications need also to include the application, interactive system and performance relating the former to the latter. Science design support requires the interactive system to do something (the application) as desired (performance). Science research acquires and validates science knowledge to support science-based design practice. Hence, the following lower-level science framework includes application, interactive system and performance.

The key lower-level concepts are shown in **Boldface** at first mention for easy identification, reference and application, but hold throughout.

8.3.4.1 Science Application

A science application can be described in many different ways for the purposes of HCI research. Here, following Dowell and Long (1989), the application is represented as objects, attributes and states. This is a standard way of representing applications and domains (Dinu and Nadkarni, 2007). Researchers are welcome to use alternative types of representation, providing the application specification is different from that of the interactive human–computer technology system. This difference is to support design by allowing either to be varied independently of the other. Whatever the approach or the framework providing structural support, design as specification and implementation inevitably involves the selection between alternative possible interactive design options. The latter are intended to achieve the same performance goals. To avoid confounding the means – the interactive system – with the ends – performance – it is important for the two to be described independently. This independence allows the means and the ends to be co-varied separately and independently. As stated, it is for this reason that researchers are welcome to use alternative types of representation to those proposed here. However, the lower-level description must be compatible with the higher-level core HCI research framework and be complete, coherent and fit for purpose.

An **Application** is described in terms of objects.

Science Objects The science application (what the interactive system does) can be described in terms of **Objects**. The latter comprise both **Physical Objects** and **Abstract Objects**. They are characterised by their attributes. Physical attributes are those of matter and energy. Abstract attributes are those of knowledge and information.

For example, phenomena associated with a teleconferencing application can be represented as objects. The latter may support the recognition of text and images over the recall of commands. The purpose may be the control of multiple communications channels. The objects and their abstract attributes may support the communication of instructions, their physical attributes supporting the visual/verbal representation of displayed information by means of language. Science objects are specified as part of the phenomena to be explained and predicted and so understood, and can be researched as such. They can also be incorporated in the development of associated design tools. Science teleconferencing technology, following the research of Barnard et al. (see 8.2), is used here to exemplify the application of the lower-level framework. This provides continuity in the support for researchers attempting to apply the specific science approach and framework.

Although representable at different levels of description, the user must at least be described for HCI research purposes at a level that relates to the transformation of science objects.

For example, a participant interacting with a teleconferencing application is described as a user, whose behaviours include receiving and replying to messages by means of recognised, rather than recalled, command instructions, as supported by science knowledge.

Science Attributes The **Attributes** of a science application object are expressed at different levels of description.

For example, characters and their configuration on a teleconferencing display are physical attributes of the object communication, expressed at one level. The meaning of the message on the display is an abstract attribute, expressed at a higher level of description.

Science Attribute States The attributes of science application objects can be represented in terms of **States**, which may change.

For example, the content and characters (attributes) of a communication (object) may change state, the content with respect to meaning and grammar, its characters with respect to size and font, and its sounds with respect to volume and frequency.

8.3.4.2 Science Interactive System

Users have aims and their associated behaviours are considered to be goal-oriented/intentional.

For example, the behaviours of a teleconference participant and the multiple communications channel application, whose purpose is to support conferencing, constitute an interactive system. Such interactive systems transform objects by producing state changes in the abstract and physical attributes of those objects. The participant and teleconferencing application may transform the object communication by changing both the attributes of its meaning and the attributes of its display. The transformation may be supported by means of recognised, as opposed to recalled, command instructions. The latter may be derived from science knowledge and used to support interactive system tool design. Behaviour is what the user does. What is done is expressed as the attribute state changes of application objects.

Users The **Behaviours** of a science **Interactive System** are both abstract and physical. **Abstract Behaviours** include the acquisition, storage and transformation of information. They represent and process information concerning application objects. Also represented are their attributes, relations and states. Further, they represent the transformations required by user goals. **Physical Behaviours** are associated with, and express, abstract behaviours.

The user, then, is represented as a system of both mental (that is, abstract) and physical (that is, overt) behaviours. User **Mental Behaviours** transform abstract application objects, represented by cognition, or express, through user **Physical Behaviours**, plans for transforming application objects.

For example, the behaviours of a teleconference participant and a multiple channel communication application, whose purpose is to support conferencing, constitute an interactive system. Interactive systems transform objects by producing state changes in the abstract and physical attributes of those objects. The participant and the teleconferencing application may transform the object communication by changing both the attributes of its meaning and the attributes of its display layout. The change may be made by means of recognised, as opposed to recalled, command instructions, as derived from science knowledge. Behaviour may be loosely understood as what the user does, in contrast with what is done (that is, attribute state changes of application objects).

Interactions Interaction of **User Behaviours** and **Computer Behaviours** is the basic unit of science HCI research. The concern here is with the interactive system, rather than with the individual behaviours of its parts.

For example, the behaviours of a participant interact with the behaviours of a teleconferencing application. The participant's behaviours influence the behaviours of the interactive system (access to communication channel selection), while the behaviours of the interactive system influence the selection behaviour of the participant (among possible appropriate selections). The design of their interaction – the participant's channel selection, the computer's presentation of possible channel selections – determines the interactive system. The latter consists of the participant and interactive teleconferencing system behaviours in their planning and control of communications supporting teleconferencing. The interaction may be the object of science-based design, favouring recognition over recall, and so design research. Hence the importance of the assignment of task goals to either the user or to the interactive computer.

For example, changing an inappropriate communications channel required in a teleconference is a goal, which can be expressed as a task goal structure of necessary and related attribute state changes. In particular, the display of the appropriate channel demands an attribute state change in the format of the display. Specifying that state change may be a task goal assigned to the participant by the recall of selection instructions, as in interaction with the behaviours of early text editor designs. Or it may be a task goal assigned to the interactive system, as in interaction with easily recognised wrap-round behaviours. Science research aims to inform such design, albeit indirectly, by seeking to understand, that is, explain and predict, associated phenomena. The assignment of the expression of the task goal of channel selection constitutes the design of the interaction of the user and interactive computer behaviours in each case. This in turn may become the object of science research.

8.3.4.3 Science Interactive System Performance

To do something (see 8.3.2 – specific science framework) derives from the relationship of an interactive system with its application. It assimilates both how well the application is performed by the interactive system – as desired – and the costs incurred by it, in performing that well. They are expressed together as performance. Costs can be further differentiated, for example, as wanted/needed/experienced/felt/valued. Desired performance is the object of design and is assumed to be indirectly derivable from science knowledge. Performance may be absolute or relative, as in a comparison to be improved upon or be equalled. Human Performance, as expressed in the literature as time and errors, relates to performance, as proposed here. Errors are behaviours that increase user costs or reduce how well the application is performed or both. The time taken by user behaviours may loosely be associated with increased behavioural user costs.

For example, a teleconference participant may be expected to make fewer errors, such as selecting an inappropriate communications channel, in a later version of the interactive system, relative to an earlier version.

User Costs Doing something as desired by means of an interactive system incurs costs for the human. Costs associated with the user are termed **User Behavioural Costs**.

For example, the behavioural costs of a participant in a teleconference attending to or selecting menu options may be experienced over time as tiredness, irritation or impatience.

User behavioural costs comprise both **Physical Costs** and **Mental Costs**.

For example, such costs might be of a teleconference participant attending to or selecting channel menu options. User behavioural physical costs may be expressed for science HCI research purposes as **Physical Workload**.

User behavioural mental behavioural costs are associated with knowing, reasoning and deciding. User behavioural mental costs may be expressed for science HCI research purposes as **Mental Workload**. Recognition behavioural costs, for example, have been shown by psychology research to be generally lower than those of recall behaviours.

For example, the physical and mental behavioural costs of a teleconference participant may be associated with channel option attention or selection.

8.3.5 Example Application of a Science Framework to a Science Approach to HCI Research

The research of Barnard et al. (2000) can be considered to constitute a science approach to HCI (see 8.2). They note that early HCI research sought to apply psychology theory to HCI design. To accommodate the increasing range of advances in computing technology, however, Barnard et al. propose new forms of deep theory, based on generic systems of interactors. Such an overlapping, layered structure of macro- and micro-theories would then serve an explanatory function for human behaviour, including human–computer interactions. The latter would inform HCI design by means of the development of engineering design tools. What potential does the Barnard et al. science approach to HCI research offer the science framework proposed here?

First, the specific science framework is for a discipline, as an academic field of study.

Potential: Barnard et al.'s science approach considers cognitive theory to belong to the scientific discipline of psychology. Their deep theory of systems interactors constitutes an instance of cognitive theory.

Second, the specific science framework is for science as understanding.

Potential: Barnard et al.'s science approach is concerned primarily with understanding as explanation. No reference is made to prediction, which is not surprising given the early stage of their research.

Third, the specific science framework is for the general problem as the design of human–computer interactions, based on science understanding.

Potential: Barnard et al.'s science approach addresses the general problem of understanding in the form of the explanation of human–computer interactions, although not so far of their prediction or their design.

Fourth, the specific science framework is for the particular scope of human–computer interaction design on the basis of science understanding to do something as desired.

Potential: Barnard et al.'s science approach is intended to address both the general problem of understanding and the particular scope of engineering tool derivation to support the design of human–computer interactions as desired.

Fifth, the specific science framework is for science research as the diagnosis of science design problems and the prescription of science design solutions, as they relate to performance for the acquisition and for the validation of knowledge to support practices.

Potential: Barnard et al.'s science approach proposes a new type of deep theory, based on systems of interactors. Validation is premature at this stage of the research, as is prediction and its indirect application to the design of human–computer interactions by the development of engineering design tools.

Sixth, the specific science framework is for science knowledge, as theories, models, laws, data, hypotheses, analytical and empirical methods and tools, and supports practices.

Potential: Barnard et al.'s science approach proposes a new type of deep theory, including models based on systems of interactors. Support for practices has yet to be addressed.

Seventh, the specific science framework is for science practices, as science-based trial and error/implement and test.

Potential: Barnard et al.'s science approach is concerned primarily with explanation and the associated theory. Given the early stage of the research, unsurprisingly no reference is made to prediction or to any details concerning a possible contribution to engineering design tools.

Conclusion: Barnard et al.'s approach to HCI as science could be further developed with respect to scientific practice of prediction and validation of their proposed theory, and also with respect to its application to the practices of HCI design by way of engineering tools. The science framework proposed here is considered to have potential for contributing to such developments.

Conclusion

This concludes the presentation of the specific science approach and the specific science framework for HCI research and their exemplification. Also presented are the science design research exemplar and the lower-level science framework.

8.4 Research Practice Assignment

The assignment comprises two sections: General and Research Design Scenarios.

8.4.1 General

- Using the science criteria presented in 8.3, select a recent paper from the HCI research literature that suggests itself to be potentially classifiable as science research, as concluded for the Barnard et al. (2000) (see 8.2).
  - Analyse the potential science research example, in the manner of 8.1 and 8.2.
  - In the light of your analysis, decide whether on balance the research example can be classified as science research or not. If so classifiable, continue with the research practice assignment. If not so classifiable, return to the beginning of the assignment and start again. Continue until a classifiable example of science research is identified.
- Apply the science framework for HCI research, presented in 8.3.2, to the research example you have classified as science.
- Create a research design exemplar, following 8.3.3 and Figure 8.1, for the research example to which you have applied the science framework.
- Re-express the research example to which you have applied the science framework at the lower level of science framework description, presented in 8.3.4. Try to use all the key concepts.

Hints and Tips

Difficult to get started?

Try reading the chapter again, while at the same time thinking explicitly about science in all its forms, whether in support of engineering or the sciences, in the development of information technology or your own professional life.

Describe your research in terms of science (of any type) before attempting to apply those of 8.1 and 8.2.

Difficult to complete?

Familiarise yourself with the concept of science as it is applied in the HCI research (and other) literature.

Note the similarities and differences between the different concepts of science identified in the HCI research literature.

Test

- Write down the titles of 8.1 and 8.3. Complete the sections in your own words.
- Propose a new and improved set of titles for 8.1 and 8.3.
- Complete the new 8.1 and 8.3 in your own words.

8.4.2 Research Design Scenarios

All the research design scenarios in 4.4.2–9.4.2 require you to characterise your own work or that of others. The same characterisation can be used for all the scenarios. The requirement, however, is repeated in each scenario to support researchers who may be completing the research practice assignments out of order and who will not have produced a characterisation at that point in the book. It is also repeated for those researchers wishing to work with a range of different characterisations. They are encouraged and supported to create such multiple characterisations.

Research Design Scenario 8.1: Characterising Your Own or Another's Approach to HCI Research

Characterise your own HCI research approach by answering the following questions, which are intended to support you in creating such a characterisation. You should call on any other relevant aspects of the assignment as required. The characterisation should preferably be of your own current project. If you are not working on a project at this time, base the characterisation on a past project. Failing that, base the characterisation on a project of your supervisor or of a colleague. In the last resort, choose a research project published in the HCI literature. The most important part of the research design scenario is the support and practice it gives researchers in planning their research. Additional hints and tips follow each question in the form of notes.

The selection of the topic or problem per se by the research is not directly supported by the assignment or more generally by the book. What is supported, however, is the manner (of science approach or of science framework) by which the topic or problem is addressed, once selected. However, the former needs to be identified to carry out the latter. Further, the selection of the approach or the framework supports the researcher in understanding the possibilities and implications for the selection of the research topic or problem. The latter is generally some combination of the following: funding available for the project, researcher's curiosity or interest, supervisor's interests and previous work, and gaps in the HCI research literature. The latter may be identified by the researcher, the supervisor or the sponsor.

1. What topic or problem of designing human–computer interactions is addressed by the research and how is that topic or problem addressed?
   Note: 'topic or problem' here should be understood widely to include any and all research activities considered to be relevant and important.

2. Which actions are performed by the research as a way of addressing the topic or problem of designing human–computer interactions?
   Note: 'actions' here should be understood widely to include any and all research activities considered to be sufficiently relevant and important.

3. What are the ways of evaluating the success or not of the actions performed by the research to address the topic or problem of designing human–computer interactions?
   Note: 'evaluating success' here should be understood widely. The particular forms of evaluation will depend on the approach taken by the research.

4. How does the research cumulate its successes in addressing the topic or problem of designing human–computer interactions?
   Note: 'cumulating successes' here should be understood widely. The particular forms of cumulating will depend on the approach taken by the research.

Research Design Scenario 8.2: Applying the Science Approach to Your Own or to Another's Approach to HCI Research

Suppose that you decide to change your current approach to HCI research in your next project to that of science. Or if your present approach is already one of science, suppose that you decide to apply the specific science approach proposed here. In both cases, apply the science approach to the earlier characterisation of your own or another's HCI research approach by answering the following questions. They are intended to support you in making such an application. Any other relevant aspects of the assignment should also be called upon as required. Additional hints and tips follow each question in the form of notes.

The selection of the topic or problem per se by the science research is not directly supported by the assignment or more generally by the book. What is supported, however, is the manner (of science approach) by which the topic or problem is addressed, once selected. However, a topic or problem needs to be identified to apply a science-based approach. Further, the latter supports the researcher in understanding the possibilities and implications for the science research of selecting the former. Science research topic selection is generally some combination of the following: funding available for the project, researcher's curiosity or interest, supervisor's interests and previous work, and gaps in the HCI research literature. The latter may be identified by the researcher, the supervisor or the sponsor.

1. What topic or problem of designing human–computer interactions on the basis of science understanding, as explanation and prediction of such interactions, is to be addressed by the research and how will that topic or problem be addressed?

Note: 'topic or problem' here should be understood widely to include any and all science research activities considered to be relevant and important.

2. Which actions are to be performed by the research as a way of addressing the topic or problem of designing human–computer interactions on the basis of science understanding as explanation and prediction of such interactions?

Note: 'actions' here should be understood widely to include any and all science research activities considered to be sufficiently relevant and important.

3. Which ways of evaluating the success or not of the actions performed by the research will be employed to address the topic or problem of designing human–computer interactions on the basis of a science understanding, as explanation and prediction, of such interactions?

Note: 'evaluating success' here should be understood widely. The particular forms of evaluation will depend on the science approach taken by the research.

4. How will the research cumulate its successes in addressing the topic or problem of designing human–computer interactions on the basis of science understanding of such interactions?

Note: 'cumulating successes' here should be understood widely. The particular forms of cumulating will depend on the science approach taken by the research.

Research Design Scenario 8.3: Applying the Science Framework to Your Own or to Another's Approach to HCI Research

Suppose that you decide to change your current planned science approach to HCI research, as you set out above, to research, supported by the science framework proposed here. The reason might be, for example, for increased rigour. In this research design scenario, apply the science framework to your proposed science approach by answering the following questions. You should also call upon any other relevant aspects of the research practice assignment as required. Additional hints and tips follow each question in the form of notes.

The selection of the topic or problem per se by the science research is not directly supported by the assignment or more generally by the book. What is supported is the manner (of science framework) by which the topic or problem is addressed, once selected. However, a topic or problem needs to be identified to apply a science framework. Further, the latter supports the researcher in understanding the possibilities and implications for the science research of selecting the former. Science research topic selection is generally some combination of the following: funding available for the project, researcher's curiosity or interest, supervisor's interests and previous work, and gaps in the HCI research literature. The latter may be identified by the researcher, the supervisor or the sponsor.

1. Which discipline, as an academic field of study, will be espoused by the conduct of the research, as supported by the science framework?
Note: additional discipline aspects should be referenced as appropriate, such as scholarliness, branch/subject area, knowledge and information/ learning.

2. How will understanding human–computer interactions be conducted by the research as supported by the science framework?
Note: additional understanding aspects should be referenced as appropriate, such as explanation and prediction.

3. What general problem of design on the basis of science understanding will be conducted by the research as supported by the science framework?
Note: additional general problem aspects should be referenced as appropriate, such as specification.

4. What particular scope of the general problem of design of human–computer interactions, to do something as desired, on the basis of science understanding, will be conducted by the research, as supported by the science framework?
Note: additional particular scope aspects of the general problem of science-based design should be referenced as appropriate, such as individual/group human interactions and interactive/embedded computer interactions, and also aspects such as to do something – actions/task – as desired – wanted, needed, experienced, felt and/or valued.

5. What research, as the diagnosis of design problems and the prescription of design solutions, as they relate to performance for the acquisition and for the validation of knowledge to support practices, will be addressed by the conduct of the research, as supported by the science framework?

Note: additional research aspects should be referenced as appropriate, such as the desired state or not of the design problems/solutions, performance as doing something as desired, acquisition as creation, and validation as confirmation.

6. What knowledge, such as theories, models, laws, data, hypotheses, analytical and empirical methods, and tools, supporting practices, will result from the conduct of the research, as supported by the science framework?

Note: additional knowledge aspects should be referenced as appropriate, such as science knowledge acquisition, validation and support for practice.

7. What practices, such as trial and error/specify, implement and test, will be involved in the conduct of the research, as supported by the science framework?

Note: additional practice aspects should be referenced as appropriate, such as science knowledge support, acquisition and validation.

9

Engineering Approach and Framework for HCI Research

This chapter presents the specific engineering approach to HCI research, including an illustration from the literature. It then presents the specific engineering framework for HCI research. The latter is followed by the engineering design research exemplar and the lower-level engineering framework. Both the exemplar and the lower-level framework are applied to the same illustration of the engineering approach taken from the literature.

9.1 Engineering Approach to HCI Research

An engineering approach to HCI research is based on the general concept of approach (see 2.2). For a more general overview of the relationship between HCI and engineering, see Card et al. (1983), Dowell and Long (1998), Rauterberg (2006) and Salter (2010).

First, an engineering approach to HCI research is a way of addressing the topic or problem of designing human–computer interactions by codifying knowledge explicitly, to support design as specification for performance that is desired.

For example, if e-shopping checkout performance were too slow, engineering design, supported by codified knowledge, would seek to speed it up by making the shopper/shopping cart interactions more effective.

Second, an engineering approach to HCI research requires the performing of actions to progress that approach to the topic or problem of designing human–computer interactions.

For example, codified knowledge support for design for performance has evolved from design guidelines to design models to design principles. All of these types of codified knowledge might be applied to making shopper/shopping interactions more effective. Performance has evolved from errors, for example, selecting a wrong shopping item, to how well the task itself is carried out, for example, completing a family shop within budget.

Third, an engineering approach to HCI research requires the evaluating of the success of the actions performed to progress that approach.

For example, if users fail to keep their family shopping within budget, the automatic scanning of items' cost can be evaluated for performance in terms of speed, errors and usability. If desired performance is achieved, then the extent to which this success is supported by codified engineering knowledge of guidelines, models or principles can also be evaluated.

Fourth, an engineering approach to HCI research requires the cumulating of the successes as a way of establishing whether the topic or problem of designing human–computer interactions has been addressed or not.

For example, successive versions of internet banking and e-shopping applications, such as they instantiate codified knowledge for performance, exemplify the cumulating of successes.

9.2 Example of an Engineering Approach to HCI Research

As an example of an engineering approach to HCI research, Blandford (2013) advances a view of engineering as the servant of design. According to the latter, the users' needs are identified outside this engineering process. This view is contrasted with HCI as comprising iterative software development life cycles. The latter address HCI engineering validation in terms of usability, utility and experience. Blandford's aim is to question the role and value of an engineering approach concerning interactive computer systems. The questioning is in the interests of a better understanding of that approach.

On what grounds might Blandford (2013) be classified as an engineering approach to HCI research?

First, an engineering approach to HCI research is a way of addressing the topic or problem of designing human–computer interactions by codifying knowledge explicitly, to support design as specification for performance that is desired.

Blandford argues that an engineering approach addresses practical problems with a view to their resolution. The latter are associated with human–computer interactions and expressed in terms of usability, utility and experience. Design for performance is implicated in these criteria and identified with the notion of being well-engineered.

Second, an engineering approach to HCI research requires the performing of actions to progress that approach to the topic or problem of designing human–computer interactions.

Blandford identifies a number of ways for an HCI engineering approach to address the design of human–computer interactions. These include researching principles, developing a phased design process, improving requirements and testing methods, and enhancing cognitive modelling. All the latter implicate the acquisition of codified engineering knowledge to support design for performance.

Third, an engineering approach to HCI research requires the evaluating of the success of the actions performed to progress that approach.

Blandford identifies both verification and validation as ways of supporting an HCI engineering approach to progress and to increase the assurance of this progression.

Fourth, an engineering approach to HCI research requires the cumulating of the successes as a way of establishing whether the topic or problem of designing human–computer interactions has been addressed or not.

Blandford reports no assessment and so no cumulating of successes.

Conclusion: On balance, Blandford's research can be classified as an engineering approach to HCI research. Most of the criteria are met. The approach is currently at a high level of description, in keeping with its aim of questioning the role and value of engineering in relation to interactive computer systems.

This classification suggests that Blandford could decide to support any of her future HCI research either on the basis of the engineering approach, presented earlier (see 2.2 and 9.1), or on the basis of the engineering framework, which follows.

9.3 Engineering Framework for HCI Research

This section covers the core framework for HCI, including HCI research, the specific engineering framework for HCI research, the engineering design research exemplar and the lower-level engineering framework.

9.3.1 Core Framework for HCI, Including HCI Research

The specific engineering framework for HCI research is based on the core framework for the discipline of HCI, including HCI research. The core framework comprises discipline, general problem, particular scope, research, knowledge and practices (see 3.4).

9.3.2 Specific Engineering Framework for HCI Research

The specific engineering framework for HCI research, such as to be applicable to an engineering approach to HCI, follows. It comprises the concepts and definitions of the core framework for the discipline of HCI, including HCI research (see 3.4), particularised for engineering. Conceptualisation to application constitutes a one-to-many mapping. Providing more than one descriptor for the same concept is a way of facilitating this mapping. To aid researchers to apply the specific engineering framework, an applications-supportive format follows. The specific engineering framework includes the main concepts, their definitional concepts and their extended definitional concepts, such as to be applicable to an engineering approach. The main concepts are presented in **Boldface** at first mention for easy identification, reference and application, but hold throughout. The definitional concepts appear in lower case. The extended definitional concepts appear in lower case and in (brackets). Each extended definition appears only once, but applies throughout, as appropriate.

The specific engineering HCI framework comprises the following:

Discipline, as an academic (that is, scholarly) field (that is, branch/subject area) of study (that is, investigation of knowledge as division of information/learning) and

Engineering, as codified knowledge (that is, explicit) to support design (that is, specification) for performance (that is, desired) and

Engineering General Problem, as the design of codified knowledge-based human–computer interactions for performance and

Engineering Particular Scope, as the design for performance of codified knowledge-based human (that is, individual/group)–computer (that is, interactive/embedded) interaction (that is, active/passive) to do something (that is, action/task) as desired (that is, wanted/needed/experienced/felt/valued) and

Engineering Research, as the diagnosis of engineering design problems (that is, not as desired) and the prescription of engineering design solutions (that is, as desired) as they relate to performance (that is, desired) for the acquisition (that is, creation) and for the validation (that is, confirmation) of knowledge to support practices and

Engineering Knowledge, as codified design guidelines/models and methods/principles both specific/general (that is, as acquired and validated by engineering research) and supports (that is, as facilitates/makes possible) engineering practices and

Engineering Practices, as specify, implement and test/specify then implement (that is, as supported by engineering knowledge acquired and validated by engineering research).

9.3.3 Engineering Framework Design Research Exemplar

The specific engineering framework for HCI research is considered to be more complete, coherent and fit for purpose than the earlier description afforded by the engineering approach (see 9.1). Hence, the engineering framework is more rigorously specified than the engineering approach and so more effectively supports thinking about and doing engineering HCI research. As the framework is more rigorous, it offers firmer support to researchers attempting to apply it. Once applied and shared, it enables researchers to build on each other's work. Engineering researchers share and build on each other's work by means of the guidelines, models and methods, and principles which they create. What is shared, then, is explicit. However, many of the researchers also claim that some aspects of their research, for example conceptualisation as in frameworks, can be shared before codification of the associated knowledge is complete. So, they also report on their work in progress within their own organisations and at conferences, for example, the ACM CHI Conference on Human Factors in Computing Systems series, both to HCI practitioners and to other researchers. The engineering framework might be expected to support further these explicit types of exchanges and so the sharing of and building on each other's work.

The latter is further supported by a summary re-expression of the engineering framework as an HCI design research exemplar. The use of the term 'exemplar' originates with Kuhn (1970). He conceives a scientific discipline as comprising a paradigm, a disciplinary matrix and shared exemplars. Building on the work of Long and Dowell (1989), Salter (2010) develops the concept of exemplar further and applies it to engineering economic systems. Here, it is applied to HCI research in general and to specific HCI research frameworks in particular. The engineering exemplar represents the complete design research cycle, which, once performed, constitutes a case study of engineering HCI research. The exemplar is intended to support researchers in the application of the engineering framework. It does so by setting out in detail what is involved in the acquisition of different kinds of engineering knowledge to support different kinds of engineering practices. The exemplar is presented in Figure 9.1. In what follows, design research concepts are Capitalised at first mention for easy identification, reference and application, but apply throughout.

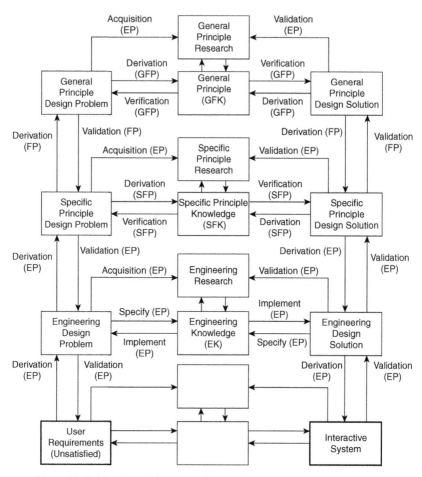

Figure 9.1 Engineering design research exemplar
Key: Engineering Knowledge as design guidelines, models and methods, principles
EP: Empirical Practice
EK: Empirical Knowledge
SFP: Specific Formal Practice
GFP: General Formal Practice
SFK: Specific Formal Knowledge as Specific Design Principle
GFK: General Formal Knowledge as General Design Principle

The four first-level boxes represent the engineering design cycle. The cycle
starts on the outer left with User Requirements (Unsatisfied) and terminates on
the outer right with an Interactive System (assumed to satisfy the user requirements). The design cycle details are not included here. First, engineering design
may involve multiple inputs. Second, the function of the figure is to represent

design research and not design per se. The design cycle, however, following the practices of the specific engineering framework for HCI research (see 9.3.2) and for present purposes, might be assumed to include a design process (the two central boxes). The latter might be further assumed to comprise some combination of specification and implementation, interspersed with iterative trial-and-error cycles.

The Blandford engineering research (see 9.2) is reused as an illustration of a possible engineering design research cycle. The latter might comprise some combination of specification and implementation, interspersed with iterative software development life cycles. The application might be associated with the redesign of an interactive e-shopping system as a result of the failure of shoppers to keep the cost of purchases within their budget. This failure constitutes undesirable performance.

The four second-level boxes represent the engineering design research cycle, starting on the left with the Engineering Design Problem and terminating on the right with the Engineering Design Solution, which solves the design problem. In terms of the Blandford research, as applied to e-shopping, the design problem might be the failure of shoppers to keep the cost of purchases within their budget. The design solution might be an interactive interface, displaying the cost of scanned items currently in the shopping cart prior to checkout.

Following the design research exemplar, the engineering design problem is Derived from, that is, formulated from, and Validated, that is, confirmed against, user requirements. The design problem is human–computer interactions not doing something as desired, that is, not desired performance. In terms of the Blandford research as applied to e-shopping, the user requirement might be not to buy goods in excess of a prescribed budget. The user requirement might be an actual requirement, but might also be a possible and plausible requirement. Note that the difference between problems and user requirements is that the latter may or may not be satisfiable in practice. The former are formulated so as to be soluble, at least in principle. Following this reasoning, an e-shopping researcher might formulate the design problem as a failure to display the cost of goods prior to checkout. The limitation of the design problem, relative to the possible and plausible user requirements, might be justified by the early stage of HCI research in designing interactive budgeting support for the shopper.

Also, following the design research exemplar, the interactive system is derived from (that is, formulated from), and validated against (that is, confirmed against), the design solution. The design solution is human–computer interactions doing something as desired, that is, desired performance. In terms of the Blandford research, as applied to e-shopping, the design solution might be an interactive interface displaying the cost of items currently in the shopping cart prior to checkout. The latter would support the shopper remaining within their prescribed budget.

Engineering Design Research Acquires, that is, creates, an expression of the design problem, for example, the failure to display the cost of hard goods to the shopper prior to checkout. The design research Validates, that is, confirms the expression against the design solution, following the latter's initial formulation. The design problem is also Implemented, that is, expressed as the Design Knowledge needed to be Tested, that is, checked against the design solution. The latter is implemented, that is, expressed as design knowledge, which is tested, that is, checked against the design problem. Note that all the engineering research processes are empirical, as is the resulting engineering knowledge. In terms of the e-shopping illustration, the engineering knowledge might take the form of design models and methods. Such engineering knowledge could be recruited to future e-shopping technology research, but would remain empirical, that is, applicable neither analytically nor without test nor with guarantee.

The four third-level boxes represent the engineering design research cycle, starting on the left with the Specific Principle Design Problem and terminating on the right with the Specific Principle Design Solution, which solves the specific principle design problem. In terms of the Blandford research, as applied to e-shopping, the specific principle design problem might be a failure to display the cost of a single hard goods article, such as CD discs, prior to checkout.

Following the design research exemplar, the specific principle design problem is derived from, that is, formulated from, and validated against, that is, confirmed against, the design problem. The processes are empirical. The specific principle design problem is human–computer interactions not doing something as desired, that is, not desired performance. In terms of the Blandford research, as applied to e-shopping, the specific principle design problem might be a failure to display the cost of a single type of hard goods article, such as CD discs, prior to checkout. The limitation of the principle design problem, relative to the design problem and to the possible and plausible user requirements, might be justified by the early stage of HCI research in designing interactive budgeting support for the shopper. The specific principle design solution would be a design, based on a codified principle, embodying the knowledge required to derive the specific principle design solution from the specific principle design problem.

Also, following the design research exemplar, the specific principle design solution is derived from, that is, formulated from, and validated against, that is, confirmed against, the design solution. The processes are empirical. The specific principle design solution is human–computer interactions doing something as desired, that is, desired performance. The specific principle design solution would be a design based on a specific principle.

Specific Principle Research acquires, that is, creates, an expression of the specific principle design problem, for example, the failure to display the cost of a single type of hard goods, such as CD discs, to the shopper prior to checkout. The specific principle research validates, that is, confirms, the expression against the specific principle design solution, following the latter's initial formulation. The specific principle design problem is also derived, that is, expressed as design knowledge in the form of a Specific Principle. The latter needs to be Verified, that is, checked against the specific principle design solution. The latter is derived, that is, expressed as design knowledge, as a specific principle, which is verified, that is, checked against the specific principle design problem. Note that the engineering research practices of acquisition and validation plus derivation and validation are empirical. However, the engineering research practices of derivation and verification, including the specific principle, are formal.

The four fourth-level boxes represent the engineering design research cycle, starting on the left with the General Principle Design Problem and terminating on the right with the General Principle Design Solution, which solves the general principle design problem. In terms of the Blandford research, as applied to e-shopping, the general principle design problem might be a failure to display the cost of three types (that is, a class) of hard goods articles, such as CD discs, books and batteries, prior to checkout. Inasmuch as the latter constitutes a class, it is general. The failure constitutes unacceptable performance, that is, not as desired.

Following the design research exemplar, the general principle design problem is derived from, that is, formulated from, the specific principle design problem. In turn, the general principle design problem is validated, that is, confirmed against the specific principle design problem. The processes are formal. The general principle design problem is human–computer interactions not doing something as desired, that is, not desired performance. In terms of the Blandford research, as applied to e-shopping, the general principle design problem might be a failure to display the cost of three types (that is, a class) of hard goods articles, such as CD discs, books and batteries, prior to checkout. The limitation of the general principle design problem, relative to the design problem and to the possible and plausible user requirements, might be justified by the early stage of HCI research in designing interactive budgeting support for the shopper. The general principle design solution derives from a General Principle embodying the knowledge required to derive the general principle design solution from the general principle design problem.

Also, following the design research exemplar, the specific principle design solution is derived from, that is, formulated from, and validated against, that is, confirmed against, the general principle design solution. The processes are formal. The general principle design solution is human–computer interactions doing something as desired, that is, desired performance.

General Principle Research acquires, that is, creates, an expression of the general principle design problem, for example, the failure to display the cost of three types (that is, a class) of hard goods, such as CD discs, books and batteries, to the shopper prior to checkout. The failure constitutes undesired performance. The general principle research validates, that is, confirms the expression against the general principle design solution, following the latter's initial formulation. The general principle design problem is also derived, that is, expressed as design knowledge in the form of the General Principle needed to be verified, that is, checked against the general principle design solution. The latter derives from design knowledge in the form of a general principle, which is verified, that is, checked against the specific principle design problem. Note that the engineering research practices of acquisition and validation plus derivation and validation are formal, that is, can be applied analytically and with guarantee.

9.3.4 Lower-Level Engineering Framework

The specific engineering framework has so far been expressed at the highest level of description. That level is of the core framework. However, to conduct and to report engineering design research and acquire/validate engineering knowledge, as suggested by the design research exemplar, a lower-level description is required. The latter is consistent with the design research exemplar.

Researchers might have their own engineering lower-level descriptions or subscribe to some more generally recognised levels (for examples of such levels, see 12.3). Such descriptions are compatible with the specific engineering framework as long as they are complete, coherent and fit for purpose, as concerns the higher-level core framework. Alternatively, and in addition, a lower-level framework description is presented in the associated chapter and design research exemplar for each type of specific HCI research framework (see 4.3.4–9.3.4).

These higher and lower levels of description need to go, respectively, from the general human to the specific website user and from the general computer to the specific tablet. The lowest level must reference engineering itself in terms of the application, for example, the codified knowledge to support the design of an interactive e-shopping system exhibits desired performance.

Following the engineering design research exemplar, researchers need to identify the design problem – as it relates to user requirements, the specific principle design problem and the general principle design problem – plus the design solution, as it relates to the interactive system. They also need to identify the specific principle design solution plus the general principle design solution, and research, as it relates to design. In addition, they need to identify the specific principle plus the general principle, and knowledge, as it relates to the design, specific principle and general principle.

These specifications need also to include the engineering application, the engineering interactive system and engineering performance, relating the former to the latter. Engineering design requires the interactive system to perform tasks (the application) as desired (performance). Engineering research acquires and validates engineering design knowledge to support engineering design practice. Hence, the following lower-level engineering framework includes application, interactive system and performance.

The key lower-level concepts are shown in **Boldface** at first mention for easy identification, reference and application, but hold throughout.

9.3.4.1 Engineering Application

An engineering application can be described in many different ways for the purposes of HCI research. Here, following Dowell and Long (1989), the application is represented as objects, attributes and states. This is a standard way of representing applications and domains (Dinu and Nadkarni, 2007). Researchers are welcome to use alternative types of representation, providing the application specification is different from that of the interactive human–computer technology system. This difference is to support design by allowing either to be varied independently of the other. Whatever the approach or the framework providing structural support, design as specification and implementation inevitably involves the selection between alternative possible interactive design options. The latter are intended to achieve the same performance goals. To avoid confounding the means – the interactive system – with the ends – performance – it is important for the two to be described independently. This independence allows the means and the ends to be co-varied separately and independently. As stated, it is for this reason that researchers are welcome to use alternative types of representation to those proposed here. However, the lower-level description must be compatible with the higher-level core HCI research framework and be complete, coherent and fit for purpose.

An **Application** is described in terms of objects.

Engineering Objects Engineering applications (what the interactive system does) can be described in terms of **Objects**. The latter comprise both **Physical Objects** and **Abstract Objects**. They are characterised by their attributes.

Physical attributes are those of energy and matter. Abstract attributes are those of knowledge and information.

For example, an e-shopping application that supports interactive real-time budgeting by shoppers can be represented for HCI research purposes in terms of objects. The abstract attributes of the e-shopping objects support the costing of items in the shopping cart. Their physical attributes support the visual/verbal representation of displayed information. The attributes concerning the items are shown on the display by means of text and images. Engineering mobile technology, as used to illustrate the approach of Blandford (see 9.2), is used here to exemplify the application of the lower-level framework. This provides continuity in the support for researchers attempting to apply the specific engineering approach and framework.

Although representable at different levels of description, the user must at least be described for HCI research purposes at a level that relates to the transformation of engineering application objects.

For example, a shopper interacting with an e-shopping application is an adult, regular user, whose behaviours include receiving and replying to messages sent to their shopping cart display.

Engineering Attributes The **Attributes** of an engineering application object are expressed at different levels of description.

For example, characters and their configuration on a shopping cart display are physical attributes of the object shopping order, expressed at one level. The costed shopping order displayed is an abstract attribute of the shopper's budget, expressed at a higher level of description.

Engineering Attribute States The attributes of engineering application objects can be represented in terms of **States**, which may change.

For example, the content and characters (attributes) of an order on an e-shopping cart display (object) may change state – the content with respect to meaning and grammar, its characters with respect to size and font.

9.3.4.2 Engineering Interactive System

Users have aims and their associated behaviours are said to be goal-oriented /intentional.

For example, the behaviours of a shopper using an e-shopping device whose purpose is to shop within their budget constitute an interactive system. Interactive systems transform objects by producing state changes in the abstract and physical attributes of those objects. The shopper and the e-shopping device may transform the object – displayed order – by changing both the attributes of its meaning and the attributes of its layout, both text and images. Behaviour is what the user does. What is done is expressed as the attribute state changes of application objects.

Users The **Behaviours** of an engineering **Interactive System** are both abstract and physical. Interactive system **Abstract Behaviours** include the acquisition, storage and transformation of information. They represent and process information concerning application objects. Also represented are their attributes, relations and states. Further, they represent the transformations required by user goals. Interactive system **Physical Behaviours** are associated with, and express, abstract behaviours.

The user, then, is represented as a system of both mental (that is, abstract) and physical (that is, overt) behaviours. User **Mental Behaviours** transform abstract application objects, represented by cognition, or express, through user **Physical Behaviours**, plans for transforming application objects.

For example, an e-shopper has the goal of maintaining the cost of the items in their shopping cart within the family budget. The e-shopper interacts with the interactive system by means of the shopping cart interface. The latter's behaviours include the transmission of information concerning the items in the shopping cart. The e-shopper acquires the cost of the items in their cart by synthesising the information displayed by the shopping cart display. They then compare it with the budgetary limits associated with their shopping goal. The e-shopper considers the attribute state changes, that is, those required by the perception and understanding of the implications for their budget of the information on the shopping cart display, as desired. That decision is expressed in the instructions given to the interactive system through overt behaviour – selecting menu options, for example. The selection and the menu options are both objects of the design process and so engineering design research. Both mental and overt user behaviours contribute to perform tasks as desired.

Interactions Interaction of **User Behaviours** and **Computer Behaviours** is the basic unit of engineering HCI research. The concern here is with the interactive system, rather than with the individual behaviours of its parts.

For example, the behaviours of an e-shopper interact with the behaviours of a budget-supporting e-shopping application. The e-shopper behaviours influence the behaviours of the interactive computer (access the total cost function). The behaviours of the interactive computer influence the selection behaviour of the e-shopper (among possible image types for item selection). The design of their interaction – the e-shopper's selection of the image function, the computer's presentation of possible image types – determines the interactive system. The latter comprises the e-shopper and the interactive computer behaviours in their planning and control of costed items. The interaction may be the object of engineering design and so design research. Hence the importance of the assignment of task goals to either the user or to the interactive computer.

For example, replacement of the inappropriate selection of a shopping cart displayed image is a goal. The latter can be expressed as a task goal structure of necessary and related attribute state changes. In particular, the field for the appropriate image demands an attribute state change in the spacing of the display. Specifying that state change may be a task goal assigned to the e-shopper, as in interaction with the behaviours of early image editor designs. Or it may be a task goal assigned to the interactive e-shopping application, as in interaction with the fill-in behaviours of later designs.

9.3.4.3 Engineering Interactive System Performance

To do something (see 9.3.2 – specific engineering framework) derives from the relationship of an interactive system with its application. It assimilates both how well the application is performed by the interactive system – as desired – and the costs incurred by it, in performing that well. They are expressed together as performance. Costs can be further differentiated, for example, as wanted/needed/ experienced/felt/valued. Performance may be absolute or relative, as in a comparison to be improved upon or to be equalled. Human Performance, as expressed in the literature as time and errors, relates to performance, as proposed here. Errors are behaviours that increase user costs or that reduce how well the application is performed or both. The time taken by user behaviours may loosely be associated with increased behavioural user costs.

For example, an e-shopper may make errors such as selecting the wrong item or exceeding their budget.

User Costs Performing tasks as desired by means of an interactive system incurs costs for the human. Costs associated with the user are termed **User Behavioural Costs**.

For example, the behavioural costs of an e-shopper selecting or attending to unfamiliar menu options may be experienced over time as tiredness, irritation or impatience.

User behavioural costs comprise both **Physical Costs** and **Mental Costs**.

For example, such costs might be keying or of attending to shopping item options.

User behavioural physical costs may be expressed for engineering design purposes as **Physical Workload**.

User behavioural mental costs are associated with knowing, thinking and deciding. User behavioural mental costs may be expressed for HCI research purposes as **Mental Workload**. Mental and physical costs are often closely associated.

For example, the physical and mental behavioural costs of an e-shopper may be associated with shopping cart menu option selection or text input.

9.3.5 Example Application of an Engineering Framework to an Engineering Approach to HCI Research

The research of Blandford (2013) can be considered to constitute an engineering approach to HCI research (see 9.2). She argues that engineering can be conceived as the servant of design. This view holds that users' needs are identified outside the engineering process. In contrast, HCI can be viewed as comprising iterative software development life cycles. The latter address HCI validation in terms of usability, utility and experience. Blandford's aim is to question the role and value of an engineering approach to advance a better understanding of that approach. What potential does the Blandford engineering approach to HCI research offer the engineering framework proposed here?

First, the specific engineering framework is for a discipline, as an academic field of study.

Potential: Blandford's engineering approach conceives HCI as an engineering discipline, for which she offers two alternative high-level views – the servant of design and iterative software development cycles. No other discipline is referenced.

Second, the specific engineering framework is for engineering as codified knowledge to support design for performance.

Potential: Blandford's engineering approach, in referencing iterative software development cycles, associates the latter with performance as usability, utility and experience. No further details are offered with respect to the relationship between usability, utility and experience and with the software development cycles. This is consistent with this type of paper, which questions the role and value of an engineering approach, the better to understand it.

Third, the specific engineering framework is for the general problem as the design of engineering human–computer interactions.

Potential: Blandford's engineering approach concerns the design of human–computer interactions and implicitly references user needs in terms of usability, utility and experience. Consistent with the high level of the paper, no details are given.

Fourth, the specific engineering framework is for the particular scope of engineering human–computer interactions for performance to do something as desired.

Potential: Blandford's engineering approach concerns the design of human–computer interactions and implicitly references performance in terms of usability, utility and experience.

Fifth, the specific engineering framework is for the diagnosis of engineering design problems and the prescription of engineering design solutions for the acquisition and for the validation of knowledge to support practices.

Potential: Blandford's engineering approach identifies a number of ways to address practical problems of the design of human–computer interactions to be acquired by HCI research. She associates verification and validation with usability, utility and experience.

Sixth, the specific engineering framework is for engineering knowledge, acquired and validated, as design guidelines/models and methods/principles both specific/general.

Potential: Blandford's engineering approach identifies a number of ways for HCI to address and to support the design of human–computer interactions. These ways include researching principles, developing a phased design process, improving requirements and testing methods and enhancing cognitive modelling. Consistent with the high level of the paper, no details are given.

Seventh, the specific engineering framework is for engineering practices, acquired and validated by research, as specify, implement and test/specify then implement.

Potential: Blandford's engineering approach contrasts the different design practices of the two views of engineering that she offers. She does not further address the issue of knowledge that supports the practices or its relationship to them with the exception of verification and validation.

Conclusion: Blandford's engineering approach to HCI research is expressed at a high level, commensurate with the questioning nature of her paper. It nevertheless meets most of the criteria for an engineering approach to HCI research. However, the approach could be further developed with respect to the relationship between performance and usability, utility and experience, and likewise for verification and validation and HCI design knowledge. Also, the concept of practical problem could be developed, for example in terms of design problem. The engineering framework proposed here is considered to have potential for contributing to such developments.

Conclusion

This concludes the presentation of the specific engineering approach and the specific engineering framework for HCI research and their exemplification.

Also presented are the engineering design research exemplar and the lower-level engineering framework.

9.4 Research Practice Assignment

The assignment comprises two sections: General and Research Design Scenarios.

9.4.1 General

- Using the engineering criteria presented in 9.3, select a recent paper from the HCI research literature that suggests itself to be potentially classifiable as engineering research, as concluded for the paper of Blandford (9.2).

  - Analyse the potential engineering research example, in the manner of 9.1 and 9.2.
  - In the light of your analysis, decide whether on balance the research example can be classified as engineering research or not. If so classifiable, continue with the research practice assignment. If not so classifiable, return to the beginning of the assignment and start again. Continue until a classifiable example of engineering research is identified.

- Apply the specific engineering framework for HCI research, presented in 9.3.2, to the research example you have classified as engineering.
- Create a research design exemplar, following 9.3.3 and Figure 9.1, for the research example to which you have applied the engineering framework.
- Re-express the research example to which you have applied the engineering framework at the lower level of engineering framework description, presented in 9.3.4. Try to use all the key concepts.

Hints and Tips

Difficult to get started?

Try reading the chapter again, while at the same time thinking explicitly about engineering in all its forms, whether in engineering or the sciences, in the development of information technology or indeed in your own professional life.

Describe your research in terms of engineering (of any type) before attempting to apply those of 9.1 and 9.2.

Difficult to complete?

Familiarise yourself with the concept of engineering as it is applied in the HCI
research (and other) literature.

Note the similarities and differences between the different concepts of engi
neering identified in the HCI research literature.

Test

- Write down the titles of 9.1 and 9.3. Complete the sections in your own
words.
- Propose a new and improved set of titles for 9.1 and 9.3.
- Complete the new 9.1 and 9.3 in your own words.

9.4.2 Research Design Scenarios

All the research design scenarios in 4.4.2–9.4.2 require you to characterise your
own work or that of others. The same characterisation can be used for all the
scenarios. The requirement, however, is repeated in each scenario to support
researchers who may be completing the research practice assignments out of
order. They may not have produced a characterisation at that point in the book.
It is also repeated for those researchers wishing to work with a range of
different characterisations. They are encouraged and supported in creating
such multiple characterisations.

Research Design Scenario 9.1: Characterising Your Own or Another's Approach to HCI Research

Characterise your own HCI research approach by answering the following
questions, which are intended to support you in creating such
a characterisation. You should call upon any other relevant aspects of the
assignment as required. The characterisation should preferably be of your
own current project. If you are not working on a project at this time, base the
characterisation on a past project. Failing that, base the characterisation on
a project of your supervisor or of a colleague. In the last resort, choose
a research project published in the HCI literature. The most important part of
the research design scenario is the support and practice it gives researchers in
planning their research. Additional hints and tips follow each question in the
form of notes.

The selection of the topic or problem per se by the research is not directly
supported by the assignment or more generally by the book. What is supported,

however, is the manner (of engineering approach or of engineering framework) by which the topic or problem is addressed, once selected. However, the former needs to be identified to carry out the latter. Further, the latter supports the researcher in understanding the possibilities and implications for the selection of the research topic or problem. The latter is generally some combination of the following: funding available for the project, researcher's curiosity or interest, supervisor's interests and previous work, and gaps in the HCI research literature. The latter may be identified by the researcher, the supervisor or the sponsor.

1. What topic or problem of designing human–computer interactions is addressed by the research and how is that topic or problem addressed?
   Note: 'topic or problem' here should be understood widely to include any and all research activities considered to be relevant and important.

2. Which actions are performed by the research as a way of addressing the topic or problem of designing human–computer interactions?
   Note: 'actions' here should be understood widely to include any and all research activities considered to be sufficiently relevant and important.

3. What are the ways of evaluating the success or not of the actions performed by the research to address the topic or problem of designing human–computer interactions?
   Note: 'evaluating success' here should be understood widely. The particular forms of evaluation will depend on the approach taken by the research.

4. How does the research cumulate its successes in addressing the topic or problem of designing human–computer interactions?
   Note: 'cumulating successes' here should be understood widely. The particular forms of cumulating will depend on the approach taken by the research.

Research Design Scenario 9.2: Applying the Engineering Approach to Your Own or to Another's Approach to HCI Research
Suppose that you decide to change your current approach to HCI research in your next piece of work to that of engineering. Or if your present approach is already one of engineering, suppose that you decide to apply the specific engineering approach proposed here. In both cases, apply the engineering approach to the characterisation of your own or another's HCI research approach (see 9.4.1) by answering the following questions. They are intended to support you in such an application. Any other relevant aspects of the

assignment should also be called upon as required. Additional hints and tips follow each question in the form of notes.

The selection of the topic or problem per se by the engineering research is not directly supported by the assignment or more generally by the book. What is supported is the manner (of engineering approach) by which the topic or problem is addressed, once selected. However, a topic or problem needs to be identified to apply an engineering approach. Further, the latter supports the researcher in understanding the possibilities and implications for the engineering research of selecting the former. Engineering research topic selection is generally some combination of the following: funding available for the project, researcher's curiosity or interest, supervisor's interests and previous work, and gaps in the HCI research literature. The latter may be identified by the researcher, the supervisor or the sponsor.

1. What topic or problem of designing, as specifying, human–computer interactions for performance, as desired, on the basis of explicit codified knowledge is to be addressed by the research and how will that topic or problem be addressed?

Note: 'topic or problem' here should be understood widely to include any and all engineering research activities considered to be relevant and important.

2. Which actions are to be performed by the research as a way of addressing the topic or problem of designing, as specifying, human–computer interactions for performance, as desired, on the basis of explicit, codified knowledge?

Note: 'actions' here should be understood widely to include any and all engineering research activities considered to be sufficiently relevant and important.

3. Which ways of evaluating the success or not of the actions performed by the research will be employed to address the topic or problem of designing, as specifying, human–computer interactions for performance, as desired, on the basis of explicit codified knowledge?

Note: 'evaluating success' here should be understood widely. The particular forms of evaluation will depend on the engineering approach taken by the research.

4. How will the research cumulate its successes in addressing the topic or problem of designing, as specifying, human–computer interactions for performance, as desired, on the basis of explicit codified knowledge?

Note: 'cumulating successes' here should be understood widely. The particular forms of cumulating will depend on the engineering approach taken by the research.

Research Design Scenario 9.3: Applying the Engineering Framework
to Your Own or to Another's Approach to HCI Research

Suppose that you decide to change your current planned engineering approach to HCI research, as set out earlier (see 9.4.2), to research, supported by the engineering framework proposed here. The reason might be, for example, for increased rigour. In this research design scenario, apply the engineering framework to your proposed engineering approach by answering the following questions. You should also call upon any other relevant aspects of the research practice assignment as required. Additional hints and tips follow each question in the form of notes.

The selection of the topic or problem per se by the engineering research is not directly supported by the assignment or more generally by the textbook. What is supported is the manner (of engineering framework) by which the topic or problem is addressed, once selected. However, a topic or problem needs to be identified to apply an engineering framework. Further, the latter supports the researcher in understanding the possibilities and implications for the engineering research of selecting the former. Engineering research topic selection is generally some combination of the following: funding available for the project, researcher's curiosity or interest, supervisor's interests and previous work, and gaps in the HCI research literature. The latter may be identified by the researcher, the supervisor or the sponsor.

1. Which discipline, as an academic field of study, will be espoused by the conduct of the research, as supported by the engineering framework?
Note: additional discipline aspects should be referenced as appropriate, such as scholarliness, branch/subject area, knowledge and information/learning.

2. How will engineering human–computer interactions be addressed by the conduct of the research as supported by the engineering framework?
Note: additional engineering aspects should be referenced as appropriate, such as explicit codified knowledge, design as specification and performance, as desired.

3. What general problem of engineering design of human–computer interaction will be addressed by the conduct of the research as supported by the engineering framework?
Note: additional general problem aspects should be referenced as appropriate, such as explicit codified knowledge, design as specification, and performance as desired.

4. What particular scope of the general problem of engineering design of human–computer interaction to do something as desired will be addressed by the conduct of the research supported by the engineering framework?

Note: additional particular scope aspects of the general problem of engineering design should be referenced as appropriate, such as individual/group human interactions and interactive/embedded computer interactions, and also aspects such as to do something – actions/task – as desired – that is, wanted/needed/experienced/felt/valued.

5. What research, as the diagnosis of design problems and the prescription of design solutions, as they relate to performance for the acquisition and for the validation of knowledge to support practices, will be addressed by the conduct of the research as supported by the engineering framework?

Note: additional research aspects should be referenced as appropriate, such as the desired state or not of design problems/solutions, performance as doing something as desired, acquisition as creation and validation as confirmation.

6. What knowledge, such as design guidelines, models and methods, and principles will result from the conduct of the research as supported by the engineering framework?

Note: additional knowledge aspects should be referenced as appropriate, such as engineering knowledge acquisition, validation and support for practice.

7. What practices, such as specify and implement/specify then implement, will be supported by the knowledge acquired or validated by the research, as supported by the engineering framework?

Note: additional practice aspects should be referenced as appropriate, such as engineering knowledge support, acquisition and validation.

10

General Approach and General Framework for HCI Research

This chapter first presents a general approach to HCI research. It then proposes a General Framework for HCI research, including a core framework, a general design research exemplar and a general lower-level framework.

10.1 General Approach to HCI Research

The general approach to HCI research is based on the general concept of approach (see 2.2) and is common to all the specific approaches to HCI research (see 4.1–9.1). The general approach follows.

First, a general approach to HCI research is a way addressing the topic or problem of designing human–computer interactions.

Second, a general approach to HCI research requires the performing of actions to progress that approach to designing human–computer interactions.

Third, a general approach to HCI research requires the evaluating of the success of the actions performed to progress that approach to designing human–computer interactions.

Fourth, a general approach to HCI research requires the cumulating of the successes as a way of establishing whether the topic or problem of designing human–computer interactions has been addressed or not.[1]

10.2 General Framework for HCI Research

The General Framework for HCI research is based on the core framework for the discipline of HCI, including HCI research (see 3.4). It is instantiated in and is common to all the specific frameworks for HCI research (see 4.3–9.3). The

General Framework includes the general design research exemplar and the general lower-level framework.

10.2.1 Core Framework for HCI, Including HCI Research

The core HCI framework, including HCI research, comprises discipline, general problem, particular scope, research, knowledge and practices (see 3.4).

The General Framework for HCI research, such as to be applicable to the general approach to HCI (see 10.1), follows.

10.2.2 General Framework for HCI Research

The General Framework for HCI research, such as to be applicable to a general approach to HCI, comprises the concepts and definitions of the core framework for the discipline of HCI, including HCI research (see 3.4). The General Framework was created by generalising over the specific frameworks for HCI research (see 4.3.2–9.3.2), which instantiate the core framework. Conceptualisation to application constitutes a one-to-many mapping. Providing more than one descriptor for the same concept is one way of facilitating this mapping. To aid researchers in applying the General Framework, an applications-supportive format follows. The General Framework includes the main concepts, their definitional concepts and their extended definitional concepts, such as to be applicable to a general approach. The main concepts are presented in **Boldface** at first mention for easy identification, reference and application, but hold throughout. The definitional concepts appear in lower case. The extended definitional concepts appear in lower case and in (brackets). Each extended definition appears only once, but applies throughout, as appropriate.

The General Framework comprises the following:

- **Discipline**, as an academic (that is, scholarly) field (that is, branch/subject area) of study (that is, investigation of knowledge as division of information/ learning) and
- **General**, as common (that is, shared) and
- **General Problem**, as the design (that is, specification) of human–computer interactions and
- **Particular Scope**, as the design of human (that is, individual/group)–computer (that is, interactive/embedded) interactions (that is, active/passive) to do something (that is, action/task) as desired (that is, wanted/needed/experienced/felt/valued) and

- **General Research**, as the diagnosis of design problems (that is, not as desired) and the prescription of design solutions (that is, as desired), as they relate to performance (that is, desired) for the acquisition (that is, creation) and for the validation (that is, confirmation) of knowledge to support practices and
- **General Knowledge**, as guidelines/models/ methods/principles (that is, as acquired and validated by research) and supports (that is, facilitates/makes possible) practices and
- **General Practices**, as trial and error/implement and/then test (that is, supported by knowledge acquired and validated by research).[2]

10.2.3 General Framework Design Research Exemplar for HCI Research

The General Framework for HCI research is considered to be more complete, coherent and fit for purpose than the description afforded by the general approach to HCI research (see 10.1). As the framework is more rigorous, it offers firmer support to researchers attempting to apply it. Once applied and shared, it enables researchers to build on each other's work. Researchers share and build on each other's work by many different means. However, exactly what is shared often remains implicit. Researchers also report on their work both internally to their companies/academic institutions and externally at conferences, for example, the ACM CHI Conference on Human Factors in Computing Systems series. The General Framework might be expected to support further these explicit types of exchanges and so the sharing of and building on each other's work.

The latter is further supported by a summary re-expression of the General Framework as a general design research exemplar. The use of the term 'exemplar' originates with Kuhn (1970). He conceives a scientific discipline as comprising a paradigm, a disciplinary matrix and shared exemplars. Building on the work of Long and Dowell/Dowell and Long (1989), Salter (2010) develops the concept of exemplar further and applies it to the engineering of economic systems. Here, this application is to HCI research in general and to specific HCI research frameworks in particular. The general design exemplar represents the complete design research cycle, which, once applied, constitutes a case study of HCI research. The exemplar is intended to support researchers in the application of the General Framework and is presented in Figure 10.1. The empty boxes are not required for the general exemplar, but are required elsewhere for some specific design research exemplars. The empty boxes have

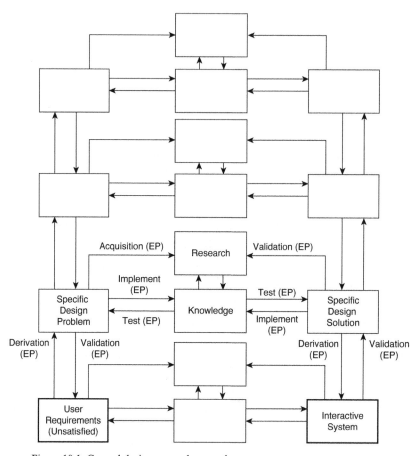

Figure 10.1 General design research exemplar
Key: EP: Empirical Practice
    EK: Empirical Knowledge

been included here for completeness and to facilitate comparison between exemplars. Design research concepts are Capitalised at first mention for easy identification, reference and application, but apply throughout.

The four first-level boxes represent the general design research cycle, starting on the outer left with User Requirements (Unsatisfied) and terminating on the outer right with an Interactive System (assumed to satisfy user requirements). The design cycle details have not been included here. First, much of design is implicit or indirect and so cannot be represented explicitly or directly. Second, the function of the figure is to represent design research and not design per se. The design cycle, however, following the practices of the General Framework for HCI research (see 10.2.2) and for present purposes, might be assumed to include a design process (the two central boxes). The latter might be further assumed to comprise some combination of specification and implementation, interspersed with iterative trial-and-error cycles.

The four second-level boxes represent the general design research cycle, starting on the left with the Specific Design Problem and terminating on the right with the Specific Design Solution, which solves the specific problem. Following the design research exemplar, the specific problem's Derivation is from, that is, formulated from, and its Validation is against, that is, confirmed against, user requirements. The specific problem is human–computer interactions not doing something as desired. The user requirements might be an actual requirement, but could also be a possible and plausible requirement. Note that the difference between problems and user requirements is that the latter may or may not be satisfiable in practice, while the former are formulated so as to be soluble, at least in principle. The limitation of the specific problem, relative to the possible and plausible user requirements, might be justified by the early stage of any associated research.

Research Acquisition formulates an expression of the specific problem. Research Validation confirms the expression against the specific solution, following the latter's initial formulation. The specific problem also undergoes an Implementation, that is, expressed as the Knowledge, needed for Test, that is, checked against the specific solution. The latter is also implemented, that is, expressed as knowledge, which is tested, that is, checked against the specific problem. Note that all the research processes are empirical, as is the resulting knowledge. Such knowledge could be recruited to future research, but would remain empirical, that is, applicable neither analytically nor without test nor with guarantee.

Finally, the specific solution derivation is formulated for inclusion in an interactive system (assumed to satisfy) the user requirements. The validation of the interactive system's inclusion is confirmed against the specific solution.

Although not included here, as not strictly required by the general design research exemplar, a General Design Problem to General Design Solution level could be added to the exemplar in the third-level empty boxes. The general problem would be derived from and validated against the specific problem. The general solution would be derived from and validated against the specific solution. The remaining components of the specific problem/solution level would remain the same, but as applicable to the general problem/general solution level.

10.2.4 Lower-Level General Framework for HCI Research

The General Framework has so far been expressed only at the highest level of description, that of the core framework. However, to conduct and to report research and to acquire/validate knowledge, as suggested by the general design research exemplar, a lower-level description is required.

Researchers might have their own lower-level descriptions or subscribe to some more generally recognised levels (for examples of such levels, see 12.3). Such descriptions are compatible with the General Framework as long as they are complete, coherent and fit for purpose as concerns the latter.

These higher and lower levels of description need to go respectively, for example, from the general human to the specific web manager and from the general computer to the specific voice-based recognition tablet. The lowest level must reference the application itself.

Following the general design research exemplar, researchers need to specify the specific problem (as it relates to user requirements), research, knowledge and specific solution (as it relates to interactive systems).

These specifications need also to include the application, interactive system and performance. The latter relates the application to the interactive system. Design requires the interactive system to do something (the application) as desired (performance). Research acquires and validates knowledge to support design practice.

The lower-level General Framework thus includes application, interactive system and performance.

The key lower-level concepts are shown in **Boldface** at first mention for easy identification, reference and application, but hold throughout.

10.2.4.1 Application

An application can be described in many different ways for the purposes of HCI research. Here, following Dowell and Long (1989), the application is represented as objects, attributes and states. This is a standard way of representing applications and domains (Dinu and Nadkarni, 2007). Researchers are welcome to use alternative types of representation, providing the application specification is different from that of the interactive human–computer technology system. This difference is to support design by allowing either to be varied independently of the other. Whatever the approach or the framework providing structural support, design as specification and implementation inevitably involves the selection between alternative possible design options. The latter are intended to achieve the same performance goals. To avoid confounding the means – the interactive system – with the ends – performance – it is important for the two to be described independently. This independence allows the means and the ends to be co-varied separately and independently. As stated, it is for this reason that researchers are welcome to use alternative types of representation to those proposed here. However, the lower-level description must be compatible with the higher-level core HCI research framework and be complete, coherent and fit for purpose.

An **Application** is described in terms of objects.

Objects The application (what the interactive system does) can be described in terms of **Objects**. The latter comprise both **Physical Objects** and **Abstract Objects**. They are characterised by their attributes. Physical attributes are those of matter and energy. Abstract attributes are those of knowledge and information. Although representable at different levels of description, the user must at least be described for HCI research purposes at a level that relates to the transformation of objects.

Attributes The **Attributes** of an application object are represented at different levels of description. The attributes of application objects can be described as having **States**, which may change.

10.2.4.2 Interactive System

Users have aims and the associated behaviours are considered to be goal-oriented/intentional. Behaviour is what the user does. What is done is expressed as the attribute state changes of application objects.

Users The **Behaviours** of an **Interactive System** are both abstract and physical. Interactive system **Abstract Behaviours** include the acquisition, storage and transformation of information. They represent and process information concerning application objects, and also their attributes, relations and states. Further, they represent the transformations required by user goals/intentions. Interactive system **Physical Behaviours** are associated with, and express, abstract behaviours.

The user, then, is represented as a system of mental (that is, abstract) and physical (that is, overt) behaviours. User **Mental Behaviours** transform abstract application objects, represented by cognition, or express, through user **Physical Behaviours**, plans for transforming application objects. Both mental and physical user behaviours contribute to doing something, as desired as wanted/needed/experienced/felt/valued.

Interactions Interaction of **User Behaviours** and **Computer Behaviours** is the basic unit of HCI research. The concern here is with the interactive system, rather than with the individual behaviours of its parts.

10.2.4.3 Interactive System Performance

To do something derives from the relationship of an interactive system with its application. It assimilates both how well the application is performed by the interactive system – as desired – and the costs incurred by it in performing that well. They are expressed together as performance. Costs can be further differentiated, for example, as wanted/needed/experienced/felt/valued. Performance may be absolute or relative, in terms of a comparison to be improved upon or to be equalled. Human Performance, as expressed in the literature as time and errors, relates to performance, as proposed here. Errors are behaviours that increase user costs or reduce how well the application is performed or both. The time taken by user behaviours may loosely be associated with increased behavioural user costs.

User Costs Doing something as desired by means of an interactive system incurs costs for the human. Costs associated with the user are termed **User Behavioural Costs**. User behavioural costs comprise both **Physical Costs** and **Mental Costs**. User behavioural physical costs are expressed as **Physical Workload** and user behavioural mental costs as **Mental Workload**. Physical and mental costs are often closely associated.

This concludes the presentation of the General Framework for HCI research, including the general design research exemplar and the general lower-level framework.

However, researchers familiar with the literature on generic frameworks must be wondering why the latter do not constitute an issue for the General Framework. In fact they do – but not one that can be resolved here and at this time. The issue must remain for future research. However, the issue needs to be addressed. The HCI research literature includes different descriptors for general frameworks, for example, generic, general, a priori and unified. The differences are small, so the frameworks together can be contrasted with specific frameworks, in the manner that the General Framework (see 3.4) is contrasted with specific frameworks (see 4.3–9.3). Following the literature, the term 'generic' is used to describe the issue.

10.3 Generic Framework Critiques

Generic frameworks have been criticised by a number of researchers. For example, Santos, Kiris and Coyle (1997) argue that frameworks are, and can never be other than, incomplete. The pace of information technology development is such that generic frameworks always lag behind and so are never completed. It is assumed that if the scope of the generic framework changes radically, it would no longer be valid, along with the HCI knowledge acquired with its support.

Elsewhere, Harris and Henderson (1999) question the feasibility of HCI generic frameworks on the grounds that they can never be complete with respect to the world to which they are intended to apply. No such ordered description of the world can succeed for long. Further, the world is inconsistent and ambiguous, so defying categorisation. Again, the incompleteness of the scope of the generic frameworks is implicated, along with the associated acquired knowledge. In similar vein, Rozanski and Haake (2003) conclude that HCI has too many different aspects, making a unified framework impossible to construct. Following a review of the generic framework literature, Rauterberg (2006) concludes that a unifying framework is very difficult to establish, if at all. Carroll (2010) may be taken to concur with this view.

All the examples argue that HCI frameworks may be incomplete with respect to their scope. The same incompleteness can be assumed to characterise HCI research frameworks, including the General Framework, since the examples do not distinguish HCI and HCI research frameworks.

The ultimate and absolute incompleteness of generic frameworks is not contested, including that of the General Framework. However, the incompleteness in practice is relative and with respect to a number of different factors. First, generic frameworks describe the world for the purposes in hand, that of supporting the acquisition and validation of HCI knowledge. A neural level of description may not be required for this purpose currently; but it may be in the future, for example for implanted interactive brain systems. If not required currently, then its absence does not constitute a relevant incompleteness at this time. If and when required, it can be added to the scope of HCI and HCI research frameworks. Further, some technology cycles may be very long and so may not pose a problem of incompleteness for long periods of time.

Second, technology is only part of the General Framework's scope, which also comprises users and applications. A radical change in any of the components might constitute a source of incompleteness for generic framework scope at some point in time. This constitutes an additional criticism of generic frameworks.

Last, HCI research takes place in HCI communities and wider national and international HCI communities. These communities are well aware of technology and other developments affecting HCI. The latter might also affect the completeness of generic frameworks. For example, the Morton et al. (1979) framework resulted from difficulties experienced by a computing technology developer to persuade non-computer professionals to use a new command-language-based interactive system. Further, Rauterberg (2006) proposes a commercial optimisation cycle involving system and user validation components. All these sources might serve to identify examples of generic framework incompleteness. Once identified, the incompleteness can be addressed. The General Framework's response to the issue of generic framework incompleteness is validation of the framework and the knowledge acquired with its support (see 11.3). Longer-term research, then, could take validation forward in terms of operationalisation, test and generalisation. Failure to validate by case study might indicate coherence or fitness for purpose as the culprit, but also completeness. If the latter, the problem could be addressed by a complete general substantive and methodological framework itself, as part of its intended application (see 14.2). Validation, then, is the primary response here to the claimed incompleteness of generic frameworks.

Conclusion

This concludes the presentation of the general approach to HCI research and the General Framework for HCI research. Also included are the core framework, the general design research exemplar and the general lower-level framework.

10.4 Research Practice Assignment

The assignment comprises two sections: General and Research Design Scenario.

10.4.1 General

- Using the criteria presented in 10.2.1, select a recent paper from the HCI research literature that suggests itself as potentially classifiable as a generic approach to HCI research.
  - Analyse the potential example of a generic approach to HCI research using the concepts of 10.2.1.
  - In the light of your analysis, decide whether on balance the research example can be classified as a generic approach or not. If so classifiable, continue with the research practice assignment. If not so classifiable, return to the beginning of the assignment and start again. Continue until a classifiable example of a generic approach is identified.
  - Apply the General Framework for HCI research presented in 10.2.2 to the example you have classified as a generic approach to HCI research.

- Construct a general design research exemplar, following 10.2.3 and Figure 10.1, for the General Framework example applied to the generic approach that you created earlier.
- Re-express the General Framework example applied to the generic approach you created earlier at the lower level of the General Framework description presented in 10.2.4.
- As concerns generic frameworks more generally, and the issue which they raise:
  - Select an HCI generic framework, either from the research literature or from those presented in 12.3.
  - Compare the selected generic framework with the General Framework for HCI research presented in 10.2.1 and 10.2.2, as concerns its completeness with respect to its scope in the manner of 12.3.
  - Note the similarities and differences between the scope of the selected HCI generic framework and of the General Framework for HCI research.
  - How many of the common scope concepts shared by the other comparison frameworks of 12.3 are also shared by your selected generic framework?

Hints and Tips

Difficult to get started?
Try reading the chapter again, while at the same time thinking explicitly about research in all its forms, whether in the arts or the sciences, in the development of information technology or, indeed, in your own professional or social life.
Describe your research in terms of generality (of any type) before attempting to apply those of 10.2.1 and 10.2.2.

Difficult to complete?
Familiarise yourself with the concept of generality as it is applied in the HCI research (and other) literature.
Note the similarities and differences between the different concepts of generality identified in the HCI research literature.

Test[3]

- Write down the titles of 10.2.1 and 10.2.2. Complete the sections in your own words.
- Propose a new and improved set of titles for 10.2.1 and 10.2.2.

- Complete the new 10.2.1 and 10.2.2 in your own words.
- Select one of the generic frameworks, which are compared with the General Framework for HCI research, from 12.3. Referencing the generic framework explicitly and the General Framework for HCI research presented in 10.4.1 and 10.4.2 from memory only, compare their scope components. Repeat until your results stabilise.

10.4.2 Research Design Scenario

Research Design Scenario 10.1: Applying the General Framework to Generalise Your Own or Another's Approaches to HCI Research
Select two or more of the approaches to HCI research that you created with respect to your own or another's research from 4.4.2–9.4.2.

- Generalise over the two or more selected approaches to HCI research, using the General Framework proposed in 10.2.
- Check for any differences between your generalisation over your two or more selected approaches and the General Framework proposed in 10.2.
- Should any such differences exist?
- In the affirmative, justify the differences. In the negative, seek their basis and either eliminate or explain.

10.5 Notes

1. Researchers may want to apply the general approach to construct specific approaches in addition to those presented in 4.1–9.1. To support such an application, a version of the general approach follows. The latter indicates the requirement for descriptors and their expansion, necessary to characterise any additional specific approach.

    The additional specific approach is marked [***] in the text for the descriptor and [*** ...] for its expansion and so specification. Application of the general approach to HCI research requires the blank descriptors and expansions to be completed by researchers to characterise any additional specific approach.

    - First, a [***] approach to HCI research is a way of addressing the topic or problem of designing [***] human–computer interactions by [***].
    - For example, [*** ...]
    - Second, a [***] approach to HCI research requires the performing of actions to progress that approach to designing [***] human–computer interaction.
    - For example, [*** ...]
    - Third, evaluating the [***] HCI research approach requires the evaluating of the success or not of the [***] actions performed by [***] to progress that approach to designing [***] human–computer interactions.

- For example, [*** …]
- Fourth, a [***] approach to HCI research requires the cumulating of the successes as a way of establishing whether the topic or problem of designing [***] human–computer interactions has been addressed or not.
- For example, [*** …]

2. It is worth reminding the reader, at this point, of the relationship between the conception of Long and Dowell/Dowell and Long (1989) and the General Framework, as proposed here. The two papers present a conception for a discipline of HCI and the design problem of HCI respectively. The conception constitutes the basis for the core framework for HCI, including HCI research (see 3.4 and 10.2). The latter in turn forms the basis for the particularisation of the specific frameworks (see 4.3–9.3), which are then generalised to form the General Framework for HCI research. The latter is re-expressed in the form of a general design research exemplar, accompanied by a general lower-level framework. For more details see 3.4.

3. The test encourages researchers to commit the approaches and frameworks to memory. Such internalisation facilitates their subsequent application.

11

Validating General Approach and General Framework for HCI Research

This chapter introduces the concept of the validation of knowledge. This is then applied to HCI knowledge acquired by HCI research. The concept of validation is applied in turn to approaches to HCI research and to frameworks for HCI research.

11.1 Validation

Validation of knowledge comprises four superordinate concepts: conceptualisation, operationalisation, test and generalisation.

The concepts are specified as follows:

- Conceptualisation of knowledge requires the expressing of the knowledge in the form of concepts, including their relations at the same and at different levels of description.
- Operationalisation of knowledge requires the making of the concepts observable and hence recordable, including their relations at the same and at different levels of description.
- Test of knowledge requires the assessing of the operationalised concepts, as expressing some form of knowledge, including their relations at the same and at different levels of description.
- Generalisation of knowledge requires the cumulating of the successfully tested operationalised concepts, as expressing some form of knowledge, including their relations at the same and at different levels of description and in particular at the highest level.

In addition, validation of knowledge also requires the applying of the following three superordinate criteria to each of the four superordinate concepts: completeness, coherence and fitness for purpose.

The criteria are specified as follows:

- Completeness requires the complete specifying of the superordinate concepts of knowledge validation, including their relations at the same and at different levels of description.
- Coherence requires the consistent specifying of the superordinate concepts of knowledge validation, including their relations at the same and at different levels of description.
- Fitness for purpose requires the correct and successful applying of the superordinate concepts of knowledge validation, including their relations at the same and at different levels of description.

When combined, the concepts and the criteria constitute a general specification of the validation of knowledge.

The general concept of validation, as applied here, was used by Long and Dowell/Dowell and Long (1989) as concerns the discipline of HCI and its design problem, respectively. However, as they themselves observe, this general concept of validation is standard and is to be found in many engineering and science textbooks. Long (1997), in his paper 'Research and the Design of Human–Computer Interactions or "What Happened to Validation?"', applies the same general concept but more widely. For example, he applies the general concept to specify the relations between HCI research and the HCI general design problem, within the particular scope of HCI to support HCI research; between cognitive science research and understanding natural and artificial forms of intelligence; between cognitive science research and the cognitive general understanding problem, within the scope of cognitive science to support cognitive science research; between the cognitive science discipline and the general understanding problem; and between cognitive science research and the design of human–computer interactions. Researchers might like to compare the differences, if any, between these sets of relations and the ones proposed here.

11.2 Validation of HCI Knowledge Acquired by HCI Research

The general specification of validation, presented in the previous section, is now expressed in particular with respect to HCI knowledge. Validation of HCI knowledge, supported by a framework for HCI research and acquired by HCI research, comprises:

- conceptualisation of HCI knowledge, which is complete, coherent and fit for purpose for
- operationalisation of HCI knowledge, which is complete, coherent and fit for purpose for
- test of HCI knowledge, which is complete, coherent and fit for purpose for
- generalisation of HCI knowledge, which is complete, coherent and fit for purpose.

The question arises as to whether the validation of HCI knowledge acquired with the support of a framework for HCI research is all-or-none (Long, 1997). If the concept of validation is not decomposed, then the validation is necessarily all-or-none. If, however, as here, the concept of validation is decomposed into superordinate concepts and their associated superordinate criteria, then validation can be partial. However, this is only with respect to the particular concepts and criteria contained in the definition and so explicitly identified. If no reference is made to the specific concepts or criteria, then validation is either all (concepts and criteria) or none (that is, less than all). What is to be avoided is the claim of partial validation without reference to its specific scope as concerns concepts and criteria.

11.3 Validation of HCI Knowledge Acquired by HCI Research Approaches

The validation of HCI knowledge acquired by HCI research approaches is presented next. It is based on the previous section. The validation includes both superordinate concepts and superordinate criteria as they relate to HCI knowledge acquired by HCI research approaches. However, although associated with the validation concepts (in brackets), the approach concepts are to be understood in the everyday language of the latter, as required by 2.2, as follows: Validation of HCI knowledge acquired by HCI research approaches comprises:

- topic or problem addressed (that is, as in conceptualisation), which makes sense (that is, as in complete, coherent and fit for purpose) for
- actions performed (that is, as in operationalisation), which makes sense (that is, as in complete, coherent and fit for purpose) for
- evaluation conducted (that is, as in test), which makes sense (that is, as in complete, coherent and fit for purpose) for
- successes cumulated (that is, as in generalisation), which makes sense (that is, as in complete, coherent and fit for purpose).

The superordinate concepts of knowledge validation are specified here as for HCI knowledge acquired by HCI research, supported by HCI frameworks (see 3.4). This is in contrast to HCI knowledge acquired by HCI approaches (see 2.2). The same concepts, however, are used only to identify the relevant associated everyday expressions for the superordinate concepts of the knowledge acquired by the HCI research approaches. This is consistent with the specification of the latter. These concepts comprise topic or problem addressed, actions performed, evaluation conducted and successes cumulated.

Case studies of the validation of HCI approaches to HCI research appear to be absent from the literature. They need to be the object of future research. However, addressing the topic or problem (as conceptualisation) of the general approach, as presented here, provides a basis for such research. This is in addition to the superordinate concepts and their relations and the superordinate criteria. Together, concepts and criteria constitute the basis on which such case studies may be conducted and assessed (see 15.2).

It could be argued that HCI knowledge acquired by research approaches and expressed in ordinary language can never be validated using the same concepts as those proposed here for frameworks. Indeed, and that is accepted. However, for as long as researchers continue to use the concept of approach to guide their work, then the possibility of the validation of the HCI knowledge thereby acquired must be admitted and addressed. However, validation needs to be expressible in the same manner as the rest of the approach description, that is to say, in ordinary or everyday language. The latter does not exclude the expression of approaches in terms which relate to those proposed here for frameworks. However, their meaning is strictly in terms of lay or ordinary language only, in the manner of the remaining approach description, as required by 2.2. The meaning is not that of the framework concepts.

11.4 Validation of HCI Knowledge Supported by General Framework for HCI Research

The General Framework is repeated here to support researchers in following and checking the details of validation.

The General Framework for HCI research (see 10.2.2) comprises the following:

Discipline, as an academic (that is, scholarly) field (that is, branch/subject area) of study (that is, investigation of knowledge as division of information/learning) and
General, as common (that is, shared) and

General Problem, as the design (that is, specification) of human–computer interactions and

Particular Scope, as the design of human (that is, individual/group)–computer (that is, interactive/embedded) interactions (that is, active/passive) to do something (that is, action/task) as desired (that is, wanted/needed/experienced/felt/valued) and

General Research, as the diagnosis of design problems (that is, not as desired) and the prescription of design solutions (that is, as desired) as they relate to performance (that is, desired) for the acquisition (that is, creation) and for the validation (that is, confirmation) of knowledge to support practices and

General Knowledge, as guidelines/models/ methods/principles (that is, as acquired and validated by research) and supports (that is, facilitates/makes possible) practices and

General Practices, as trial and error/implement and/then test (that is, supported by knowledge acquired and validated by research).

The general concept of framework (see 3.1) is conceptualised in terms of HCI research (see 3.2), and current frameworks are illustrated (see 3.6). The complete set of specific frameworks is presented in 4.3.2–9.3.2. The General Framework is reproduced here to support the expression of the validation of HCI knowledge acquired by HCI research.

It is important to note that frameworks for HCI research can only be validated by research that is attempting to acquire HCI design knowledge or to validate already acquired HCI design knowledge. In other words, they cannot be evaluated separately from the research for which they provide a support structure, other than in terms of the criteria of completeness and coherence; but not fitness for purpose. Hence the need for case studies of such research – studies that have yet to be conducted (see 15.2). Note further that there are two basic ways of validating frameworks by conducting research. In the first, the same framework is applied to acquire or to validate at least two different examples of HCI knowledge, for example, two models, two methods or a model and a method. This is a within-framework-between-knowledge validation. In the second, two different frameworks are used to acquire or to validate the same example of HCI knowledge, for instance, a model or a method. This is a between-framework-within-knowledge validation. Both basic ways of validating frameworks require case studies, which have yet to be conducted.

The validation of HCI knowledge, supported by a General Framework for research (see 10.2), is expressed as follows: validation of HCI knowledge, supported by a General Framework for HCI research, comprises:

- conceptualisation of HCI knowledge that is complete, coherent and fit for purpose for
- operationalisation of HCI knowledge that is complete, coherent and fit for purpose for
- test of HCI knowledge that is complete, coherent and fit for purpose for
- generalisation of HCI knowledge that is complete, coherent and fit for purpose.

As concerns the validation of HCI knowledge, the General Framework for HCI research can only be considered at this time as being conceptualised. It is only complete with respect to its particular scope. It is not coherent and fit for purpose for being operationalised. Nor is it complete, coherent and fit for purpose for being tested. Nor is it complete, coherent and fit for purpose for being generalised.

Case studies of HCI research would be needed to make good these shortcomings of framework validation. They should be the object of future research. However, conceptualisation of the General Framework, as presented here, provides a basis for, and proposes, superordinate concepts and their relations. In addition, it proposes superordinate criteria by which such case studies may be conducted and assessed. The latter and associated assessments are required for the validation of any proposed General Framework for HCI research. Such a conceptualisation of a General Framework for HCI research appears currently to be absent from the research literature (see 15.1). The absence is particularly critical as concerns superordinate concepts and their relations, as well as superordinate criteria.

However, even without such case studies, frameworks can be assessed for completeness against other HCI frameworks (see 12.3). Frameworks can also be assessed against HCI knowledge, which typically take the form of theories acquired or validated by the use of other frameworks (see 13.3). Each framework has its own scope and these scopes may differ. For example, the scope of a framework for single user and single computer interactions would be incomplete with respect to the scope of a framework for computer-supported cooperative work interactions. The reverse, however, would not necessarily be the case.

Conclusion

This concludes the presentation of the validation of HCI knowledge, as acquired by HCI research. The concept of validation is applied in turn to approaches to HCI research and to frameworks for HCI research.

11.5 Research Practice Assignment

The assignment comprises two sections: General and Research Design Scenarios.

11.5.1 General

- Has the validation of HCI knowledge been involved in your research or in research with which you are familiar or how you think about validation?
  - If so, characterise the type of validation and describe how it has been involved.
  - If validation has not been involved in the research, why do you think this is so?
  - Do you think that this omission is important or not?
- Search the HCI literature for an alternative definition of the validation of HCI knowledge to that offered in 11.2.
  - Compare the alternative definition of validation with that presented in 11.2 and note the similarities and differences.
  - Are any of these similarities and differences shared by the type of validation involved in your research or in research with which you are familiar or how you think about validation? If so, consider why this might be the case.
- Search the HCI literature for an alternative definition of the validation of HCI knowledge acquired by HCI research approaches to that offered in 11.3.
  - Compare the alternative definition of validation with that presented in 11.3 and note the similarities and differences.
  - Are any of these similarities and differences shared by the type of validation involved in your research or in research with which you are familiar or how you think about validation? If so, consider why this might be the case.
- Search the HCI literature for an alternative definition of the validation of HCI knowledge supported by a generic framework (see 12.3), acquired by HCI research, to that offered in 11.4.
  - Compare the alternative definition of validation with that presented in 11.4 and note the similarities and differences.
  - Are any of these similarities and differences shared by the type of validation involved in your research or in research with which you are familiar or how you think about validation? If so, consider why this might be the case.

Hints and Tips

Difficult to get started?

Try reading the chapter again, while at the same time thinking explicitly about the validation of knowledge in all its forms, whether in the arts or the sciences, in the development of information technology or, indeed, in your own professional or social life.

Describe your research in terms of validation (of any type) before attempting to apply those of 11.2 and 11.3.

Difficult to complete?

Familiarise yourself with the concept of validation, as it is applied in the HCI research (and other) literature.

Note the similarities and differences between the different concepts of validation identified in the HCI research literature.

Test[1]

- List and specify from memory the four superordinate concepts of validation. Also, from memory:
  - Apply the four superordinate concepts of validation to HCI research approaches (see 11.3).
  - Apply the four superordinate concepts of validation to the General Framework for HCI research (see 11.2).
- List and specify from memory the three superordinate criteria of validation. Also, from memory:
  - Apply the three superordinate criteria of validation to HCI research approaches (see 11.3).
  - Apply the three superordinate criteria of validation to the General Framework for HCI research (see 11.2).

11.5.2 Research Design Scenarios

Research Design Scenario 11.1: Validating an HCI Framework from the Research of Others

- Select an approach to HCI research that you created to complete the initial research design scenarios of 4.4.2–9.4.2.
  - For illustrative purposes only, such an approach might be in the manner of the craft approach of Balaam et al. (2015) (see 6.2).

- Select a framework listed in 12.3 with which you are familiar or which you consider to be in need of validation.[2]
  - For illustrative purposes only, such a framework might be in the manner of that of Shneiderman (1983) (see 12.3.3).
  - Select from the chosen framework a limited number of concepts. The concepts should be of the more important ones and at least two to be related, either at the same or at different levels of description.
  - For illustrative purposes only, such concepts might be in the manner of *Objects*, *Representations*, *Actions* and *Performance*, as they appear in the Shneiderman framework (see 12.3.3).
- Applying the approach selected earlier, sketch a plan for a research project whose aim is to validate some aspect(s) of the selected framework. The plan should specify the stages/phases of the research to be conducted, although at a high level of description. The latter should be restricted to the concepts selected and so can only be selective and partial.
  - For illustrative purposes only, such a sketch of the plan for a project might take the form of research by Balaam et al. (2015) – see 6.2. The latter reports four phases of a design and research project. These include user-engagement sensitisation, user-centred design, development/deployment and in-the-wild assessment of a mobile phone application. The latter is called FeedFinder, a location-mapping mobile application for breastfeeding women.
  - The scope of the validation should be from one or more different examples of HCI knowledge, for example models, methods or performance/other claims. Is the framework able to accommodate the piece(s) of knowledge/claims? Again, the application of the framework can only be selective and so partial, as only some of its concepts are involved.
  - For illustrative purposes only, such a research project sketch of a plan might be of the Shneiderman framework (see 12.3.3), being validated by the craft approach of Balaam et al. (see 6.2). The framework might be represented by the concepts of *Objects*, *Representations*, *Actions* and *Performance*. The validation aim might be to test the Shneiderman framework *Performance* claim that application of the selected concepts results in *Reduced Memory Load*.
  - Do your best to include as many superordinate concepts of validation in your plan (see 11.4) as appropriate. In the event that you cannot apply one or more concepts, identify and record the reason.
  - Do your best to include as many superordinate criteria of validation in your plan (see 11.4) as appropriate. In the event that you cannot apply one or more criteria, identify and record the reason.

- Search the HCI research literature to establish whether any attempts have been made to validate the framework you selected for this research design scenario.
  - In the affirmative, compare the published instance(s) of framework validation with your validation. Identify the similarities and differences.
- Finally, consider how your illustrative project plan for validation might be improved.

Research Design Scenario 11.2: Validating an HCI Theory from the Research of Others

- Select an approach to HCI research that you created to complete the initial research design scenarios of 4.4.2–9.4.2.
  - For illustrative purposes only, such an approach might be in the manner of the craft approach of Balaam et al. (see 6.2).
  - Select an HCI theory listed in 13.3 with which you are familiar or which you consider to be in need of validation.[3]
  - For illustrative purposes only, such a theory might be in the manner of that of external cognition (see 13.3.1.1).
  - Select from the chosen theory a limited number of concepts. The concepts should be of the more important ones and at least two to be related, either at the same or at different levels of description.
  - For illustrative purposes only, such concepts might be in the manner of *Externalisation, Annotation and Cognitive Tracing*, as they appear in external cognition theory (see 13.3.1.1).
- Applying the approach selected earlier, sketch a plan for a research project whose aim is to validate some aspect(s) of the selected theory. The plan should specify the stages/phases of the research to be conducted, although at a high level of description. The latter should be restricted to the concepts selected and can only be selective and so partial.
  - For illustrative purposes only, such a sketch of the plan for a project might take the form of research by Balaam et al. (see 6.2). The latter reports four phases of a design and research project. These include user-engagement sensitisation, user-centred design, development/deployment and in-the-wild assessment of a mobile phone application. The latter is called FeedFinder, a location-mapping mobile application for breastfeeding women.
- The scope of the validation should be from one or more different examples of HCI knowledge, for example, models, methods or performance/other claims. Is the theory able to accommodate the piece(s) of knowledge/claims? Again,

the application of the theory can only be selective and so partial, as only some of its concepts are involved.

- For illustrative purposes only, such a research project sketch of a plan might be of the external cognition theory being validated by the craft approach of Balaam et al. (see 6.2). The theory might be represented by the concepts of *Externalisation*, *Annotation* and *Cognitive Tracing*. The validation aim might be to test the external cognition theory *Performance* claim that application of the selected concepts results in *Reduced Memory Load*.
- Do your best to include as many superordinate concepts of validation as possible in your plan (see 11.4) as appropriate. In the event that you cannot apply a concept, try to identify the reason.
- Do your best to include as many superordinate criteria of validation in your plan (see 11.4) as appropriate. In the event that you cannot apply a criterion, try to identify the reason.
- Search the HCI research literature to establish whether any attempts have been made to validate the theory you selected for this research design scenario.
  - In the affirmative, compare the published instance(s) of theory validation with your illustrative plan. Identify the similarities and differences.
- Finally, consider how your plan might be improved.

11.6 Notes

1. The test encourages researchers to commit the approaches and frameworks to memory. Such internalisation facilitates their subsequent application.
2. Validation properly belongs in Chapter 11. However, the HCI frameworks of other researchers are not presented until Chapter 12. Research Design Scenario 11.1 requires reference to HCI frameworks. To support researchers in completing this particular research design scenario, the latter is presented in both chapters. This gives the researchers the option of completing the scenario as most suits them. Alternatively, researchers might like to complete the design scenario twice to help them memorise the concepts and so to facilitate their application.
3. Validation properly belongs in Chapter 11. However, the HCI theories of other researchers are not presented until Chapter 13. Research Design Scenario 11.2 requires reference to HCI theories. To support researchers in completing this particular design scenario, the latter is presented in both chapters. This gives the researchers the option of completing the scenario as most suits them. Alternatively, researchers might like to complete the design scenario twice to help them memorise the concepts and so to facilitate their application.

12

Assessing General Framework against Other HCI Frameworks

This chapter assesses the General Framework for HCI research for completeness against other frameworks for HCI. Overall, the General Framework is considered to be complete, although this depends much on the coherence of individual concepts. This assessment, however, does not constitute a validation of the General Framework. It is nevertheless indicative of its comparability with other HCI frameworks with respect to its completeness. The frameworks are further considered as concerns their dissemination in the HCI research literature. The General Framework is then assessed for its accommodation of the factors that appear to influence the success of framework dissemination.

12.1 General

The General Framework for HCI research is assessed against other HCI frameworks. The aim of the assessment is to establish whether or not the General Framework is complete, and so comparable with respect to these frameworks. The General Framework is considered complete if it is able to classify all the key concepts of a comparison HCI framework. The classification categories comprise the same concept with the same descriptor, the same concept with a different descriptor and a different (but coherent) concept with a different descriptor. Individual concepts are assessed as present, and so classified as complete, or absent, and so classified as incomplete. The General Framework itself can be assessed overall as complete, generally complete, partially complete or incomplete, depending on the completeness of its individual concepts.

For example, the concept of application in the General Framework would be classified as complete with respect to the concept of application in a comparison HCI framework. It is the same concept with the same descriptor. Likewise, the concept of application in the General Framework would be classified as complete with respect to the concept of domain in a comparison HCI framework. It is the same concept with a different descriptor. Last, the concept of application in the General Framework would be classified as complete with respect to the concept of e-shopping in a comparison framework. It is a different, but coherent, concept with a different descriptor. In this case, the coherence derives from the superordinate relations of application to 'e-shopping'.

The assessment does not constitute a validation of the General Framework nor the knowledge acquired by means of its application. However, the assessment is indicative as to the comparability of the General Framework with other HCI frameworks, at least as concerns its completeness. It is also suggestive as to the potential of the General Framework for both types of validation: framework and knowledge.

Superordinate and subordinate relations are reciprocal. That is, if the General Framework concept is subordinate to that of a comparison framework, the concept of the latter is considered to be superordinate to that of the former. For example, if 'application' is superordinate to 'e-shopping', then 'e-shopping' is subordinate to 'application'. Coherence, then, between the frameworks is also reciprocal for such concepts. That is, if most of the General Framework concepts are coherent with those of a comparison framework, then the related concepts of the latter are coherent with those of the former.

The most rigorous assessment would have applied the same superordinate criteria proposed for validation – that is, completeness, coherence and fitness for purpose – for each of the four superordinate concepts of conceptualisation, operationalisation, test and generalisation. However, the General Framework has only been conceptualised, so only this superordinate criterion can be assessed (see 11.4). In addition, the concepts of the comparison frameworks are generally not identified explicitly by their proposers. Further, most of the frameworks are for HCI, rather than for HCI research, although the latter may be implied. The coherence and fitness for (design research) purpose of the latter, then, cannot be reliably established. Hence, it can only constitute an indicative basis for the assessment of the General Framework.

As a result, the assessment is selective, but systematic and informal. It is selective, because although it includes completeness, it does not include coherence (in general) or fitness for purpose. It is systematic, because the criteria for completeness are explicit. Also, they are applied consistently to the relations between the concepts of the General Framework and the key concepts of the comparison HCI frameworks. Last, the assessment is informal, where formal would mean reliably replicated by different but appropriate other researchers. This is not the case.

As well as the assessment of the General Framework for completeness against other HCI frameworks (and the reverse), each framework is also considered as concerns its dissemination in the HCI research literature. Dissemination is understood to include the framework's disseminators, as well as the dissemination's content, media and means. The framework's relative dissemination success is also considered for the light it sheds on the large number of frameworks in the HCI research literature and their, at best, modest dissemination. Such a historical perspective and consideration is currently absent from the research literature. The review of HCI framework dissemination, however, is not intended to be a definitive history to make good the deficit. That would be beyond the scope of the book. Rather, the review seeks insights into the origins and development of the frameworks. The aim is to identify the factors that appear to influence the success of their dissemination and to which the General Framework needs to accommodate.

12.2 General Framework Assessment

The core framework for HCI research constitutes the basis for the General Framework for HCI research (see 3.4–3.5). The General Framework for HCI research itself is presented in 10.2.2. It instantiates the core framework, as expressed by the specific frameworks (see 4.3–9.3), and also by the associated design research exemplars (see Figures 4.1–9.1) and by the specific lower-level frameworks (see 4.3.4–9.3.4). All these sources may provide support for the assessment of General Framework concepts against those of other HCI frameworks.

HCI frameworks for research support the acquisition and validation of HCI knowledge by research. For example, there are a number of different computer-supported cooperative work frameworks. The latter, against which the General Framework is assessed, are those having currency in the HCI literature in terms of citations, replications, validation and case studies.[1]

It is a matter of judgement as to whether, in some cases, a specific research contribution should be assessed as a theory or as a framework, as here. Morton et al.'s (1979) paper explicitly proposes a framework, as indicated by its title – 'Interacting with the Computer: A Framework', and similarly for Kuutti's (1996) paper 'Activity Theory as a Potential Framework for Human–computer Interaction Research'. However, in-the-wild theory proposals, such as those presented by Rogers (2012), constitute, or are intended to constitute, a theory. There is no explicit framework, although an implicit framework cannot be excluded. Likewise with human values theory (Harper et al., 2008). Consequently, the latter two references are considered as theories, rather than as frameworks.

The General Framework is repeated here to support researchers in following and checking the details of the assessment.

The General Framework for HCI research comprises the following:

Discipline, as an academic (that is, scholarly) field (that is, branch/subject area) of study (that is, investigation of knowledge as division of information/learning) and

General, as common (that is, shared) and

General Problem, as the design (that is, specification) of human–computer interactions and

Particular Scope, as the design of human (that is, individual/group)–computer (that is, interactive/embedded) interactions (that is, active/passive) to do something (that is, action/task) as desired (that is, wanted/needed/experienced/felt/valued) and

General Research, as the diagnosis of design problems (that is, not as desired) and the prescription of design solutions (that is, as desired) as they relate to performance (that is, desired) for the acquisition (that is, creation) and for the validation (that is, confirmation) of knowledge to support practices and

General Knowledge, as guidelines/models/ methods/principles (that is, acquired and validated by research) and supports (that is, facilitates/makes possible) practices and

General Practices, as trial and error/implement and/then test (that is, supported by knowledge acquired and validated by research).

12.3 Assessment of General Framework for HCI Research against Other Frameworks

The assessment of the General Framework for HCI research against individual other frameworks follows.

12.3.1 Morton et al. (1979) Interacting with the Computer: A Framework

Summary
The Morton et al. (1979) framework was prompted by the introduction in the 1970s of the interactive computer. It is, then, perhaps the earliest framework of its kind. The main aim of the framework is to describe the behavioural

phenomena of people interacting with the newly introduced computers, and also to apply the models and methods of cognitive psychology, including linguistics, to the better understanding of these phenomena.

On the basis of observational studies of computer users at work, Morton et al. conclude that the information technology industry's model of human–computer interaction is essentially computer-centric and, on occasion, also designer-centric. The resulting interactive systems are difficult to understand and to use. This is clearly demonstrated by a number of observational studies (Long et al., 1980, 1982).

Morton et al. propose an alternative to the information technology industry's model. The alternative is one in which 'systems match people' rather than 'people match systems'. That is, the systems are user-centric. They argue that cognitive psychology research is well placed to characterise and to understand such a mismatch between people and computers. Understanding is to be achieved by the use of empirical tools. The latter include field and laboratory studies and conceptual tools, such as models and representations, for example, block interaction, information structures and state transition models. The resultant output to designers is intended to support more user-centric design. Consistent with the paper's title, the research required to acquire and to validate such an output is neither included nor specified.

Key Concepts
The key concepts of the Morton et al. framework are presented in *Italics*, and the related main General Framework concepts (see 3.4 and 10.2.2) are presented in **Boldface.**

- *Scope* (as *People, Computers, Systems, Interactions, Behavioural Phenomena* and *Performance*) – **Particular Scope.**
- *Cognitive Science* (as *Psychology* and *Linguistics*) – **Discipline**, and *Output to Designers* (as *User-Centric*) – **General Problem** and **Knowledge.**
- *Tools* (as *Empirical Tools/Methods – Field Studies, Observational Studies, Laboratory Studies*) and (as *Conceptual Tools – Models* as *Block Interaction, Information Structures, State Transition*) – **Research, Knowledge** and **Practices.**
- *Representations* (as *Domain – Computer Representation*) and (as *Problem – User Knowledge, Computer, Interface, General Systems, Machines, Procedures*; as *Natural Language – Lexical, Syntactic* and *Semantic*; as *Mismatch People/Computers*) – **Research** and **Knowledge.**

Assessment
Since the Morton et al. framework comprises a science framework and the concept of its application (*Output to Designers*), the related General

Framework concepts can also be found in the specific framework instantiations (for applied see 7.3 and for science see 8.3). In addition, the related General Framework concepts may also be referenced in the associated design research exemplars (for applied see Figure 7.1 and for science see Figure 8.1).

The General Framework does not reference specific lower-level concepts, such as *Models* and *Representations*, as proposed by Morton et al. These concepts, such as the *Block Interaction*, the *Information Structures* and the *State Transition Models*, are all different concepts with different descriptors, compared with those of the General Framework. The superordinate concepts of **Research** and **Knowledge** (see 3.4 and 10.2.2), however, are coherent as concerns the *Models* and *Representations*.

With respect to the framework of Morton et al., the General Framework is considered to be generally complete. However, the completeness is much dependent on the coherence between the two sets of concepts. It is not considered as complete, to allow for the possibility of disagreement as to which concepts form part of the Morton et al. framework, and also, which of those concepts are key. Unlike the General Framework, all the concepts of Morton et al. are not explicitly identified.[2]

Dissemination
Concerning the dissemination of the Morton et al. framework, the HCI research literature suggests the disseminators are limited to the framework's creators, for example Barnard (1991) and Long (1987), but not Morton, who subsequently changed research field. The dissemination content consists of the application of a few highly selective concepts and their illustration, plus the general concept of applied cognitive psychology. Note that the latter is not exclusive to the framework. The dissemination media comprise research papers. The dissemination means consist essentially of using the framework for illustrative purposes and as the basis for other frameworks. There is no evidence of any case studies attempting to validate the original framework.

12.3.2 Card, Moran and Newell (1983) *The Psychology of Human-Computer Interaction*

Summary
Card et al. (1983) propose a model of the user interacting with the computer, entitled the 'model human processor' (MHP). It is an information-processing-type model, following the psychology of the time. The aim is to understand

human behaviour as explanation and prediction of human behavioural phenomena. It constitutes one of the earliest cognitive models intended to support HCI engineering in the design of human–computer interactions. MHP comprises three interacting systems: perceptual, cognitive and motor, each with its own memory and processor.

In addition, Card et al. develop a family of models, known by the acronym GOMS. This stands for: Goals – desired aims to be achieved by the user; Operators – cognitive processes and physical actions needed to achieve the user's goals; Methods – steps and procedures to carry out the cognitive processes and physical actions required to achieve the user's goals; and Selection rules – by which the user is able to select the best method for achieving their goals. The family of methods supports the systematic expression of task performance at different levels of description. The task-level model (TLM) is at the highest and the keystroke-level model (KLM) is at the lowest level of description.

The framework, then, supports the recruitment of the models and findings of psychology to support the design of interactive systems.

Key Concepts
The key concepts of the Card et al. framework for HCI are presented in *Italics*, and the related main General Framework concepts (see 3.4 and 10.2.2) are presented in **Boldface.**

- *Scope* (as *People, User, Human Behaviour, Phenomena, Computers, Interactions* and *Performance*) – **Particular Scope**.
- *Psychology* (as *Findings, Understanding, Explanation* and *Prediction*) – **Discipline**.
- *Engineering* and *Design* – **Discipline** and **General Problem.**
- *Models* (as *Cognitive Model, Information Processing Model, Model Human Processor* (*MHP*) – *Perceptual, Cognitive* and *Motor*, all with *Own Memory* and *Processor*) – **Research** and **Knowledge**.
- *GOMS Model Family*, as *Goals – Desired User Aims, Achievement* and *User*; as *Operators – Cognitive Processes* and *Physical Actions, Achievement*; as *Methods – Steps* and *Procedures* for *User Goals* and as *Selection Rules – Best Method Selection* for *Achievement User Goal, Speed and Errors*), *Levels of Description* (from *Task-Level* to *Keystroke-Level Model*) – **Research, Knowledge** and **Practices**.

Assessment
Since the Card et al. framework comprises both an applied and a science framework, the related General Framework concepts can also be found in the

specific framework instantiations (for applied see 7.3 and for science see 8.3). In addition, the related General Framework concepts may also be referenced in the applied design research exemplar (see Figure 7.1) and the science design research exemplar (see Figure 8.1).

The General Framework does not reference the specific *MHP* and *GOMS* models and their associated representations. They are all different concepts with different descriptors. However, the superordinate concepts of **Research**, **Knowledge** and **Practices** (see 3.4 and 10.2.2) are coherent concerning both models.

With respect to the framework of Card et al., the General Framework is considered to be generally complete. However, the completeness is much dependent on the coherence between the two sets of concepts. It is not considered as complete, to allow for the possibility of disagreement as to which concepts form part of the framework and, of those concepts, which are key. Like the General Framework, concepts are explicitly identified, at least in terms of the *MHP*, the *GOMS* and the *Family of Task Models*.[3]

Dissemination

Concerning the dissemination of the Card et al. framework, apart from the creators, the primary disseminators appear to be fellow research group members. The dissemination content consists of the *MHP* and the *GOMS models* and the overall concept of psychology, supporting the engineering of interactive systems. The dissemination media comprise research papers, book chapters and the original book. The dissemination means consist of case studies, applying the different models.

12.3.3 Shneiderman (1983) Direct Manipulation: A Step beyond Programming Languages

Summary

As its name suggests, Shneiderman's (1983) framework has a very specific scope – human–computer interactions involving direct manipulation. The framework addresses a style of interaction which, although introduced in the 1980s, continues to be popular. However, HCI is necessarily implicated more generally, both explicitly and implicitly. Little reference is made to HCI research per se as the acquisition and validation of HCI knowledge, although a theoretical understanding of the novel information technology is offered. The framework is based on the ease with which people manipulate physical objects in their everyday lives. The framework assumes that a comparable ease can be built into interactive systems design by means of direct manipulation. The latter is of digital/virtual objects, such as buttons, icons and line drawings.

Shneiderman proposes three basic principles for such design. First, digital object representations and their associated actions should be continuous, so reducing the users' memory load. Second, such actions should be rapid, reversible and incremental. They should also be followed by immediate feedback, designed to support error recovery. Third, such actions should be embodied physically. The framework has been very popular for its ability to describe and rationalise direct manipulation as a successful and enduring style of interaction.

Key Concepts

The key concepts of the Shneiderman framework are presented in *Italics*, and the related main General Framework concepts (see 3.4 and 10.2.2) are presented in **Boldface**.

- *Scope* (as *People, Everyday Lives, Interface, Computers, Interactive Systems, Novel Information Technology, Direct Manipulations, Interactions/Style* and *Performance*) – **Particular Scope**.
- *Software Engineering* – **Discipline**.
- *Design* (as *Engineering*; *Theoretical Understanding*; *Design* and *Principles*) – **Discipline** and **General Problem**.
- *Objects* (as *Digital/Virtual* – *Buttons, Icons, Line Drawings*; as *Physical*) – **Research** and **Knowledge**.
- *Representations* (as *Continuous* – to reduce *Memory-Load*) – **Research** and **Knowledge**.
- *Actions* (as *Direct Manipulation* with *Immediate Feedback*; as *Controllable/ Reversible/Incremental/Physical*) – **Research** and **Knowledge**.
- *Performance* (as *Easy to Manipulate/Remember/Learn/Master*; as *Speed and Errors*) – **Research, Knowledge** and **Practices**.

Assessment

Since Shneiderman's framework includes *Design*, the related General Framework concepts can also be found in the specific framework instantiations of craft (see 6.3) and of engineering (see 9.3). In addition, the related General Framework concepts may also be referenced in the craft design research exemplar (see Figure 6.1) and the engineering design research exemplar (see Figure 9.1).

The General Framework does not reference the specific *Representations* of *Controllable, Reversible, Incremental, Physical Representations*. However, these concepts are coherent with respect to **Research** and **Knowledge** (see 3.4 and 10.2.2). This leaves the conclusion concerning the completeness of the General Framework unaffected.

With respect to the framework of Shneiderman, the General Framework is considered to be generally complete. However, the completeness is much dependent on the coherence between the two sets of concepts. It is not considered as complete, to allow for the possibility of disagreement as to which concepts form part of the Shneiderman framework and, of those concepts, which are key. Unlike the General Framework, the concepts of Shneiderman are not all explicitly identified.[4]

Dissemination

Concerning the dissemination of the Shneiderman framework, the primary disseminator is the creator of the framework. The dissemination content consists mainly of the three basic principles for direct manipulation interface design and their exemplification. The dissemination media comprise research papers, book chapters and books. The framework continues to be a popular way of thinking about direct manipulation. The dissemination means consist largely of informally demonstrating the framework's application to design. Other aspects of framework validation, however, appear absent.

12.3.4 Long (1987) Cognitive Ergonomics and Human-Computer Interaction

Summary

Long first proposes a general framework that relates work, as tasks, to knowledge, as science. Work is decomposed into tasks, which are analysed to produce an acquisition representation. The latter is then generalised by science in the process of acquiring related knowledge. The associated general representation is used to produce an application representation, which is synthesised in its application to tasks.

Long then uses the framework to model traditional ergonomic tasks. The latter include the operation of machinery and the inspection of items in the manufacturing process. The models are in terms of sciences, such as psychology and physiology. Tasks are analysed to produce a laboratory simulation, which is generalised by the sciences for the purposes of acquiring related knowledge. The generalisation is then particularised in the form of guidelines, which are synthesised for application to the traditional ergonomic tasks.

Last, the framework is used to model cognitive ergonomics in the form of HCI tasks. These include, for example, online shopping, computer-aided design and information manipulation and enquiry. The framework is also used to model associated sciences, for example, cognitive psychology and linguistics. HCI tasks are analysed to produce a laboratory simulation, which is generalised by the sciences. The latter generalisation is particularised in the form of guidelines, which are synthesised for application to HCI tasks, such as word processing and videotex search.

The framework and models are exemplified by the HCI tasks of online shopping, computer-aided design and information manipulation and enquiry. It is suggested how guidelines resulting from such research might be used by designers to increase the usability of interactive systems by reducing the cognitive incompatibility between users and computers.

The key concepts of the Long framework are presented in *Italics*, and the related main General Framework concepts (see 3.4 and 10.2.2) are presented in **Boldface**.

Key Concepts

* *Scope* (as *Work, Tasks, People, Computers, Interactions, Cognitive In/ Compatibility*) – **Particular Scope**.
* *Sciences* (as *Ergonomics – Operation, Inspection, Cognitive Psychology, Cognitive Ergonomics – Online Shopping, Computer-Aided Design, Information Manipulation* and *Enquiry*) – **Discipline** and **General Problem**.
* *Laboratory Simulation, Knowledge, Guidelines, Application* – **Research, Knowledge** and **Practices**.
* *Representations* (as *Acquisition and Application, General* and *Particular, Analysis* and *Synthesis*) – **Research** and **Knowledge**.

Assessment

Since Long's framework references *Science* in general and *Cognitive Psychology* in particular, the related General Framework concepts, based on the core framework, can also be found in the specific framework instantiations (see applied 7.3 and science 8.3). In addition, the latter concepts may also be referenced in the applied design research exemplar (see Figure 7.1) and the science design research exemplar (see Figure 8.1).

The General Framework does not reference the specific *Representations* of *Acquisition* and *Application*. However, these concepts are coherent with those of **Research** and **Knowledge** (see 3.4 and 10.2.2), so leaving the conclusion concerning the completeness of the General Framework unaffected.

With respect to the framework of Long, the General Framework is considered to be generally complete, although the completeness is much dependent on the coherence between the two sets of concepts. It is not considered as complete, to allow for the possibility of disagreement as to which concepts form part of the Long framework and, of those concepts, which are key. Unlike the General Framework, the concepts of Long are not all explicitly identified.[5]

Dissemination

Concerning the dissemination of the Long framework, the disseminators are limited to the creator of the framework and Barnard (1991). The dissemination content consists of the illustrative application of the framework to examples of emerging technology of the time. The dissemination media comprise research papers and a book chapter. The dissemination means consist largely of illustrative examples of the framework's application to organise thinking about psychology and its relationship to design.

12.3.5 Long and Dowell (1989) Conceptions of the Discipline of HCI: Craft, Applied Science, and Engineering; Dowell and Long (1989)Towards a Conception for an Engineering Discipline of Human Factors

Summary

This conception constitutes the basis for the core framework (see 1.6 and 10.2.1), and so for the General Framework for HCI research (see 3.4). As concerns the General Framework's main concepts, the latter are complete with respect to the conception. There are differences at the lower level of framework description, but all are coherent with the higher level. No further comparison, then, is required for the purposes in hand. The framework has been included here only to complete the listing and to locate it historically.

Dissemination

Concerning the dissemination of the Long and Dowell/Dowell and Long (1989) conception, the primary disseminators are the framework creators, and other collaborators belonging to their research group. The dissemination content consists of the application of the framework and the address of some aspects of validation. The dissemination media comprise essentially research papers. The dissemination means consist largely of case studies, primarily involving conceptualisation, but also, to a much lesser extent, operationalisation.

12.3.6 Barnard (1991) Bridging between Basic Theories and the Artefacts of Human–Computer Interaction

Summary

Barnard (1991) begins by reviewing the bridging required to relate cognitive theory to the behaviours observed in human–computer interactions. Such bridging, he argues, is one of the many types of bridging needed, if science is to support the design of interactive systems. Barnard proposes a framework to bridge this gap, based on Long (1987 and 1989 – see also 12.3.4). He develops further the idea that tasks are analysed to produce an acquisition (he prefers the term 'discovery') representation. The latter is generalised (he prefers 'assimilated') by the sciences, and in particular cognitive psychology. The tasks are then particularised (he prefers 'contextualised') to produce an application representation. The latter is synthesised for application to tasks. He argues that such a framework, comprising bridging, discovery and application representations, is potentially valuable. It facilitates specification of comparison between, and evaluation of, the many different paradigms and practices operating in the field of HCI.

Barnard then expands the discovery representation to include assumptions leading to the design of observational, experimental and scenario studies. The application representation is expanded, in turn, to include a family of cognitive task models. The latter comprise goal formation and action, expressed in terms of process configuration, procedural knowledge, record contents and dynamic coordination and control. Finally, the cognitive science representation is expanded in terms of a model – interacting cognitive subsystems. The latter includes its principles of operation and the HCI phenomena which it characterises. The characterisation comprises the behaviours observed in human–computer interactions.

According to Barnard, the ultimate impact of basic theory, such as the interacting cognitive subsystems model, on design can only be indirect, that is, through explicit application representations. Alternative and additional forms of such representations, he argues, need to be created, developed and evaluated. On this view, the direct theory-based product of an applied science HCI is not an interface design. It is an application representation capable of providing principled support for reasoning about designs.

Key Concepts

The key concepts of the Barnard framework are presented in *Italics*, and the related main General Framework concepts (see 3.4 and 10.2.2) are presented in **Boldface**.

- *Scope* (as *People, Behaviour, Computers, Systems, Tasks* and *Interactions*) – **Particular Scope**.
- *Cognitive Psychology* (*Applied Science*) *Paradigm, Basic Theory, Comparison, Evaluation* – **Discipline**.
- *Principled Design Support, Design* (as *Direct/Indirect, Reasoning*) – **General Problem** and **Research**.
- *Representations* (as *Bridging – Discovery, Assimilation, Contextualisation and Synthesis*) – **Research** and **Knowledge**.
- *Research Studies* (as *Observational, Experimental* and *Scenario); Models* (as *Cognitive Task Models – Goal Formation* and *Action,* as *Process Configuration, Procedural Knowledge, Record Contents*; *Dynamic Coordination* and *Control,* as *Cognitive Models – Interacting Cognitive Subsystems*) – **Knowledge** and **Practices**.

Assessment

Since Barnard's framework comprises a science framework and the concept of applied (*Design Support*), the related General Framework concepts can also be found in the specific core framework instantiations of applied (see 7.3) and science (see 8.3). In addition, the related General Framework concepts may also be referenced in the specific applied design research exemplar (see Figure 7.1) and the science design research exemplar (see Figure 8.1).

The General Framework does not reference some of the specific higher-level representations proposed by Barnard, such as *Discovery, Assimilation, Contextualisation* and *Synthesis*. However, these can be accommodated by **Research** and **Knowledge** (see 3.4 and 10.2.2), with which they are coherent. The General Framework also does not reference the specific lower-level *Cognitive Task Models*, comprising *Goal Formation* and *Action,* expressed in terms of *Process Configuration, Procedural Knowledge, Record Contents* and *Dynamic Coordination. Interacting Cognitive Subsystems* is one such *Cognitive Task Model,* which is not referenced by the General Framework. However, these specific lower-level concepts can be accommodated by **Knowledge**, with which they are coherent, so leaving the conclusion concerning completeness unaffected.[6]

Dissemination

Concerning the dissemination of the Barnard framework, the only disseminator appears to be the framework's creator. The dissemination content consists of the application of the framework to underpin different aspects of cognitive modelling. The dissemination media comprise research papers and book chapters. The dissemination means consist largely of the successive development of cognitive models, for example, the interacting cognitive subsystems model.

12.3.7 Kuutti (1996) Activity Theory as a Potential Framework for Human-Computer Interaction Research

Summary

'Activity theory' originated with the Russian psychologists Vygotsky (1962) and Leontiev (1978 and 1989). It attempts to understand human behaviour in terms of everyday interactions, with things and people within their developmental, cultural and historical context. Operations (having conditions) support actions (having goals), which support activities (having motives). Activities are mediated by artefacts, which are both physical and abstract. Abstract artefacts support psychological and social activities (Bannon and Bodker, 1991). These basic concepts have been further developed for the specific activity of work. For example, Engeström (1990) added the concepts of tools, rules, community and division of labour.

Activity theory has been taken up by HCI in many different forms, and also with many different extensions and modifications. It could have been assessed in 13.3, as an HCI theory or group of theories. However, it is included here because Kuutti's (1996) framework is proposed specifically as a potential framework for HCI research. Kuutti extended the activity hierarchical structure, for example, to show how computer technology can be used to support different activities at different levels. Further, Nardi (1996) also used the framework to elicit new design concerns. In addition, Gonzalez (2006) inserted the concept of engagement, between action and activity. Engagement comprises five types: requests, projects, problems, events and recurrents. Activity theory continues to propagate itself in HCI in many different forms.

The origins and developments of activity theory are assessed here together with Kuutti's framework, as they have a common basis.

Key Concepts

The key concepts of Kuutti's potential activity theory framework are presented in *Italics*, and the related main General Framework concepts (see 3.4 and 10.2.2) are presented in **Boldface**.

- *Scope* (as *Things* and *People – Individuals* and *Groups/Teams*, *Networked Computers*, *Everyday Interactions*, *Interactions*, *Performance*, *Human Behaviour*) – **Particular Scope**.

- *Social* and *Organisational Psychology* (as *Framework, Activity Theory –
  Understanding,* as *Developmental, Cultural* and *Historical Context*) –
  Discipline.
- *Group Technology Support* (as *Application*) – **General Problem** and
  Practices.
- *People's Work Behaviour* (as *Operations – Conditions*; *Supporting Actions –
  Goals*; *Supporting Activities – Motives*; *Engagements –* as *Requests,
  Projects, Problems* and *Recurrents* and as *Tools, Rules, Community,
  Division of Labour, Different Activities* at *Different Levels*) – **Research** and
  Knowledge
- *Artefacts* (as *Physical* and *Abstract Interactive*; *Networked Computers –
  Psychological* and *Social Activities*) – **Particular Scope, Research** and
  Knowledge.

Assessment

Since activity theory, as embodied in the potential HCI framework of Kuutti,
presumes some application to design, the related General Framework concepts can also be found in the applied framework instantiation (see 7.3) and
may also be referenced in the applied design research exemplar (see Figure
7.1).

Although *Group Working* and *Networked Computers* are included in the
scope of the General Framework, along with concepts such as *Operations,
Actions* and *Activities*, the particular concept of *Engagement* and its associated
types, as *Requests, Projects, Problems* and *Recurrents*, are absent from its
lower-level framework. These concepts are all different concepts with different
descriptors. However, the superordinate concepts of **Particular Scope,
Research** and **Knowledge** (see 3.4 and 10.2.2) are coherent with respect to
Engagement and its associated types, hence leaving the conclusion concerning
completeness unaffected.

With respect to the framework of Kuutti, the General Framework is considered
to be generally complete. However, the completeness is much dependent on the
coherence between the two sets of concepts. It is not considered as complete, to
allow for the possibility of disagreement as to which concepts form part of the
Kuutti framework and, of those concepts, which are key. Unlike the General
Framework, the concepts of the Kuutti framework are not all explicitly identified.[7]

Dissemination

Concerning the dissemination of the Kuutti framework, the disseminator is the
creator of the framework, with occasional support from other researchers. The

dissemination content consists of the application of the framework, but often only in the form of illustrations. The dissemination media comprise research papers and book chapters. Validation of the framework does not seem to be addressed.

12.3.8 Olson and Olson (2000) Distance Matters

Summary
The Olson and Olson (2000) framework was a timely response to the increased networking of interactive computers and the resultant redistribution of work, tasks and activities. They propose a framework for HCI collaboration technology with the four key concepts: common ground, coupling of work, collaboration readiness and collaboration technology readiness. Other frameworks were also proposed at about the same time and with a similar scope, but with different and/or additional concepts. For example, Bacon and Fitzgerald (2001) proposed a systematic framework for the field of information systems, and De Souza, Barbosa, and Prates (2001) proposed a semiotic engineering approach to HCI. The Olson and Olson framework is carried forward here in preference to the other frameworks for further consideration, as concerns its dissemination, as it is better known.

Key Concepts
The key concepts of the Olson and Olson framework are presented in *Italics*, and the related main General Framework concepts (see 3.4 and 10.2.2) are presented in **Boldface**.

- *Scope* (as *Interactive Computers, Networking, Work, Distribution of Work*) – **Particular Scope**.
- *Collaboration Technology* (as *Common Ground, Coupling of Work, Collaboration Readiness* and *Collaboration Technology Readiness*) – **Particular Scope**, **Research** and **Knowledge.**

Assessment
Since the Olson and Olson framework, as applied to HCI, presumes some application to design, the related General Framework concepts can also be found in the applied core framework instantiation (see 7.3) and in the applied design research exemplar (see Figure 7.1).

Although the concepts of *Technology* and *Collaboration* are included in the scope of the General Framework, specific concepts, such as *Common Ground, Coupling of Work, Collaboration Readiness* and *Collaboration*

Technology Readiness, are absent. The superordinate concepts of **Particular Scope**, **Research** and **Knowledge** (see 3.4 and 10.2.2) are coherent with respect to these concepts, so leaving the conclusion concerning completeness unaffected.

With respect to the Olson and Olson framework, the General Framework is considered to be generally complete. However, the completeness is much dependent on the coherence between the sets of concepts. It is not considered as complete, to allow for the possibility of disagreement as to which concepts form part of the Olson and Olson framework and, of those concepts, which are key. Unlike the General Framework, all the concepts of the framework are not individually identified and explicitly specified.[8]

Dissemination

The disseminators of the Olson and Olson framework seem to be themselves. The dissemination content consists of the application of the framework, generally in illustrative form only. The dissemination media comprise primarily the original research paper. The dissemination means include occasional referencing by others. Validation of the framework has not been addressed.

12.3.9 Rauterberg (2006) HCI as an Engineering Discipline: To Be or Not To Be!?

Summary
Rauterberg begins by defining HCI broadly and by considering its past and possible future. Next, he defines the disciplines of science and engineering and their development. He then reviews the design paradigms of design and engineering. Academic knowledge, he argues, involves abstraction and concrescence, as well as explanation and prediction. Rauterberg then defines the scope of HCI, following Dowell and Long (1989). The latter includes the worksystem and the work domain, including their context. He considers the need for a scientific language, its definition and its support for consensus.

Rauterberg goes on to consider the possibility of a coherent research line. The latter is expressed in terms of a framework, its triangulation (validation) of design knowledge, the interactive system and empirical validation. Last, Rauterberg considers the relationship of HCI with industry and the system validation cycle. He concludes that to become an engineering discipline, HCI needs a well-specified interaction space which includes problems, a coherent taxonomy, a rigorous validation method, a coherent scientific language to achieve consensus and a research line to develop validated design knowledge.

Key Concepts

The key concepts of the Rauterberg framework are presented in *Italics*, and the related main General Framework concepts (see 3.4 and 10.2.2) are presented in **Boldface**.

- *Scope* (as *People* and *Computers* as a *Worksystem, Work Domain, Context, Interactions* and *Performance*) – **Particular Scope**.
- *Science* (as *Abstraction, Concrescence, Explanation* and *Prediction*); *HCI* (as *Past, Present, Future, Coherent Scientific Language, Consensus*) – **Discipline**.
- *Engineering* (as *Design, Development, Paradigm*) – **Discipline** and **General Problem**.
- *Models*, as *Interactive Worksystem, Work Domain* – **Research** and **Knowledge**.
- *Research Line* as *Coherence, Framework, Triangulation* (as *Academic Validation Cycle – Design Knowledge, Interactive System, Empirical Validation*) – **Research**, **Knowledge** and **Practices**.
- *Industrial Relationship* (as *System Validation Cycle, Interaction Space of Problems, Coherent Taxonomy, Rigorous Validation*) – **Discipline** and **Research.**

Assessment

Since Rauterberg's framework comprises *Science, Engineering* and *Design*, the related General Framework concepts can also be found in the specific core framework instantiations – applied (see 7.3), science (see 8.3) and engineering (see 9.3). In addition, the related General Framework concepts may also be referenced in the design research exemplars of applied (see Figure 7.1), of science (see Figure 8.1) and of engineering (see Figure 9.1).

Although the discipline concepts of *Science, Engineering* and *Design* are included in the scope of the General Framework, the higher-level concept of *Concrescence* is not. Perhaps the concept of operationalisation is the nearest equivalent. Some specific lower-level concepts are also absent, for example, *Worksystem* and *Work Domain*. Their equivalents in the General Framework are interactive system and application, respectively. The superordinate concepts **Research** and **Knowledge** (see 3.4 and 10.2.2), however, are coherent, so leaving the conclusion concerning completeness unaffected.

With respect to the Rauterberg framework, the General Framework is considered to be generally complete, although the completeness is much dependent on the coherence between the two sets of concepts. This is not surprising, since both frameworks have a common basis (Long and Dowell/Dowell and Long,

1989). It is not considered as complete, to allow for the possibility of disagreement as to which concepts form part of the Rauterberg framework and, of those concepts, which are key. Unlike the General Framework, the concepts of the Rauterberg framework are not all explicitly identified.[9]

Dissemination

Concerning the dissemination of the Rauterberg framework, the only disseminator appears to be the creator of the framework. The dissemination content consists largely of the referencing of the framework with respect to other research published in the literature. The dissemination media to date comprise primarily the original research paper. The dissemination means include largely proposals for future research.

12.3.10 Carroll, Kellogg and Rosson (1991) The Task-Artifact Cycle in Designing Interaction

Summary

Carroll et al. (1991) propose a programme for HCI. This includes design rationale as a framework and as a theory. The function of the latter is to integrate research and practice. Design rationale supports a detailed description of the history and meaning of an artefact. Carroll et al. argue that the most effective role for science in HCI design, for example applied cognitive science, is to interpret designs being used in practice. The interpretation is then codified as the knowledge implicit in those designs. The latter could be applied explicitly in subsequent designs. Further, importing these insights into HCI design would constitute essentially theory-based design. This proposal is considered to constitute an expansion of craft practice.

Carroll et al. argue that artefacts can be understood as theories and that HCI design and development can be supported by analysis of the artefacts. Implemented designs, once considered as knowledge, are claimed to be both sufficiently complete and precise enough for the purpose of design support. Artefacts address all the issues required by their specification, synthesising ideas from any source or origin. A design might apply ideas from GOMS (Card et al., 1983) as concerns keystroke-level interactions, and also ideas from activity theory (Nardi, 1996) as concerns cultural practices, and ideas from social psychology (McGrath, 1991) as concerns how users learn to trust systems such as internet banking. Last, designs are tested in practice, that is, people use the implemented interactive systems for desired purposes. Users are able to evaluate the success of the interactive systems for themselves.

Design rationale is proposed as the framework for such theories. The latter is intended to integrate HCI craft practices with applied social and cognitive science. The aim is to support those practices to make them more efficient. The main criterion for such synthesis is its compatibility with the practices and values of HCI designers. The concept and method of scenario design is proposed for this purpose.

Carroll (2010) Conceptualising a Possible Discipline of Human-Computer Interaction

Carroll (2010) proposes concepts additional to those presented in Carroll et al. (1991). Given the title of the paper ('conceptualisation' here means the same as 'framework' for the purposes in hand), the concepts have been included in the interests of completeness. According to Carroll, the scope of HCI includes work, play, leisure, education and other non-work activities. However, effectiveness, he argues, is not an appropriate criterion for their performance. Further, Carroll requires that HCI practices be specified empirically. Codified formal methods are to be applied in a similar manner.

Craft practice is the primary paradigm for technology innovation. Carroll goes on to argue that craft knowledge is objectified less, and proceduralised more, by craft practice than by applied science or engineering. HCI science provides an explicit foundation for engineering models. The latter should be sought in the practices of scientists, engineers and designers. Craft practice, applied science and engineering should function together as a mutually supportive ensemble of disciplinary models.[10]

Key Concepts

The key concepts of the Carroll et al./Carroll framework are presented in *Italics*, and the related main General Framework concepts (see 3.4 and 10.2.2) are presented in **Boldface**.

- *Scope* (as *People, Computers, Interactive Systems, Artefacts, Context, Interactions, Work, Play, Leisure, Education, Non-work Activities, Performance, Effectiveness, Other Criteria*) – **Particular Scope** and **Research**.
- *Disciplinary Models, Ensemble, Science* (as in *Applied Social* and *Cognitive Science* – support for *Design Practice, Empirical*); *Craft* (as *Practice, Design, Knowledge, Objectified, Proceduralised, Codified Formal Methods*); *Engineering*; *HCI* – *Programme, Framework, Technology Innovation*) – **Discipline**, **General Problem** and **Knowledge**.

- *Knowledge* (as *Theory, Codification, Integration, Application*); *Research* (as *Analysis, Claims Extraction*); *Artefact* (as *HCI Technology*); *Practice* (as *Design, Development, Implementation*) – **Research**, **Knowledge** and **Practices**.
- *Task-Artefact Cycle* (as *Task, Psychology of Tasks, Artefact in Situation of Use, Cycle*) – **Research** and **Knowledge**.
- *Design Rationale* (as *Design, Rationale, Claims Identification*) – **Research**, **Knowledge** and **Practices**.
- *Scenario-Based Design* (as *Design, Scenario, Representation, Method, User Questions*) – **Research**, **Knowledge** and **Practices**.

Assessment

Since the Carroll et al./Carroll framework references science as applied social and cognitive science (as support for *Design Practices*), the related General Framework concepts can also be found in the specific core framework instantiations of craft (see 6.3), of applied (see 7.3) and of science (see 8.3). In addition, the related General Framework concepts may also be referenced in the design research exemplars of craft (see Figure 6.1), of applied (see Figure 7.1) and of science (see Figure 8.1).

The General Framework does not reference some of the specific representations proposed, such as *Craft Practice* as expressed in terms of the *Task-Artefact Cycle, Design Rationale* and *Scenario-Based Design*. However, craft design has its own specific framework (see 6.3), along with applied design (see 7.3), science design (see 8.3) and engineering design (see 9.3) and the associated design research exemplars. Further, all the concepts are coherent with the superordinate concepts of **Discipline**, **General Problem** and **Research**. The General Framework also does not reference the specific lower-level concepts of the *Task-Artefact Cycle*, expressed as *Psychology of Tasks, Artefact in Situation of Use, Cycle, of Design Rationale*, as *Rationale, Claims Identification* and of *Scenario-Based Design*, as *Scenario* and *User Questions*. The superordinate concepts of **Research** and **Knowledge** (see 3.4 and 10.2.2), however, are coherent, so leaving the conclusion concerning completeness unaffected.

With respect to the Carroll et al./Carroll framework, the General Framework is considered to be generally complete, although the completeness is much dependent on the coherence between the two sets of concepts. It is not considered as complete, to allow for the possibility of disagreement as to which concepts form part of the Carroll et al./Carroll framework and, of those concepts, which are key. Unlike the General Framework, the concepts of the comparison framework are not all explicitly identified, although many are so identified.

Dissemination

Concerning the dissemination of the Carroll et al./Carroll framework, apart from the creators, the primary disseminators are fellow research group members and other researchers. The dissemination content consists of the task-artefact cycle and design rationale and their relation to craft practice. The dissemination media comprise research papers and book chapters. The dissemination means consist of case studies published by other researchers.

12.4 Dissemination of HCI Frameworks for Research

The preceding assessment of the General Framework against other HCI frameworks prompts two questions of interest to researchers attempting to apply frameworks in their work. First, why do there appear to be so many frameworks? The ten frameworks discussed in this chapter constitute a minority of the frameworks published in the HCI research literature. Second, why does the dissemination of frameworks, given the time period examined, seem so modest? The assessment offers a unique historical perspective within which to review the HCI frameworks. Such a perspective is currently absent from the HCI research literature.

Conducting the extensive analysis of the research literature required to produce a definitive answer to these two questions is beyond the scope of this book. However, the number of frameworks assessed, and the time period covered by the assessment, present an opportunity to identify, informally but systematically, some of the factors involved. The latter are of general interest to HCI researchers, but also of particular interest concerning the extent to which the General Framework takes or might take account of these factors.

The dissemination of frameworks is essential to their application and to their uptake in general. It is an appropriate criterion, then, by which to attempt to identify the factors affecting their number and dissemination. The latter is first defined generally and then applied specifically to HCI research frameworks.

12.4.1 Dissemination in General

Dissemination can be generally defined as the spreading of ideas widely. Dissemination involves agents, content, media and means. Agents are the 'who' of dissemination. They carry out the dissemination, that is, the spreading of the ideas widely. Content is the 'what' of dissemination, that is, the ideas that are spread widely. Media is the 'where' of dissemination, that is, the type of communication in which the ideas are expressed and spread widely. Means is the 'how' of dissemination, that is, the structure of the expression of the ideas that are spread widely.

12.4.2 Dissemination of HCI Frameworks for Research

Following the general definition of dissemination, the specific dissemination of HCI frameworks for research can be defined as the spreading of HCI frameworks widely. Dissemination of HCI frameworks involves researchers as the agents, frameworks as the ideas, papers and books as the media and applications, and case studies as the means (see also 12.1).

In terms of the frameworks assessed against the General Framework, Barnard (1991) and Carroll (2010) both constitute researchers proposing frameworks to support HCI research. They propose the bridging framework and the task-artefact cycle framework respectively. Their framework proposals are both published in HCI research journals. Barnard's framework takes the form of a model. Carroll's framework takes the form of a method.

12.4.3 Dissemination Success

Dissemination success expresses how widely the idea of an HCI framework is spread. Informal but systematic evaluation of the dissemination success of the frameworks assessed here realises the opportunity to identify some of the factors involved in that success. The General Framework for HCI research can be further considered in terms of these factors.

One way of evaluating the dissemination success of the frameworks assessed for HCI research is to divide them into two groups; for example, one of well-disseminated frameworks and the other of less well-disseminated frameworks. Each group can then be analysed for the factors judged to be associated with dissemination success or its lack thereof. Ideally and for this purpose, all the frameworks would be rank-ordered on the basis of individual book and paper publications and their associated citations. However, such an approach is beyond the scope of this book and its requirements here. Instead, recent and well-recognised HCI textbooks were consulted, by which to make the well/less well dissemination division. The textbooks are those authored by Rogers, Sharp and Preece (2011) and Rogers (2012). The number of reference appearances of a framework was taken to be a rough indication of the success of its dissemination. Only those reference appearances related to framework dissemination are taken into account, and not simply any publication authored by the framework creator. The results of this evaluation follow. The frameworks are ordered by date within the two divisions.

The well-disseminated HCI frameworks for research are Card et al. (1983), Shneiderman (1983), Long and Dowell/Dowell and Long (1989), Barnard (1991) and Carroll et al. (1991)/Carroll (2010). Each is considered in turn for the factors favouring well-disseminated HCI frameworks for research.

The less well-disseminated HCI frameworks for research are Morton et al. (1979), Long (1987), Kuutti (1996), Olson and Olson (2000) and Rauterberg (2006). Each is considered in turn for the factors favouring less well-disseminated HCI frameworks for research.

12.4.4 Factors Contributing to the Dissemination Success of Individual HCI Frameworks for Research

Individual frameworks from each group are now considered for factors judged to be associated with dissemination success or lack thereof.

12.4.4.1 Well-Disseminated HCI Frameworks for Research
Card et al. (1983) The Card et al. (1983) publication was the first HCI book to address human–computer interaction, the engineering of such interactions and how the science of cognitive psychology might support such engineering. These three firsts, in timely book form, guarantee its appearance in any HCI textbook references, including those of Rogers et al. (2011) and Rogers (2012). This conjunction of factors, however, is unique.

A more general factor favouring the dissemination of the framework is the clear specification of the concepts of the HCI framework in the form of the MHP model (model human processor) and the GOMS model (goals, operators, methods and selection rules). A further factor is the difference between the high-level discipline science/engineering frameworks with respect to that of the low-level models. The last factor is the conceptualisation and operationalisation case-study publication of the framework by researchers other than its authors, for example, John and Gray (1995), Atwood, Gray and John (1996) and Teo and John (2008).

Shneiderman (1983) Shneiderman's (1983) framework is for direct manipulation, comprising continuous digital object representations and rapid, reversal and incremental actions. The framework has found favour with HCI textbooks. The latter include those of both Rogers et al. (2011) and Rogers

(2012), in particular with respect to their address of the extensive developments characterising graphical use interface (GUI) technology. Shneiderman's use of the framework, as the starting point for further theoretical developments and applications (Shneiderman 1998, 2010), constitutes, by association, an additional factor favouring the framework's dissemination.

Long and Dowell/Dowell and Long (1989) The Long and Dowell/Dowell and Long (1989) conception appears in the Roger's HCI theory textbook (Rogers 2012), but not in Rogers et al. (2011). Factors more strongly supporting its dissemination, however, include well-specified concepts and, in particular, the glossary appended to the later Dowell and Long (1998). Another factor supporting dissemination includes the combination of a high-level discipline framework and a low-level human–computer interaction framework. Last, two key factors in its dissemination were its subsequent development by the authors, for example, Dowell (1998) and Long (2002, 2010), and its application and case-study publication by other researchers, for example, respectively, Rauterberg (2006) and Wild (2010), and also, in particular, researchers from their own research group, for example, Denley and Long (2001), Long and Timmer (2001), Long and Monk (2002), Long and Brostoff (2002), Hill (2010), Long (2010) and Salter (2010).

Barnard (1991) The Barnard (1991) framework appears in the Roger's (2012) HCI theory textbook, but not in Rogers et al. (2011). Factors more strongly supporting its dissemination, however, include well-specified concepts, in particular those of the lower-level interacting cognitive subsystems model, and also the inclusion of the higher-level science and applied science framework. An additional dissemination factor was its subsequent application by the author and his collaborators: Barnard and May (1999) and Barnard et al. (2000).

Carroll et al. (1991)/Carroll (2010) The Carroll et al. (1991)framework appears in the references of Roger's (2012) HCI theory textbook, but not in Rogers et al. (2011). However, the Carroll (2010) framework is likely to be too recent for publication in either. Factors more strongly supporting its dissemination include well-specified concepts. These include in particular those of the lower-level task-artefact cycle framework and the design rationale theory, as compared with the discipline level of science and craft. Both framework and theory have been well disseminated by the first author and his collaborators in publications (Carroll et al., 1991, 1995, 2003). There has also been some dissemination by other researchers, for example, Gregoriades and Sutcliffe (2005).

This completes the characterisation of the well-disseminated frameworks for HCI research, and the identification of factors judged to be associated with dissemination success. These factors include reference by well-rated text-books, clear specification of framework concepts, their specification at both high and low framework levels, subsequent development and application by the authors, and application and case-study publication by other researchers.

12.4.4.2 Less Well-Disseminated HCI Frameworks for Research

Morton et al. (1979) The Morton et al. (1979) framework does not appear in the references of either the textbook of Rogers et al. (2011) or the HCI theory book of Rogers (2012). There has been no development of the original frame-work by the authors, other than in much-modified forms. The latter retain only the overall applied science orientation (Long, 1987 and Barnard, 1991). The framework does contain well-specified model concepts. Those included are the block interaction, the information structures and the state transition models. However, their application is only illustrative and low level. Further, the models are not specifically related to the higher-level applied science orienta-tion. There have been no published case studies by either the authors or other researchers, so no attempts at framework validation. The failure to identify individual framework concepts has not supported any such validation.

Long (1987) The Long (1987) framework does not appear in the references of either the textbook of Rogers et al. (2011) or the HCI theory book of Rogers (2012). There has been no development of the original framework by the author, other than in a form that retains essentially only the overall applied science aspects, as one possible orientation for HCI (Long and Dowell, 1989). Further, the framework's exemplification is only illustrative, for example, Gilligan and Long (1984) and Buckley (1989). There has been no application to research or published case studies by either the authors or other researchers, although the framework was further adopted and developed by Barnard (1991). The framework was used to introduce and to organise an edited book on cognitive ergonomics and human–computer interaction (Long and Whitefield, 1989). However, this does not count as a research application that addresses validation.

Kuutti (1996) The Kuutti (1996) potential framework for human–computer interaction appears in the references of both the Rogers et al. (2011) and the Rogers (2012) textbooks. In spite of these references, there seems to have been no further specific development of the original extended hierarchical structure proposed by the author. Search of the HCI research literature suggests there to be no complete application or published case studies of the original potential framework by the author or by other researchers. Validation of the framework, then, has not been addressed.

Olson and Olson (2000) The scope of the Olson and Olson (2000) framework is primarily collaboration technology. The framework appears in the references of both the Rogers et al. (2011) and the Rogers (2012) textbooks. In spite of these references, there seems to have been no further specific development of the collaboration structure proposed originally. There also seems to be no complete application or published case studies of the original framework by the authors or by other researchers, and so no address of validation.

Rauterberg (2006) The Rauterberg (2006) framework is not referenced either by Rogers et al. (2011) or by Rogers (2012). It might have appeared somewhat late for either. There has been no development of the original framework by the author. The framework is supported by much referencing of the literature, but little exemplification in terms of its possible application. There appears to have been no application to research or published case studies by either the author or other researchers, so no address of validation.

This completes the characterisation of the less well-disseminated frameworks for HCI research, along with the identification of factors judged to be associated with lack of dissemination success. The latter factors include no reference by well-rated textbooks (with the exception of Kuutti, 1996 and Olson and Olson, 2000), no individual identification or clear specification of framework concepts, no specification of framework concepts at high and at low levels, and also no subsequent development and application by authors and no application and case-study publication by other researchers, and so no address of validation.

12.4.5 Dissemination Success and the General Framework

The General Framework can now be assessed for its likely ability to accommodate the factors that have been identified as being judged to be associated with successful and less successful HCI framework dissemination. A strong claim can be made for factors to which the General Framework is already accommodated in its present state of development. These include the clear specification of framework concepts which, unlike the remaining frameworks (with the exception of Dowell and Long, 1998), are individually and uniquely identified. Further, the concepts of the General Framework are specified at both high and low levels – those of the core framework and the lower-level framework respectively. Only a less strong claim can only be made for factors that the General Framework has been made ready to accommodate by dint of the detailed and comprehensive support provided to researchers for its application. This support includes validation of, and case studies for, the General Framework, the design research exemplar and the research practice assignments, including research design scenarios.

12.5 Summary and Observations

The General Framework has been assessed for completeness against a wide and representative range of other HCI frameworks. The assessment is intended to indicate whether or not the General Framework is comparable to other HCI frameworks, at least as concerns completeness, and so shows potential for validation. The assessment is considered a success. It classifies all the key concepts of the comparison frameworks in terms of the concepts of the General Framework. The latter is considered generally complete with respect to the former in all cases considered. However, the completeness is much dependent on the coherence between the General Framework and the comparison framework concepts. It is not considered as complete, to allow for the possibility of disagreement as to which concepts form part of the other HCI frameworks and, of those concepts, which are key.

The assessment prompts a number of observations.

First, the assessment confirms the currency of frameworks for HCI in terms of the range and number of frameworks available for comparison. Only the better-known and more explicit frameworks are used in the assessment, for example, Card et al. (1983) and Carroll (2010). Many lesser-known frameworks could also have been assessed, for example Ng (2002). Frameworks implied by very well-known and popular publications could also have been included, for example, Nielsen (1993) and Norman (1986, 2010). It is not possible, however, to assess either of the latter two categories of framework for the purposes in hand. The framework concepts are either insufficiently complete, and so partial, or insufficiently explicit, and so difficult to identify.

Second, the assessment shows there to be essentially no limit to the concepts that appear in the frameworks, for example, the *Conceptual Tools* of Morton et al. (1979), the *Direct Manipulation* of Shneiderman (1983), the *Cognitive Incompatibility* of Long (1987), the *Interacting Cognitive Subsystems* of Barnard (1991), the *Operations Having Conditions* of Kuutti (1996), the *Collaboration Technology Readiness* of Olson and Olson (2000) and the *Concrescence* of Rauterberg (2006). Consistent with this finding, the majority of frameworks include concepts not appearing in other frameworks, for example, the

Model Human Processor of Card et al. (1983) and the *Task-Artefact Cycle* of Carroll et al. (1991).

Third, the assessment confirms the need for, and the importance of, completeness for evaluating any framework claiming generality, as is the case of the General Framework. For example, compare the marked differences in concepts between the Kuutti (1996) framework and the Barnard (1991) framework.

Fourth, the assessment shows that completeness as a criterion for evaluating the General Framework is much dependent on coherence. Such dependence was expected for different concepts having different descriptors, for example, *Application* from the General Framework and *Education* from the Carroll (2010) framework, where the former is superordinate to the subordinate latter.

However, even the same concept with the same descriptor may have different lower-level expressions implicating coherence. For example, the General Framework's *Performance* is a concept that also appears in many other frameworks: Morton et al. (1979), Card et al. (1983), Kuutti (1996), Rauterberg (2006) and Carroll (2010). However, its decomposition varies from Morton et al.'s *Mismatch People/Computers* to Card et al.'s *Speed/ Errors* and *Achievement* to Shneiderman's *Easy to Manipulate* and in particular to Carroll's *Not Effectiveness*. All these different expressions are subordinate to *Performance*. Similarly for the same concept with a different descriptor. For example, the General Framework's *Application* is a concept appearing in other frameworks with a different descriptor – *Domain* in Morton et al., *Work* in Long, and *Work Domain* in Rauterberg. The different descriptor may be at the same or at a different level of description. In the latter case, expressions may vary, but remain subordinate to the original, so maintaining coherence.

Fifth, the assessment confirms the appropriateness of its being selective, systematic and informal. The selectivity derives from the current states of development of the General Framework and the comparison frameworks. Included are completeness and coherence, as it supports the former. Excluded are coherence in general and fitness for (HCI design research) purpose. Although the assessment is systematic, its systematisation is not helped by the failure of comparison frameworks to identify explicitly the concepts of which they are composed, and to define them fully in the manner of the General Framework and, in particular, to distinguish HCI and HCI research. In some cases, the concepts (typically key concepts) belonging to the comparison framework are clearly specified, for example, the *Model Human Processor* for Card et al. (1983), *Direct Manipulation* for Shneiderman (1983) and the *Task-Artefact Cycle* for Carroll et al. (1991). In other cases it is less clear, for example, *User Centric* (Morton et al., 1979),

Paradigm (Barnard, 1991) and *Consensus* (Rauterberg, 2006). The latter concepts can only be included with confidence once the comparison frameworks make explicit claim to them. The same goes for the formality of comparison frameworks.

Sixth, the assessment prompts the possible application of coherence relations, other than superordinate/subordinate, as criteria in support of completeness or in general and per se. Such relations might include those of equivalence, hierarchy and generification. However, these relations have been excluded from the present assessment. Their inclusion is considered to be premature.

Last, a number of factors are identified and judged to be associated with well-disseminated and less well-disseminated frameworks. The General Framework is strongly claimed to accommodate some of the factors in its present state. It is less strongly claimed to be ready to accommodate others. In both cases, the accommodation is a result of the support for its application and validation, as provided here.

Conclusion

This concludes the assessment of the General Framework for HCI research for completeness against other frameworks for HCI. Overall, the General Framework is considered to be generally complete, although this depends much on the coherence of individual concepts. The frameworks are further considered as concerns their dissemination in the HCI research literature. The General Framework is assessed for its accommodation of the factors that appear to influence the success of framework dissemination.

12.6 Research Practice Assignment

The assignment comprises two sections: General and Research Design Scenarios.

12.6.1 General

- Search the HCI research literature for an additional framework not presented in 12.3.
  - Compare the selected additional framework with the General Framework for HCI research (see 10.2.2) and in the manner of 12.3.1–12.3.10.

- Note any general similarities and differences between the main concepts of the selected additional framework and the main concepts of the General Framework for HCI research (see 10.2.2).
- Select a second framework from those listed in 12.3.1–12.3.10. How many of the common main concepts of the second framework are also shared by the selected additional framework?

Hints and Tips

Difficult to get started?

Try reading the chapter again, while at the same time thinking explicitly about the main differences between the assessment frameworks, compared with the General Framework for HCI research. Note the differences as you go along.

Consider the explicit or implicit framework used by your research in terms of the main concepts of the General Framework for HCI research (see 10.2.2).

Difficult to complete?

Familiarise yourself with the concepts of framework and assessment as they are applied in the HCI research (and other) literature.

Note the similarities and differences between the different concepts of framework and assessment identified in the HCI research literature.

Test[11]

- Select one of the frameworks that are compared with the General Framework for HCI research from 12.3.1–12.3.9.
  - Referencing the framework explicitly from source and referencing only from memory the General Framework for HCI research (see 10.2.2), repeat the assessment.
  - Check the result of your assessment with that presented here.
  - Repeat until the results are comparable. Rationalise any differences.

12.6.2 Research Design Scenarios

Research Design Scenario 12.1: Validating an HCI Framework from the Research of Others

- Select an approach to HCI research which you created to complete the initial research design scenarios of 4.4.2–9.4.2.

- For illustrative purposes only, such an approach might be in the manner of the craft approach of Balaam et al. (2015) (see 6.2).
- Select a framework listed in 12.3 with which you are familiar or which you consider to be in need of validation.[12]
  - For illustrative purposes only, such a framework might be in the manner of that of Shneiderman (1983) (see 12.3.3).
  - Select a limited number of concepts from the chosen framework. The concepts should be of the more important ones and at least two to be related, either at the same or at different levels of description.
  - For illustrative purposes only, such concepts might be in the manner of *Objects*, *Representations*, *Actions* and *Performance*, as they appear in the Shneiderman framework (see 12.3.3).
- Applying the selected approach, sketch a plan for a research project whose aim is to validate some aspects(s) of the selected framework. The plan should specify the stages/phases of the research to be conducted, although at a high level of description. The latter should be restricted to the concepts selected and so can only be selective and partial.
  - For illustrative purposes only, such a sketch of the plan for a project might take the form of research by Balaam et al. (2015) (see 6.2), which reports four phases of a design and research project. These include user-engagement sensitisation, user-centred design, development and in-the-wild deployment/assessment of a mobile phone application called FeedFinder, a location-mapping mobile application for breastfeeding women.
  - The scope of the validation should be from one or more different examples of HCI knowledge, for example, models, methods or performance/other claims. Is the framework able to accommodate the piece(s) of knowledge/claims? Again, the application of the framework can only be selective and so partial, as only some of its concepts are involved.
  - For illustrative purposes only, such a research project sketch of a plan might be of the Shneiderman framework (see 12.3.3), being validated by the craft approach of Balaam et al. (see 6.2). The framework might be represented by the concepts of *Objects*, *Representations*, *Actions* and *Performance*. The validation aim might be to test the Shneiderman framework *Performance* claim that application of the selected concepts results in *Reduced Memory Load*.
  - Do your best to include as many superordinate concepts of validation in your plan (see 11.4) as appropriate. In the event that you cannot apply one or more concepts, identify and record the reason.

- Search the HCI research literature to establish whether any attempts have been made to validate the framework you selected for this research design scenario.
  - In the affirmative, compare the published instance(s) of framework validation with your validation. Identify the similarities and differences.
- Finally, consider how your illustrative project plan for validation might be improved.

Research Design Scenario 12.2: Applying a Generic Framework to Your Own or to Another's Approach to HCI Research

Suppose that you decide to change your current approach to HCI research to research supported by a generic framework for increased rigour. Select a generic framework from those presented in this chapter, for example Carroll et al. (1991) (see 12.3.10). However, any framework would do. Apply the selected framework to one of the characterisations of your own or another's approach to HCI research created in the initial research design scenarios (see 4.4.2–9.4.2).

The application should assume some illustrative project, taking the form of the sketch of a plan, as a context. The illustrative project could be based on your own current project. If you are not working on a project at this time, base the project plan on a past one. Failing that, base the illustrative project on that of your supervisor or of a colleague. In the last resort, base the illustrative sketch of a plan on a project published in the HCI literature, for example Balaam et al. (2015) (see 6.2), although other projects would do as well. The most important part of the research design scenario is the support and practice it gives researchers to apply frameworks to their own research. Complete the scenario with the help of the questions that follow later. Any other relevant aspects of the research practice assignment should also be called upon as required. Additional hints and tips follow each question in the form of notes.

The selection of the topic or problem per se by the research is not directly supported by the assignment or more generally by the book. What is supported is the manner (of framework) by which the topic or problem is addressed, once selected. However, a topic or problem needs to be identified to apply a framework. Further, the latter supports the researcher in understanding the possibilities and implications of the research of selecting the former. The latter is generally some combination of the following: funding available for the project, researcher's curiosity or interest, supervisor's interests and previous work, and gaps in the HCI research literature. The latter may be identified by the researcher, the supervisor or the sponsor.

In the light of the topic or problem, the selected approach and the selected framework:

1. Which discipline, as an academic field of study, will be espoused by the conduct of the research, as it appears in the illustrative plan and as supported by the generic framework?
Note: additional discipline aspects should be referenced as appropriate, such as scholarliness, branch/subject area, knowledge and information/learning.

2. How will HCI, as human–computer interaction, be effected by the conduct of the research, as it appears in the illustrative plan and as supported by the generic framework?
Note: additional aspects should be referenced as appropriate, such as those generic to the framework.

3. What general problem of human–computer interaction design will be addressed by the conduct of the research, as it appears in the illustrative plan and as supported by the generic framework?
Note: additional general problem aspects should be referenced as appropriate, such as specification.

4. What particular scope of the general problem of human–computer interaction design to do something as desired will be addressed by the conduct of the research, as it appears in the illustrative plan and as supported by the generic framework?
Note: additional particular scope aspects of the general problem of design should be referenced as appropriate, such as individual/group human interactions and interactive/embedded computer interactions.

5. What research, as the diagnosis of design problems and the prescription of design solutions, as they relate to performance for the acquisition and for the validation of knowledge to support practices, will be addressed by the conduct of the research, as it appears in the illustrative plan and as supported by the generic framework?
Note: additional research aspects should be referenced as appropriate, such as the desired state or not of design problems/solutions, performance as doing something as desired, acquisition as creation and validation as confirmation.

6. What knowledge will result from the conduct of the research, as it appears in the illustrative plan and as supported by the generic framework?
Note: additional knowledge aspects should be referenced as appropriate, such as knowledge acquisition, validation and support for practice.

7. What practices, such as specify and implement/specify then implement, will be supported by the knowledge acquired or validated by the research as it appears in the illustrative plan, as supported by the generic framework?

Note: additional practice aspects should be referenced as appropriate, such as knowledge support, acquisition and validation.

12.7 Notes

1. Additional guidance in the selection of frameworks to be assessed was also sought in relevant HCI research literature. The latter include Rogers et al. (2011), Rogers (2012) and Cockton (2014).

2. Assessing the General Framework for HCI research for completeness in this way also supports the reverse assessment, that is, the completeness of the Morton et al. framework with respect to the General Framework. The assessment does not contribute to the promise of the latter with respect to validation, nor to the knowledge that may have been acquired with its support. However, it does contribute to a more comprehensive consideration of frameworks more generally. The same holds for all the other HCI frameworks against which the General Framework is compared.

   The Morton et al. framework is essentially high level, for example, *Empirical and Conceptual Tools*, and *Models* and *Representations*. It is accompanied by low-level illustrations, for example, instances of *Dynamic Models*. The two levels would need to be more systematically related, for example, in the manner in which the framework for a discipline of HCI (see 3.4) is related to the lower-level framework (see 3.5). Instantiation of the relationship can be found in 10.2.2. For a more complete conceptualisation of the Morton et al. framework, it needs to be more explicit about the concepts themselves, in particular their identification, and also about the relations between the concepts at both the same and at different levels of description, in the manner of 3.4–3.5 and the General Framework instantiation (see 10.2.3). Last, its application in research, as the acquisition and validation of HCI knowledge, needs to be specified and implemented, following the General Framework (see 10.2.2).

   The Morton et al. framework is only high level as concerns its design application. The concept is limited to the *Output to Designers*. The latter is not further developed. Completeness would require additional concepts and their relations at the same and at different levels of description, in the manner of the General Framework (see 10.2.3). In addition, the framework is for 'interacting with the computer' rather than for HCI research per se. There is scant reference to the latter as concerns the *Output to Designers*. In particular, there is no reference to validation of the associated knowledge in the manner of 3.4 and 10.2.2.

   These observations, however, take nothing from Morton et al. as concerns the early date of the framework's publication – 1979, perhaps the earliest of its kind.

3. Assessing the General Framework for HCI research for completeness in this way also supports the reverse assessment, that is, the completeness of the Card et al. framework against the General Framework. The same holds for all the other HCI frameworks against which the General Framework is compared.

The Card et al. framework is perhaps the most complete framework of its kind. Not surprisingly, it is considered complete with respect to the General Framework. Indeed, it is more detailed, longer and with more extended exemplification. However, the following points are in order.

First, although the *Goals* of the *GOMS Model* are expressed as the *Aims of the User* in terms of *Desired States*, the latter concept is developed further by the General Framework. The development concerns the application, expressed as objects, attributes and states (see 10.2.4).

Second, the concept of *Performance* is also developed further by the General Framework (see 10.2.4) than the *Speed and Errors* concept as espoused by Card et al. Performance in the former comprises both how well the application is performed and the user costs expended in achieving that level of performance.

Last, the Card et al. framework is more supportive of *Evaluation* as a *Practice* than of *Design*. This is somewhat akin to the General Framework, it must be said (see 14.1–14.2). No concept of validation of the framework, however, is referenced with respect to the HCI knowledge acquired by research for either *Evaluation* or *Design*. A more complete conceptualisation would require these points to be addressed in the manner of the design research exemplar (see 10.2.3 and Figure 10.1).

4. Assessing the General Framework for HCI research for completeness in this way also supports the reverse assessment, that is, the completeness of the Shneiderman framework against the General Framework. The same holds for all the other HCI frameworks against which the General Framework is compared.

The Shneiderman framework concerns primarily *Direct Manipulation Interactions*. The focus, then, is on lower-level descriptions of the *Interface*, as referenced (but with less specificity) in 3.4. As a result, there is less focus on the higher-level descriptions. For a more complete conceptualisation of the Shneiderman framework, it needs to be more explicit about the relations between the concepts at both the same and at different levels of description, for example, in the manner of 3.4–3.5 and the General Framework (see 10.2.2). Further, it needs additional address of HCI research, in particular the validation of the associated knowledge (see Figure 10.1 and 11.4). The overall focus, however, is consistent with the claimed scope of the framework itself, that is, *Direct Manipulation*.

5. Assessing the General Framework for HCI research for completeness in this way also supports the reverse assessment, that is, the completeness of the Long framework against the General Framework. The same holds for all the other HCI frameworks against which the General Framework is compared.

The Long framework is essentially high level, for example, *Cognitive Psychology* and *Ergonomics* and *Representations* as *Acquisition* and *Application*. The latter are accompanied by low-level illustrations of computerised tasks such as online shopping, computer-aided design and information manipulation and enquiry. Framework higher and lower levels of description would need to be systematically related, for example, as the General Framework main concepts (see 10.2.2) are related to the lower-level concepts (see 10.2.4). Instantiations of the relationship can be found in 10.2.3. For a more complete conceptualisation of the Long framework, it needs to be more explicit about the relations between the concepts at both the same and at different levels of description, and also the associated instantiations in the manner of the General Framework. In addition, the framework is for cognitive ergonomics and human–computer interaction, rather than for the research of either. So, its application to research as the acquisition and validation of HCI knowledge needs to be more completely specified and implemented, for example, following the General Research design exemplar (see 10.2.3) in addition to the validation proposal (see Figure 10.1 and 11.4).

6. Assessing the General Framework for HCI research for completeness in this way also supports the reverse assessment, that is, the completeness of the Barnard framework against the General Framework. The same holds for all the other HCI frameworks against which the General Framework is compared.

     The Barnard framework is essentially high level, for example, *Cognitive Psychology*, *Representations* and *Studies*, but with detailed *Cognitive* and *Cognitive Task Models*. The two levels would need to be more systematically related, for example, in the manner in which the higher-level concepts (see 3.4) are related to the lower-level descriptions (see 3.5). Instantiations of the relationship can be found in 10.2.2 for the General Framework. For a more complete conceptualisation of the Barnard framework, it needs to be more explicit about the relations between the concepts at both the same and at different levels of description. Last, its application in research as the acquisition and validation of HCI knowledge needs to be specified and implemented, for example, following the General Framework design research exemplar (see Figure 10.1 and 10.2.3).

7. Assessing the General Framework for completeness in this way also supports the reverse assessment, that is, the completeness of the Kuutti framework against the General Framework. The same holds for all the other HCI frameworks against which the General Framework is compared.

     The Kuutti framework is both high level, for example, *Developmental*, *Cultural* and *Historical Context*, but also low level, for example, *Operations* and *Supporting Actions*. The two levels would need to be more systematically related, for example, in the manner in which the higher-level General Framework discipline (see 3.4) is related to the associated lower-level framework (see 3.5). Instantiations of the relationship can be found in 10.2.2. For a more complete conceptualisation of the Kuutti framework, it needs to be more explicit, as concerns research, about the relations between the concepts at both the same and different levels of description and the associated instantiations. Last, its application in research, as the acquisition and validation of HCI design knowledge, needs to be specified and implemented, for example, following the General Framework design exemplar (see 10.2.3) in addition to the validation proposal (see Figure 10.1 and 11.4).

8. Assessing the General Framework for completeness in this way also supports the reverse assessment, that is, the completeness of the Olson and Olson framework against the General Framework. The same holds for all the other HCI frameworks against which the General Framework is compared.

     The Olson and Olson framework has a high and a low level – for example, *Collaboration Technology* and *Common Ground*, respectively. The two levels would need to be more systematically related, for example, as the General Framework discipline (see 3.4) is related to the lower-level framework (see 3.5). For a more complete conceptualisation, the framework needs to be more explicit as concerns research, and also about the relations between the concepts at both the same and at different levels of description and the associated instantiations. Lastly, its application in research, as the acquisition and validation of HCI design knowledge, needs to be specified and implemented, for example, following the General Framework design exemplar (see 10.2.3) in addition to the validation proposal (see Figure 10.1 and 11.4).

9. Assessing the General Framework for completeness in this way also supports the reverse assessment, that is, the completeness of the Rauterberg framework against

the General Framework. The same holds for all the other HCI frameworks against which the General Framework is compared.

The Rauterberg framework is essentially high level, for example, *Triangulation* and *Industrial Relationship*, accompanied by low-level illustrations in the form of references to the HCI literature. It is unclear how well the two levels are related, since concepts differ from reference to reference. The two levels would need to be identified in detail and systematically related, for example, in the manner in which the higher-level General Framework discipline (see 3.4) is related to the lower-level framework for a discipline of HCI (see 3.5). Instantiations of the relationship can be found in 10.2.3–10.2.4. For a more complete conceptualisation of the Rauterberg framework, it needs to be more explicit about the concepts themselves, and also their relations at both the same and at different levels of description (see 3.4) and the associated specific framework instantiations. Last, its application in research, as the acquisition and validation of design knowledge in a *Research Line*, could be usefully assessed in detail against the general design research exemplar (see Figure 10.1).

10. Assessing the General Framework for HCI research for completeness in this way also supports the reverse assessment, that is, the completeness of the Carroll et al./ Carroll framework against the General Framework. The same holds for all the other HCI frameworks against which the General Framework is compared.

The Carroll et al./Carroll framework is both high and low level, for example, *Applied Cognitive Science* and *Claims Extraction* respectively. The two levels are generally well related, as in the case of the *Task-Artefact Cycle* and *Claims Extraction*, which are extensively illustrated, for example, in the Training Wheels case study. However, the highest level of *Applied Cognitive Science* might be more systematically related to the lower level of *Claims Extraction*, as the General Framework (see 3.4) is related to the lower-level framework descriptions for a discipline of HCI (see 3.5). Instantiations of the relationship can be found here (see 10.2.3–10.2.4). For a more complete conceptualisation of the comparison framework, it needs to be more explicit about the concepts themselves and their relations at both the same and at different levels of description and the associated instantiations. Last, its application in research, as the acquisition and validation of *Design Knowledge* as part of the *Programme for HCI*, might be usefully assessed in detail against the general design research exemplar (see Figure 10.1).

11. The test encourages researchers to commit the approaches and frameworks to memory. Such internalisation facilitates their subsequent application.

12. Validation properly belongs in Chapter 11. However, the HCI frameworks of other researchers are not presented until this chapter (see 12.3.1–12.3.10). Research Design Scenario 11.1 requires reference to both. To support researchers in completing this particular research design scenario, the latter is presented in both chapters. This gives the researchers the option of completing the scenario as meets their need. Alternatively, researchers might like to complete the design scenario twice to help them memorise the concepts and so to facilitate their application – see also Note 11.

13

Assessing General Framework against HCI Theories

This chapter assesses the General Framework for HCI research for coherence against HCI theories. The assessment concerns the key concepts of the HCI theories, although other concepts are also referenced. The concepts of the General Framework are assessed as generally coherent. The assessment does not constitute a validation of the General Framework. However, it does show promise for such validation. The outcome is also indicative as to the potential of the General Framework to support research that aims to develop such theories.

13.1 General

The General Framework for HCI research is assessed against current HCI theories. The aim of the assessment is to establish whether or not the General Framework is coherent with respect to these theories. The General Framework is considered coherent if it is able to classify all the key concepts of a comparison HCI theory. The classification categories comprise the same concept with the same descriptor; the same concept with a different, but coherent, descriptor; and a different concept with a different, but coherent, descriptor. Individual concepts are assessed as coherent or not coherent. The General Framework itself can be assessed as coherent, generally coherent, partially coherent or non-coherent, depending on the coherence of its individual concepts.

For example, the concept of application in the General Framework would be classified as coherent with respect to the concept of application in a comparison HCI theory. It is the same concept with the same descriptor. Likewise, the concept of application in the General Framework would be classified as coherent with respect to the concept of domain in a comparison HCI theory. It is the same concept with a different descriptor. Last, the concept of application in the General Framework would be classified as coherent with respect to the concept of e-shopping in a comparison HCI theory. It is a different, but coherent, concept with a different, but coherent, descriptor. The assessment does not constitute a validation of the General Framework nor the knowledge acquired by means of its application. However, the assessment supports the suggestion that the framework shows promise for such validation. The assessment also indicates the General Framework's potential to support research that aims to develop such theories.

Superordinate and subordinate relations are reciprocal. That is, if the General Framework concept is subordinate to that of a comparison theory, the concept of the latter is superordinate to that of the former. For example, if 'application' is superordinate to 'e-shopping', then, 'e-shopping' is subordinate to 'application'. Coherence, then, between the General Framework and the HCI theories is also reciprocal for such concepts. That is, if most of the General Framework concepts are coherent with respect to those of a comparison HCI theory, then the related concepts of the latter are coherent with respect to those of the former.

The most rigorous assessment would have applied the same criteria proposed for validation, that is, completeness, coherence and fitness for purpose, for each of the four superordinate concepts of conceptualisation, operationalisation, test and generalisation. However, the General Framework has only been conceptualised, so only this superordinate criterion can be assessed (see 11.4). In addition, the concepts of the comparison theories are not, in general, identified explicitly by their proposers. The coherence and fitness for (design research) purpose of the theories, then, cannot be reliably established. Hence, it can only constitute an indicative basis for the assessment of the General Framework.

As a result, the assessment is selective, but systematic and informal. It is selective because although it includes coherence, it does not include completeness (see 12.3) or fitness for purpose (see 15.2). It is systematic because the criteria for coherence are explicit, and also because they are applied consistently to the relations between the concepts of the General Framework and the key concepts of the comparison HCI theories. Last, the assessment is informal, where formal would mean reliably replicated by different and appropriate other researchers, which is not the case.

13.2 General Framework Assessment

The basis of the General Framework for HCI research, to be assessed against HCI theories, is presented and exemplified in terms of its core framework (see

3.4). The General Framework itself is presented in 10.2.2. It instantiates the core framework (see 4.3.1–9.3.1). It also instantiates the associated design research exemplars (see Figures 4.1–9.1) for each of the specific HCI research frameworks. All these sources are relevant to the assessment of the General Framework against HCI theories.

The HCI theories included in the assessment claim to have acquired HCI knowledge. The latter, however, with very few exceptions, have not been validated, for example, the theories of computer-supported cooperative work. Theories against which the General Framework is assessed are those having currency in the HCI literature in terms of citations, replications and case studies.[1]

It is a matter of judgement as to whether, in some cases, a specific piece of research should be assessed as a theory, as here, or as an HCI framework for research (see 12.3). In-the-wild theory proposals, such as those presented by Rogers (2012), obviously constitute or are intended to constitute theory, and likewise with human values theory (Harper et al., 2008). Consequently, the latter two publications are considered as theories, rather than as frameworks. Morton et al.'s (1979) proposal is obviously a framework, as indicated by its title – 'Interacting with the Computer: A Framework'. However, Kuutti's (1996) 'Potential Framework for HCI Research' could have been assessed as either a framework or a theory, as in activity theory. The critical requirement here, however, is that the General Framework be assessed both for completeness with respect to the HCI frameworks and coherence with respect to the HCI theories.

The General Framework is repeated here to support researchers following and checking the details of the assessment.

The General Framework for HCI research comprises the following:

- **Discipline**, as an academic (that is, scholarly) field (that is, branch/subject area) of study (that is, investigation of knowledge as division of information/ learning) and
- **General**, as common (that is, shared) and
- **General Problem**, as the design (that is, specification) of human–computer interactions and
- **Particular Scope**, as the design of human (that is, individual/group)–computer (that is, interactive/embedded) interactions (that is, active/passive) to do something (that is, action/task) as desired (that is, wanted/needed/experienced/felt/valued) and
- **General Research**, as the diagnosis of design problems (that is, not as desired) and the prescription of design solutions (that is, as desired) as they

relate to performance (that is, desired) for the acquisition (that is, creation) and for the validation (that is, confirmation) of knowledge to support practices and

• **General Knowledge**, as guidelines/models/ methods/principles (that is, as acquired and validated by research) and supports (that is, facilitates/makes possible) practices and

• **General Practices**, as trial and error/implement and/then test (that is, supported by knowledge acquired and validated by research).

13.3 Assessment of General Framework for HCI Research against HCI Theories

The assessment of the General Framework for HCI research against individual/ groups of theories follows.

13.3.1 Extended Cognitive Theories

Extended cognitive theories include external cognition, distributed cognition and ecological cognition. These theories further develop earlier models of cognition. In general, they assign a more important role to the environment in support of perception and action

13.3.1.1 External Cognition Theory

Summary External cognition theories are a loosely related set of theories, which include among others those of Larkin and Simon (1987), Scaife and Rogers (1996) and Wright, Fields and Harrison (2000). These theories comprise both explicit and implicit concepts. Further, the theories differ as concerns scope, level of description, research origins and validation. It is not appropriate, then, to compare the General Framework against each of these individual theories. However, the theories share a set of concepts which generally characterise external cognition. The General Framework, then, can be compared with the latter for coherence.

External cognition attempts to relate the cognitive processes used when people interact with computers to the external representations involved in those interactions. It has been demonstrated that different representations may be more or less effective in supporting such cognitive processes. Command languages versus icons is a good example, the latter generally providing the more effective support. For example, external cognition claims to offer designers ways of reducing memory load. Recommended strategies to this end include externalisation of knowledge by the use of interactive tools, including annotation and cognitive tracing. Specific design dimensions include re-representation, graphical constraint, explicitness, visibility and dynalinking.

Key Concepts The key concepts of external cognition are presented in *Italics* and the related main General Framework concepts (see 13.2) are presented in **Boldface**.

- *Scope* (as *People, Computers, Interactions, Environment* and *Performance*) – **Particular Scope**.
- *External Cognition* (as *Research*) – **Discipline** and **Research**.
- *External Cognition* (as *Design – Application*) – **General Problem** and **Practices**.
- *Strategies* and *Tools* for *Reducing Memory Load* (as *Externalisation, Annotation* and *Cognitive Tracing*) – **Research** and **Knowledge**.
- *Dimensions* (as *Re-representation, Graphical Constraint, Explicitness, Visibility* and *Dynalinking*) – **Research** and **Knowledge**.

Assessment Since external cognition presumes its application to design, the related General Framework concepts can also be found in the applied framework instantiation (see 7.3) and may also be referenced in the applied design research exemplar (see Figure 7.1).

The General Framework, then, is considered to be generally coherent with respect to the theories of external cognition. The General Framework fails to reference some of the specific lower-level representations proposed by the theories, such as *Strategies* and *Tools*. However, these concepts are accommodated by **Research** and **Knowledge**. The General Framework fails to reference additional specific lower-level concepts of *Memory Load Reduction* (as *Externalisation, Annotation* and *Cognitive Tracing*) and *Dimensions* (as *Re-representation, Graphical Constraint, Explicitness, Visibility* and *Dynalinking*). However, these concepts can also be accommodated by **Research** and **Knowledge**. For both representations and other concepts, however, the accommodating General Framework concepts are superordinate and so coherent with respect to those of the comparison theories.

13.3.1.2 Distributed Cognition Theory

Summary The key concepts of distributed cognition theory include the cognitive system, comprising all sources of cognition. They also include the environment, comprising all environmental sources of cognition (Hutchins,

1995; also see 13.3.1.1). The aggregate, together with external cognition, characterises distributed cognition. However, the *Environment* already appears in external cognition. Further, Nardi (2002) claims that distributed cognition is difficult to apply, as there is no set of explicit concepts with which to analyse and organise the data. For these reasons, no further comparison is made of the General Framework against distributed cognition theory. As a result, there is no change to the associated conclusions as concerns external cognition, with respect to coherence.

13.3.1.3 Ecological Cognition Theory

Summary Ecological cognition theories are a loosely related set of theories, which originate in those of Gibson (1966 and 1979). They are further developed in the theories of Vicente and Rasmussen (1990), Woods (1995) and Kirsh (2001). These latter comprise a wide range of both explicit and implicit concepts. Further, they differ as concerns scope, level of description, application to research and validation. It is not appropriate, then, to compare the General Framework with these individual theories. However, they share a set of general concepts sufficient to differentiate ecological theory from others. The General Framework, then, is compared with the latter for coherence.

The scope of ecological cognition theory is the interaction of people with their environment. A basic feature of the latter is its invariant structures and how they support human perception and action, for example, as in ecological constraints and affordances. Ecological constraint refers to the invariant structures in the environment. Affordance refers to their potential for human perception and action. Together they support interaction with both physical and virtual worlds. Interactive interfaces may be both ecological and hierarchical (with entry points). Affordances can be discovered empirically or created and applied to support design.

Key Concepts The key concepts of ecological cognition are presented in *Italics* and the related main General Framework concepts (see 13.2) are presented in **Boldface.**

- *Scope* (as *People, Computers, Interactions, Environment* and *Performance*) – **Particular Scope.**
- *Ecological Psychology* (as *Research*) – **Discipline** and **Research.**
- *Design* (as *Application*) – **General Problem** and **Practices.**
- *Invariant Structures* (as *External Ecological Constraints – Perceptual* and *Action Affordances, Ecological Cognition*) – **Research** and **Knowledge.**

• *Interfaces* (as *Ecological, Hierarchical*, with *Entry Points*) – **Knowledge**.

Assessment Since ecological cognition theories comprise both applied and science concepts, the related General Framework concepts can also be found in the specific core framework instantiations of applied (see 7.3) and of science (see 8.3). In addition, the related General Framework concepts may also be referenced in the design research exemplars of applied (see Figure 7.1) and of science (see Figure 8.1).

The General Framework is considered to be generally coherent with respect to ecological cognition theory. The General Framework fails to reference some of the specific lower-level representations proposed by the theory. The latter include, for example, *Invariant Structures* (as *External Ecological Constraints* and *Perceptual and Action Affordances*). However, the concepts can be accommodated by **Research** and **Knowledge**. The General Framework also fails to reference the specific lower-level concepts as *Interfaces* (as *Ecological, Hierarchical*, with *Entry Points*). However, these concepts can be accommodated by **Knowledge**. In the cases of both representations and other concepts, however, the accommodating General Framework concepts are superordinates and so coherent with respect to those of the comparison theories.

13.3.2 Social Theories

Social theories include situated action and computer-supported cooperative work (CSCW). In different ways, these theories attempt to introduce social factors into the research and design of interactive systems, which involve people interacting with other users, either directly or indirectly. The interaction is usually via a computerised communications link.

13.3.2.1 Situated Action Theory

Summary According to Suchman (1987), situated action (which she would not consider as traditional theory) has its origins in cultural anthropology. She argues that it is necessary to take account of the historical and cultural aspects of the relations between and among people to understand how they interact with one another and the environment, and also how they might be supported by computers, as a technological base for applications. This understanding needs to include actions having structures, resources, contexts and constraints. All these are afforded by physical and social circumstances. Understanding involves further 'analysing how people use their circumstances (including historical, cultural, social and physical) to achieve intelligent action'. Suchman contrasts this with 'attempting to abstract action away from its circumstances'. She goes on to argue that it is not so much that people do not use plans to support their activities and performance, but rather that the plans are highly contingent on the state of the environment, and also on the past and present planned and situated actions and interactions associated with their implementation. Ng (2002) develops this point further by proposing a theoretical framework for understanding the relationship between situated action and planned action in information retrieval contexts.

Key Concepts The key concepts of situated action are presented in *Italics* and the related main General Framework concepts (see 13.2) are presented in **Boldface.**

- *Scope* (as *People, Computers, Interactions, Environment, Contexts, Circumstances, Performance*) – **Particular Scope.**
- *Cultural Anthropology, Situated Action* (as *Understanding*) – **Discipline.**
- *Technology Support* (as *Application*) – **General Problem** and **Practices.**
- *Circumstances* (as *Historical, Cultural, Social, Physical*) – **Discipline** and **Knowledge.**
- *Actions* (as *Planned/Situated*, having *Structures, Resources, Constraints* and *Contexts)* – **Research** and **Knowledge.**

Assessment Since situated action presumes some application to design, the related General Framework concepts can also be found in the specific applied core framework instantiation (see 7.3) and may also be referenced in the applied design research exemplar (see Figure 7.1). The General Framework is considered to be generally coherent with respect to situated action theory. The General Framework fails to reference some of the specific higher-level representations, such as *Cultural Anthropology, Situated Action* (as *Understanding*) and *Circumstances* (as *Historical, Cultural, Social, Physical*). However, the concepts can be accommodated by **Discipline** and **Knowledge.** The General Framework also fails to reference the specific lower-level concepts as *Actions* (as *Planned/Situated*, having *Structures, Resources, Constraints* and *Contexts*). However, these concepts can be accommodated by **Research** and **Knowledge.** In the cases of both representations and other concepts, however, the accommodating General Framework concepts are superordinates and so coherent with respect to those of the comparison theory.

13.3.2.2 CSCW Theory

Summary The scope of computer-supported cooperative work (CSCW) theories is primarily the social and organisational aspects of networked interactive systems. The concern here is how the latter can be developed to support collaborative working, for example, users organised into groups or into teams. In their time, social, organisational and sociological psychologies have each contributed to this undertaking. McGrath (1991) proposed four modes of team/ group work behaviour: inception, problem-solving, conflict resolution and execution. Each mode has three functions: production, group well-being and member support. Aspects of social theories are claimed to have contributed to the design of group support systems for communication, decision-making, coordination, brainstorming and conferencing. Specific behaviours involved in group working have been identified, such as loafing, lurking and self-promoting.

Key Concepts The key concepts of CSCW are presented in *Italics* and the related main General Framework concepts (see 13.2) are presented in **Boldface**.

- *Scope* (*People*, as *Individuals* and *Groups/Teams*, *Networked Computers*, *Interactions*, *Performance*) – **Particular Scope**.
- *Social*, *Organisational*, *Sociological Psychology* (as *Understanding*) – **Discipline**, and *Group Technology Support* (as *Application*) – **General Problem** and **Practices**.
- *Modes* (as *Inception*, *Problem-Solving*, *Conflict Resolution* and *Execution*) – **Research** and **Knowledge**.
- *Functions* (as *Production*, *Group Well-Being* and *Member Support*) – **Research** and **Knowledge**.

Assessment Since CSCW presumes some application to design, the related General Framework concepts can also be found in the specific applied framework instantiation (see 7.3) and may also be referenced in the applied design research exemplar (see Figure 7.1).

The General Framework is considered to be generally coherent with respect to CSCW theory. The General Framework fails to reference some of the specific higher-level representations proposed by the theory, such as *Social*, *Organisational*, *Sociological Psychology* (as *Understanding*) and *Group Technology Support* (as *Application*). However, the concepts can be accommodated by **Discipline**. The General Framework also fails to reference the specific lower-level concepts as *Functions* (as *Production*, *Group Well-Being* and *Member Support*). However, these concepts can be accommodated by **Research** and **Knowledge**. For both representations and other concepts, however, the accommodating General Framework concepts are superordinate and so coherent with respect to those of the comparison theory.

13.3.3 Miscellaneous Theories

The following miscellaneous theories are included for completeness of the listing and to exemplify the ongoing development of HCI theory. They are combined, because none makes such a critical contribution to that development such as to impact the assessment of the General Framework for coherence. They are also generally too recent to be well formed and continue to undergo development.

13.3.3.1 Ethnography Theory

Summary Ethnomethodology studies how people live their lives. The method is borrowed from sociology and is bottom-up, allowing concepts to be discovered in the data. The focus is social, historical and cultural. Ethnographic accounts (or theories) are intended to result. Ethnomethodology has been used in HCI to characterise often complex work practices, such as underground train control (Heath and Luff, 1991) and air traffic management (Bentley et al., 1992). The characterisation is largely descriptive, offering an informal understanding of the work practices studied. Little substantive theory has resulted to date, and also little specific support for interactive system design. The concept of theory may even be alien to much of this research.

Nothing in the General Framework opposes the application of the ethnographic method. Indeed, the opposite. The method has been used informally to provide the basis for modelling emergency services coordination (Hill 2010, applying concepts shared with the core framework – see 10.2.1). The modelling requires the mapping of the concepts resulting from the method analysis to those of the General Framework. The latter, then, is able to support any further developments of the ethnographic method and so ethnographic account/theory.

13.3.3.2 Grounded Theory

Summary Grounded theory is not a substantive theory as such. Rather, it is a method by which such theories may be developed on the basis of data and its analysis (Glaser and Strauss, 1967). The data and analysis comprise three types of coding: open coding (of categories, properties and dimensions), axial coding (of details and subcategories) and selective coding (integrating the products of open and axial coding). The resulting theory is of the original data set. For an example of the application of grounded theory to HCI see Salisbury (2014) (5.2 and 5.3.5). Many versions of grounded theory now exist, some of which have been adopted by HCI research.

Nothing in the General Framework opposes the application of the grounded theory method. Indeed, the opposite is true. It has been used informally to model players' engagement with video games (Salisbury, 2014), which has been applied to form the basis for illustrating the approaches and frameworks presented here (see 5.2 and 5.3.5 respectively). The modelling requires the mapping of the concepts resulting from the method analysis to those of the General Framework. The latter, then, is able to support any further developments of the grounded theory method, and also the grounded theory that results from the application of the method.

13.3.3.3 Design Theory

Summary Design has been a central feature of HCI since its beginning. Design as craft practice, using experience as implicit knowledge, is one form it has taken (see 6.3). Design as engineering, using codified explicit knowledge, is another form (see 9.3). Acquiring user requirements and supporting user-centred design has resulted in design heuristics and design guidelines. The latter offer informal design support, although perhaps not expressed as design theory as such (Winograd, 1997).

Ideas for the construction of design theory per se have been sought outside HCI, including in design, the arts and the humanities (Lowgren and Stolterman, 2004). Or at least, ideas have been put forward of how to think about design theory. Various types of design engagement have been proposed, including, for example, worth-sensitive design (Cockton, 2006) and inclusive design (Vanderheiden, 2008). However, at this time little or no distinctive HCI design theory has resulted against which the General Framework can be assessed for coherence.

However, nothing in the General Framework opposes the application of the new design theory concepts, such as they have been developed to date, for example, worth-sensitivity and inclusivity. The General Framework concept of performance is coherent with respect to both. The modelling requires the mapping of the concepts to those of the General Framework. The latter, then, is able to apply and to support any further developments of design theory, sharing its aim of acquiring explicit design knowledge.

13.3.3.4 Human Values Theory

Summary Human values theory has extended the scope of HCI to people's private social lives, rather than to just their work lives, as some earlier theories. It has developed on the basis of technology's support for personal communication, as conducted by means of the smartphone, tablet and pad. Its concern is with life goals and style and their meaning, rather than just with tasks and activities.

The launch of human values theory was very much an HCI community, rather than discipline, affair (Harper et al., 2008). To date, it has produced no theory as such, although Harper et al. proposed the addition of 'understand' as the first stage of the user-centred research and design process. The latter comprises study, design, build and evaluate. Indeed, its commitment to explicit theory, in the manner of the General Framework, and the form that it might take, remains unclear.

Nothing in the General Framework opposes the application of the new human values theory concepts, such as they have been developed to date, for example, life goals and style and their meaning. They are all coherent with the General Framework's concept of performance. The modelling requires the mapping of the concepts to those of the General Framework. The latter is then able to apply and support any further developments of human values theory.

13.3.3.5 Technology as Experience Theory

Summary For some time now, user experience has vied with user-friendliness and usability as the most popular criterion for successful interactive system design and evaluation. It can be argued that it has generally replaced the latter, especially with practitioners.

A detailed and thoroughly exemplified specification is offered by McCarthy and Wright (2004). They propose four key threads which, woven together, make up our lived experience. The first is compositional – the meaning of the experience, including its values and making sense thereof. The second is sensual – the engagement of the experience by means of vision, hearing, touch, taste and smell. The third is emotional – the feeling of the experience in terms of love/hate, like/dislike, fun/misery. The last is spatio-temporal – the unfolding of the experience in terms of time/duration, place/location. The threads are claimed to be able to support the thinking of designers in their design practice. As yet, there is no technology as experience theory and so no application of it.

Nothing in the General Framework opposes the application of any new technology as experience theory concepts, such as they have been developed to date, for example, the four threads. They are coherent with the General Framework's concept of performance and the lower-level framework description more generally. The modelling requires the mapping of the concepts to those of the General Framework. The latter is, then, able to apply and to support any further developments of technology as experience theory.

13.3.3.6 Critical Theory

Summary Critical theory conceives knowledge as essentially personal, social, political and cultural. When applied to human–computer interaction design, it comprises the understanding, interpretation and everyday practices of the intended users of the technology. Following Carroll (1991; see also 12.3.9), Bardzell, Bolter and Lowgren (2010) argue that an expert reading of interactive designs is able to expose useful HCI design insights. Knowledge of HCI design, and the important contributions that have been made to it, constitute the basis for critical theory.

Elsewhere, Bardzell (2009) has proposed four kinds of contribution that critical theory can make to the practice of HCI design. The first is informing the present design process. The second is resisting or innovating that design process. The third is developing and adapting critical theory relevant to the HCI design process. The last is critiquing interaction designs that expose the consequences of the design.

Nothing in the General Framework opposes the application of any new critical theory concepts, such as they have been developed to date, for example, the four kinds of contribution cited. They are coherent with the General Framework's concept of performance and the lower-level framework description more generally. The modelling requires the mapping of the concepts to those of the General Framework. The latter is then able to apply and to support any further developments of critical theory.

13.3.3.7 In-the-Wild Theory

Summary In-the-wild theory is derived from studying people's interactions with technology in the context in which they are performed, for example, in the home or in a public space (Hutchins, 1995). As concerns HCI, the studies may focus on valued life goals or styles, for example, reducing energy consumption or improving people's health. Applications are developed that are intended to support the attainment of these goals. The technology is then implemented and installed, in the location where it is to be used. Follow-up studies observe the success or failure of the installed technology, and also the extent to which people adapt it to suit their personal requirements. Evolutionary design may then be pursued. To date, little or no in-the-wild theory as such has been reported in the research literature, although additional other theories have been proposed, for example, embodiment and ecological rationality (Rogers, 2012).

Nothing in the General Framework opposes the application of any new in-the-wild theory concepts, such as they have been developed to date, for example, valued life goals and styles. They are compatible with the General Framework's concept of performance and the lower-level framework description more generally. The modelling requires the mapping of the concepts to those of the General Framework. The latter, then, is able to apply and to support any further developments of in-the-wild theory.

13.4 Summary and Observations

The General Framework has been assessed for coherence against a wide and representative range of HCI theories. The aim of the assessment is to establish whether or not the General Framework has the potential to support research that aims to develop such theories. The assessment is considered a success. It classified all the main concepts of the comparison theories with respect to coherence in terms of the concepts of the General Framework. The latter, then, is considered generally coherent with respect to the former. Coherence here is expressed in terms of superordinate and subordinate relations between the two sets of concepts.

The General Framework is not considered as coherent, to allow for the possibility of disagreement as to which concepts form part of the HCI theories and, of those concepts, which are key. The assessment does not constitute a validation of the General Framework nor the knowledge acquired by means of its application. However, it shows promise for such validation. Rather, the assessment is indicative of the potential of the General Framework to support research that aims to develop such theories.

The assessment prompts a number of observations.

First, the assessment confirms the currency of theories for HCI with respect to the range and number of the theories available for comparison. Only the better-known theories are used in the assessment, for example, external cognition theory (Scaife and Rogers, 1996; Wright et al., 2000), CSCW theory (McGrath, 1991) and technology as experience theory (McCarthy and Wright, 2004). Many lesser-known theories could also have been assessed.

Second, the assessment shows there to be essentially no limit to the concepts that appear in the HCI theories, for example, *Actions* (as *Planned/Situated*, having *Structures*, *Resources*, *Constraints* and *Contexts*) from situated action (see 13.3.2.1) and *Modes* as *Inception*, *Problem-Solving*, *Conflict Resolution* and *Execution* and *Functions* as *Production*, *Group Well-Being* and *Member Support* from CSCW theory (see 13.3.2.2). This wide range of concepts underlines the need for coherence between the latter and any framework, such as the General Framework, which aims to support the research needed to develop the associated theories.

Third, the assessment confirms the need for, and the importance of, coherence between HCI theories and any framework, such as the General Framework, that aims to support the research needed to develop these theories. For example, compare the differences in concepts between the General Framework, external cognition theory and design theory.

Fourth, the assessment prompts the possible application of coherence relations other than superordinate and subordinate in general and/or per se. Such relations might include those of equivalence, hierarchy and generification. However, these relations are not considered to be appropriate for the present assessment.

Fifth, the assessment shows how modest the development and uptake of HCI theories turn out to be in many of the cases referenced as such by HCI textbooks (Rogers, 2012). These include, in particular, human values theory, critical theory and in-the-wild theory.

Last, the assessment confirms the appropriateness of its being selective, systematic and informal. The selectivity derives from the current state of development of the General Framework and the comparison HCI theories. Included is coherence between the two sets of concepts. Excluded are completeness (see 12.3) and fitness for (design research) purpose (see 15.2). Although the assessment is systematic, its systematisation is not supported by the failure of comparison theories to identify explicitly the concepts of which they are composed and to define them fully (in the manner of the General Framework); likewise, and in particular, to distinguish HCI and HCI research. In some cases, the concepts (typically main concepts) belonging to the comparison theories are easily identified, for example, the *Invariant Structures* of ecological cognition theory (see 13.3.1.3), the *Situated Action* of situated action theory (see 13.3.2.1), the *Groups/Teams* of CSCW theory (see 13.3.2.2), the *Complex Work Processes* of ethnography theory (see 13.3.3.1) and the *Open/Axial/Selective Coding* of grounded theory (see 13.3.3.2). In other cases, it is less clear, for example, *Graphical Constraint* of external cognition theory (see 13.3.1.1), *Entry Points* of ecological cognition (see 13.3.1.3) and *Meaning* of human values theory (13.3.3.4). The latter concepts can only be included with confidence once the comparison theories make explicit claim to them and define them clearly. The same goes for the formality of comparison theories.

Conclusion

This chapter assesses the General Framework for HCI research for coherence against HCI theories. The concepts of the General Framework are assessed as generally coherent. The assessment does not constitute a validation of the General Framework. However, it does show promise for such validation. The outcome is also indicative as to the potential of the General Framework to support research that aims to develop such theories.

13.5 Research Practice Assignment

The assignment comprises two sections: General and Research Design Scenarios.

13.5.1 General

- Search the HCI research literature for an additional theory not presented in 13.3.
  - Compare the selected additional theory with the General Framework for HCI research (see 10.2.2), in the manner of the assessment presented in 13.3.1 and 13.3.2.
  - Note any general similarities and differences between the main concepts of the selected additional theory and the main concepts of the General Framework for HCI research (see 10.2.2).
- Select a second theory from those listed in 13.3.1 and 13.3.2. How many of the common main concepts of the second theory are also shared by the selected additional theory?

Hints and Tips

Difficult to get started?

Try reading the chapter again, while at the same time thinking explicitly about the differences between the theories compared with the General Framework for HCI research. Note the differences as you go along.

Consider the explicit or implicit theory used by your research in terms of the main concepts of the General Framework for HCI research (see 10.2.2).

Difficult to complete?

Familiarise yourself with the concepts of theory and assessment, as they are applied in the HCI research (and other) literature.

Note the similarities and differences between the different concepts of theory and assessment identified in the HCI research literature.

Test[2]

- Select one of the theories that are compared with the General Framework for HCI research from 13.3.1 and 13.3.2.
- Referencing the theory explicitly and referencing only from memory the General Framework for HCI research (see 10.2.2), repeat the assessment. Check the result of your assessment with that presented here.
- Repeat until the results are comparable. Rationalise any differences.

13.5.2 Research Design Scenarios

Research Design Scenario 13.1: Validating an HCI Theory
from the Research of Others

- Select an approach to HCI research that you created to complete the initial research design scenarios of 4.4.2–9.4.2.
  - For illustrative purposes only, such an approach might be in the manner of the craft approach of Balaam et al. (2015) (see 6.2).
  - Select an HCI theory from 13.3.1 or 13.3.2 with which you are familiar or which you consider to be in need of validation.[3]
  - For illustrative purposes only, such a theory might be in the manner of that of external cognition (see 13.3.1.1).
  - Select a limited number of concepts from the chosen theory. The concepts should be of the more important ones and at least two to be related, either at the same or at different levels of description.
  - For illustrative purposes only, such concepts might be in the manner of *Externalisation*, *Annotation* and *Cognitive Tracing*, as they appear in external cognition theory (see 13.3.1.1).
- Applying the selected approach, sketch a plan for a research project whose aim is to validate some aspect(s) of the selected theory. The plan should specify the stages/phases of the research to be conducted, although only at a high level of description. The latter should be restricted to the concepts selected and can only be selective and so partial.
  - For illustrative purposes only, such a sketch of the plan for a project might take the form of research by Balaam et al. (2015) (see 6.2), which reports four phases of a design and research project. These comprise user-engagement sensitisation, user-centred design, development and in-the-wild deployment/ assessment of a mobile phone application called FeedFinder, a location-mapping mobile application for breastfeeding women.
  - The scope of the validation should be from one or more different examples of HCI knowledge, for example models, methods or performance/other claims. Is the theory able to accommodate the piece(s) of knowledge/ claims? Again, the application of the theory can only be selective and so partial, as only some of its concepts are involved.
  - For illustrative purposes only, such a research project sketch of a plan might be of the external cognition theory being validated by the craft approach of Balaam et al. (see 6.2). The theory might be represented by the concepts of *Externalisation*, *Annotation* and *Cognitive Tracing*. The validation aim might be to test the external cognition theory *Performance* claim that application of the selected concepts results in *Reduced Memory Load*.

- Do your best to include as many superordinate concepts of validation as possible in your plan (see 11.4), as appropriate. In the event that you cannot apply a concept, try to identify the reason.
- Do your best to include as many superordinate criteria of validation in your plan (see 11.4) as appropriate. In the event that you cannot apply a criterion, try to identify the reason.
- Search the HCI research literature to establish whether any attempts have been made to validate the theory you selected for this research design scenario.
  - In the affirmative, compare the published instance(s) of theory validation with your illustrative plan. Identify the similarities and differences.
- Finally, consider how your plan might be improved.

Research Design Scenario 13.2: Applying to HCI Theory Your Own or Another's Approach to HCI Research

Suppose that you decide to change the HCI theory informing your current approach to research to a different theory (from 13.3.1–13.3.2), for example, as being more appropriate or being better validated. Select a different theory from the object or motivator of your current approach from those presented in 13.3.1–13.3.2. Then apply your own or, if you prefer, another's approach to the selected theory, as suggested later. Any other relevant aspects of the research practice assignment should also be called upon as required. Additional hints and tips follow each question in the form of notes.

The selection of the topic or problem per se by the research is not directly supported by the assignment or more generally by the book. What is supported is the manner (of theory) by which the topic or problem is addressed, once selected. However, a topic or problem needs to be identified to apply a theory. Further, the latter supports the researcher in understanding the possibilities and implications for the research of selecting the former. Research topic selection is generally some combination of funding available for the project, researcher's curiosity or interest, supervisor's interests and previous work, and gaps in the HCI research literature. The latter may be identified by the researcher, the supervisor or the sponsor.

In the light of the selected topic or problem, your own or another's approach to research and the selected theory:

1. What topic or problem of designing human–computer interactions is to be addressed by the research approach and how will that topic or problem be addressed with respect to the selected theory?

Note: 'topic or problem' here should be understood widely to include any and all research activities considered to be relevant and important.

2. Which actions are to be performed by the research approach as a way of addressing the topic or problem of designing human–computer interactions with respect to the selected theory?

Note: 'actions' here should be understood widely to include any and all research activities considered to be sufficiently relevant and important.

3. Which ways of evaluating the success or not of the actions performed by the research approach will be employed to address the topic or problem of designing human–computer interactions with respect to the selected theory?

Note: 'evaluating success' here should be understood widely. The particular forms of evaluation will depend on the approach taken by the research.

4. How will the research approach cumulate its successes in addressing the topic or problem of designing human–computer interactions with respect to the selected theory?

Note: 'cumulating successes' here should be understood widely. The particular forms of cumulating will depend on the approach taken by the research.

13.6 Notes

1. Additional guidance in the selection of theories to be assessed was also sought in relevant HCI research publications, for example, Rogers et al. (2011), Rogers (2012) and Cockton (2014).
2. The test encourages researchers to commit the approaches and frameworks to memory. Such internalisation facilitates their subsequent application.
3. Validation properly belongs in Chapter 11. However, the HCI theories of other researchers are not presented until this chapter (see 13.3). Research Design Scenario 11.1 requires reference to both. To support researchers in completing this particular research design scenario, the latter is presented in both chapters. This gives the researchers the option of completing the scenario as most suits their need. Alternatively, researchers might like to complete the design scenario twice to help them memorise the concepts and so to facilitate their application – see also Note 2.

14

Methodological Component for General Framework

HCI frameworks, including the General Framework, are largely substantive in nature at this time. This is in spite of some lesser reference to practices and methods. Knowledge, however, is both methodological and substantive, hence the requirement for a greater methodological component for such frameworks. Suggestions are made as to the research needed to develop a greater methodological component, for the General Framework and other such generic frameworks. In this way, the requirement could be met.

14.1 Methodological Framework Requirement

Knowledge, at the highest level of description, comprises substantive (or declarative) and methodological (or procedural) components. The former expresses the 'what' and the latter the 'how' of knowledge, as acquired and validated by HCI research. An HCI researcher, then, might expect to find in the literature either separate substantive and methodological HCI research frameworks or integrated such frameworks. However, examination of the other frameworks used to assess the General Framework (see 12.3) indicates that all the frameworks are largely substantive in nature, for example, Morton et al.'s (1979) scope of *Cognitive Science, Tools* and *Representations*, Card et al.'s (1983) scope of *Psychology, Models* and *Levels of Description*, Shneiderman's (1983) scope of *Software Engineering, Objects, Representations, Actions* and *Performance* and Kuutti's (1996) scope of *Social* and *Organisational Psychology, People's Work Behaviour* and *Artefacts*. The General Framework is no different in this regard, with its scope of *Discipline, General Problem, Particular Scope, Research* and *Knowledge*. However, *Practice*, as the exception, is also included (see 3.4 and 10.2.2).

Although some frameworks make more reference to practices and methods than others (see 12.3), in general substantive reference is greater than that of methodological reference. Examples of framework practice and method referencing include Morton et al.'s (1979) *Laboratory Studies* and *Field Studies*, Long's (1987) *Laboratory Simulation*, Carroll et al.'s (1991) *Theory* as *Codification*, *Integration* and *Application* and *Design Practice* as *Proceduralised*, Barnard's (1991) *Research Studies* and Rauterberg's (2006) *Academic Evaluation Cycle*, *Empirical Validation*, *System Validation* and *Rigorous Validation*. Most of this research appears to be referencing research practice rather than design practice. However, it is not always clear, and some research clearly references design practice, for example, Carroll et al. (1991).

The General Framework for HCI research references both design and research practices, consistent with the distinction. However, the latter is the primary concern here. Design practices supported by knowledge acquired and validated by research satisfy user requirements with an interactive system. HCI design practices are taken to include some combination of specifying and implementing human–computer interactions, interspersed with iterative trial-and-error cycles (see 10.2.3 and Figure 10.1). Design practices may also include the diagnosis of design problems and the prescription of design solutions.

Research practices, following the General Framework design research exemplar, are taken to include the diagnosis of design problems and the prescription of design solutions (see 3.4 and 10.2.2). Also included are derivation and validation (as they relate to user requirements), acquisition and validation (as they relate to the specific problem and specific solution), and implementation and test (as they also relate to the specific problem and specific solution – see 10.2.3).

In addition, some theories make mention of practices and methods (see 13.3), for example, external cognition and ecological cognition theories' *Design* (as *Application*), situated action theory's account of *Situated Action* (as *Understanding*), CSCW theory's *Social*, *Organisational*, *Sociological Psychology* (as *Understanding*), grounded theory's *Open-*, *Axial-* and *Selective-Coding*, and critical theory's *Expert Reading*.

The allusion to practices and methods made by frameworks and theories may be explicit or implicit, as an assumption that is associated with the design of interactive systems. Two forms of practice are distinguished – research practice and design practice, both including methods. Generally, practice is assumed to involve the application of knowledge to do something as intended. Research practice applies knowledge to acquire and to validate HCI knowledge. Design practice applies knowledge to specify interactive systems in response to unsatisfied user requirements. Researchers are no doubt wondering how the two sorts of practice relate in general.

First, HCI research and HCI design practices have much in common, for example, they share some methods (Dix, 2010). Both may use task analysis, observational study and empirical evaluation. However, research and design practices also differ in many ways, for example as concerns methods. Research experimental studies may be very different from the user-centred methods used by designers to specify an interactive system. Likewise, the same user-centred design methods (see 14.2.1) may be very different from research structured analysis and design methods (see 14.2.3).

Second, none of the comparison frameworks or theories, however, makes clear how or why or with what guarantee the knowledge acquired by research practice should constitute the knowledge applied by design practice. However, this assumption is made by most of the comparison HCI frameworks and theories. This is the case whether the application involved is a framework, for example, Shneiderman (1983), Barnard (1991) and Carroll et al., 1991), or a theory, for example, McCarthy and Wright (2004) and Rogers (2012). Rauterberg's (2006) framework, however, is an exception, suggesting how knowledge acquired by research practice and knowledge applied by design practice might be commonly grounded. The latter would be effected by a research line comprising both academic and empirical evaluation. The common grounding of research and design practice, as concerns the knowledge acquired by the former and applied by the latter, is the object of the research/design issue raised and addressed here.

Third, according to the General Framework, within the concept of a discipline, HCI research acquires and validates knowledge. This supports practices solving the general HCI problem of design with the particular scope of human–computer interactions. The HCI knowledge comprises design problems, their design solutions, and the acquired knowledge transforming the former into the latter. An HCI design problem is an aspect of interactive system performance that is not as desired. An HCI design solution is the problem expression of the interactive system performance that is desired in the satisfaction of user requirements.

In contrast, design practices comprise specifying and implementing human–computer interactions in the form of an interactive system. In so doing, they may include the application of the acquired knowledge that transforms the design problem into a prescription of a design solution. This is the case if the design problem is implicated in the user requirements for, and in, the corresponding interactive system itself. Thus, the research knowledge acquisition and the design knowledge application are commonly grounded in design problems, design solutions and the knowledge transforming the former into the latter. This common grounding is made clear in the General Framework design research exemplar (see 10.2.3 and Figure 10.1).

Fourth, in contrast to HCI design practice and following the HCI design research exemplar, research practice empirically derives a specific design problem from possible user requirements. The specific design problem is expressed as an interactive system whose performance is not as desired. The problem selected is assumed to be soluble, although subsequent research might show it not to be so. Contradictory or impossible user requirements are not selected as design problems, as they are known in advance not to be soluble. The specific design problem is empirically validated against the possible user requirements from which it is derived. Research empirical practice comprising empirical implementation and test of the design problem and empirical implementation and test of the (initially putative) design solution is conducted iteratively, that is, until the knowledge supporting the transformation of the specific design problem to the specific design solution is successful. The resulting knowledge might take different forms as a function of the guarantee they offer. For example, design principles (see 9.3.3, Figure 9.1) might offer the highest guarantee. Design guidelines (see 7.3.3, Figure 7.1) might offer a medium guarantee. Design heuristics (see 6.3.3, Figure 6.1) might offer the lowest guarantee. Last, a possible interactive system corresponding to the original possible user requirements is empirically derived. It is also empirically validated against the original specific design solution. Here, 'empirical' means by trial and error, using any implicit or explicit methods.

Fifth, in contrast to HCI research practice, HCI design practice specifies and implements interactive systems in response to user requirements. All design methods referenced by the specific frameworks (see 4.3.2–9.3.2) have a stage in which the design is specified and in which design knowledge might be applied. Design knowledge applied in the creation of the specification might be implicit or explicit. If explicit, the knowledge might or might not have been acquired by HCI research. If acquired by HCI research, then it would be applied in the case of a design problem identified among user requirements to specify a corresponding design solution, expressed in terms of the interactive system.

However, in both comparison frameworks and theories, the substantive component is greater than the methodological component, in particular as concerns research practice. It is accepted that the appropriate substantive/ methodological balance cannot be specified a priori. It is further accepted that in a well-formed framework or theory, the balance of substantive and methodological knowledge might be asymmetric, and correctly so as concerns fitness for (design) purpose. However, this is not the case with current frameworks and theories, or at least has not yet been shown to be the case. In addition, advancing the methodological component is one way of advancing our knowledge of an appropriate and correct asymmetry, should one be appropriate.

In the meantime, the need for a greater methodological research practice contribution to HCI frameworks, including to the General Framework proposed here, constitutes a methodological framework requirement. It is not possible here or at this time to meet this requirement. That remains for future research. What can be done, however, is to suggest how a methodological component might be constructed and integrated with the General Framework, and also integrated with other frameworks, as part of that future research. A similar methodological component could likewise be added to any or all of the comparison HCI theories as required (see 13.3).

14.2 Meeting Methodological Framework Requirement

The research framework and theory elements that reference practices and methods are in many respects very different (see above). However, they have common aspects. The latter, in some cases, may even be identical to the elements appearing in HCI design practices and methods. The latter, then, could form the starting point for meeting the methodological framework requirement identified here. The design practices and methods could form the basis of HCI research methods for the acquisition and validation of knowledge. The basis would then support the expression of the methodological component of an HCI research framework. There are three relevant types of such design practices and methods: user-centred, structured analysis and design, and research structured analysis and design. Each is briefly described, along with its potential for contributing to meeting the methodological framework requirement.

14.2.1 User-Centred Design Methods

User-centred design methods are generally implicit in part, informal and incompletely specified. As a result, there are many different such methods. However, for present purposes, they have sufficient common features to constitute a type of method.

For example, according to Life (2018) and more generally, user-centred design can be broken down into stages.

The first stage identifies the tasks that users are to perform using the interactive system being designed. The environmental and organisational context for use is also analysed. The emphasis is user-centred, focusing on user needs elicited by means of communication and by observation of existing task performance. The second stage specifies user requirements, in addition to the technological and organisational constraints. The latter limit the range of possible designs, and thus also desired task performance. The third stage proposes an initial design intended to satisfy the user requirements. The fourth and last stage evaluates a simulated or implemented interactive system for usability, effectiveness or other performance criteria. The design method is iterative, any or all stages being repeated as required.

Similarly, Sharp, Rogers and Preece (2007) identify the four main stages of iterative user-centred design, as follows. First, identification of user needs, expressed in terms of user experience. Second, the creation of alternative designs to meet that experience. Third, the implementation of interactive systems, which embody those designs. Last, the evaluation of the experience offered by the implementation of the interactive systems. Again, the design method is iterative, any or all stages being repeated as required.

As a final example of user-centred design methods, Harper et al. (2008) propose the addition of a stage of understanding to precede the stages of studying, designing, building and evaluating iteratively.

User-centred design methods have the potential to contribute to the creation of the methodological component for an HCI research framework. However, they might be best suited to the more implicit, more informal and less completely specified frameworks, for example, frameworks that set store by craft practice (see Carroll, 2010). The compatibility is likely to be better than with more structured design methods more alien to such craft practice. To be developed into research practice, the methods would need to be appropriately refined, such as to relate to the substantive component of a framework. The methods, as well as being conceptualised, would also need to have the potential to be correctly operationalised, tested and generalised.

14.2.2 Structured Analysis and Design Methods

Structured analysis and design methods are generally more explicit, less informal and more completely specified than those of user-centred design. These structured methods approach design top-down, based on information derived bottom-up from analyses of existing systems and tasks. Design progresses from general features of existing tasks and interactive systems to the specific details of the to-be-designed task and systems. In addition, these methods are often associated with parallel software engineering design methods, including the exchange of design products such as those associated with the user interface.

An example of such methods is MUSE: Method for Usability Engineering (Lim and Long, 1994). MUSE consists of three phases, each divided into stages. The first phase is the information elicitation and analysis phase. It involves the collection and analysis of user and task information to support later design decisions. The second phase – user requirements – identifies the user requirements of the to-be-designed interactive system in terms of performance. Using this information and the task models from the initial phase, a conceptual design is created. The latter is agreed with the software engineering design team. Next, the agreed conceptual design is divided into those tasks to be performed using the interactive system under development, and those performed using other devices. An allocation of function between user and interactive system is then conducted. The third and final phase is the design specification phase. The conceptual design is decomposed further to create a device-specific, implementable specification, including error recovery. The user interface is then evaluated and developed iteratively further. Once finalised, the interface design is passed to the software engineering design team for implementation.

Structured analysis and design methods have the potential to contribute to the creation of the methodological component for an HCI research framework. However, they might be best suited to the more explicit, less informal and more completely specified frameworks, for example, frameworks that set much store by research coherence, triangulation and validation (for example, Rauterberg, 2006). The compatibility is likely to be better than with user-centred design methods, which do not address these aspects explicitly (for example, Life, 2018).

A second structured analysis and design method is STUDIO: STructured User-interface Design for Interaction Optimisation (Browne, 1994). STUDIO is composed of five stages, further divided into steps. The first stage is the project proposal and planning stage. It concerns the case for the project, based on cost–benefit analysis and a quality assurance plan. The second stage, termed user requirements analysis stage, involves the collection of information to inform later design. The stage consists of steps that describe the plan for data collection, the data collection itself, the task analysis validation and the documentation. The third stage, the task synthesis stage, uses information from the previous stage to create an initial user interface design. The third stage consists of five steps – user support (user manual), style guide, task synthesis, design specification, and formative evaluation. The fourth stage is usability engineering and refines the task synthesis design by means of iterative prototyping, audit and evaluation by users. The fifth and final stage is that of the user interface development. The designs are passed to the software implementers, issues of integration are addressed, acceptance testing is conducted and final reporting completed.

The third, and final, structured analysis and design method is GUIDE: Graphical User Interface Design and Evaluation (Redmond-Pyle and Moore, 1995). GUIDE is composed of six processes. The first process defines the users and the usability requirements. User class descriptions characterise each type of user. Usability requirements are listed with criteria for their subsequent evaluation. The second process includes modelling and agreeing the user tasks, and also creating scenarios to inform prototyping and later user testing. The third process involves modelling the system objects as viewed by the user and producing a user glossary and a graphical user interface (GUI) style guide. The fourth design GUI process creates an initial interface design. The fifth process produces a prototype, which is evaluated by users and then iteratively refined. The sixth, and final, process evaluates the design against the earlier usability requirements.

Individual structured methods differ in many ways – for example, use of terminology, level of proceduralisation, inclusion of design knowledge and specific design products. However, they support similar design transformations, leading to broadly comparable user interface specifications. These common aspects can be generalised. Such a general model has been proposed by Middlemass and Long (2005).

The top level of the general model derives from analysis of the three structured methods, that is, MUSE, STUDIO and GUIDE, and is expressed in terms of a general task model, as specified by MUSE (Lim and Long, 1994). The method comprises seven stages: plan project, prepare groundwork, specify detailed tasks, specify high-level design, document functional requirements, refine design and implement user interface. In turn, prepare groundwork is decomposed into: establish requirements, examine systems, decompose tasks, identify usability needs, scope task-level system, analyse domain and verify models. Also, refine design is decomposed into an iteration over detail design and evaluate design.

General structured methods may be more complete than individual such methods. For this reason, the former may be preferred to the latter for constructing a methodological component, as the basis for better supporting HCI research frameworks. The methods would need to be appropriately refined, such as to relate to the substantive component of a framework. As well as being conceptualised, they would also need to have the potential to be correctly operationalised, tested and generalised.

14.2.3 Research Structured Analysis and Design Methods

Research structured methods are compatible with substantive research frameworks. For example, Stork (1999) enhanced MUSE (see earlier) as required by his research strategy of applying the particular research conception of Long and

Dowell/Dowell and Long (1989). The concepts of the latter are *Italicised* at first mention for easy identification, reference and application, but apply throughout. The MUSE scope, processes and notations are used by the enhanced method, entitled MUSE/R (MUSE for Research).

MUSE has three phases. The first phase is the information, elicitation and analysis phase, the second is the conceptual design phase and the third is the detailed design phase. The first phase of MUSE involves the analysis of existing systems, including task operationalisations, their domains and their generalisations. For MUSE/R, these stages are re-scoped to operationalise concepts from the Long and Dowell/Dowell and Long (1989) conception – the specific *Structures* and *Behaviours* of the *Extant Worksystems*, their *Structural* and *Behavioural Costs*, their *Domain* and the *Quality* of their *Work*. Thus, the first stages of the first phase of MUSE/R operationalise specific current designs, expressed according to the application of the research conception. The final stages of the first phase of MUSE and the first stages of the second phase involve the specification of user needs. For MUSE/R, these stages are re-scoped to operationalise the specific *Design Problem*. The final stages of the second and third stages of MUSE/R involve the specification of the *Interactive System* and documentation of the design rationale. For MUSE/R, these stages are re-scoped to operationalise the specific *Design Solution* and the previously acquired design knowledge applied to develop the specific design solution. The method has been appropriately refined by Stork, such as to relate to the substantive component of the conception which he applied. The method, as well as being conceptualised and correctly operationalised, would need to have the potential for being tested and generalised.

Longer-term research could build on MUSE/R to develop a methodological component for the General Framework proposed here. The conception used by Stork would be replaced by the General Framework, which would in turn be operationalised, tested and generalised, consistent with the requirements of validation (see 11.4). The resulting component would meet the methodological framework requirement in the form of an integrated substantive and methodological framework to acquire and to validate substantive and methodological HCI knowledge.

Conclusion

This concludes the presentation of suggestions concerning the reasons for developing, and the research needed to develop a greater methodological component for the General Framework. Design methods are proposed as a starting point for such research. The latter include user-centred, structured analysis and design, and research structured analysis and design methods. Any such methodological component could also be integrated with other such generic frameworks.

14.3 Research Practice Assignment

The assignment comprises two sections: General and Research Design Scenarios.

14.3.1 General

- Select an HCI research framework, either from the research literature or from those presented in 12.3.
  - Compare the selected framework with the General Framework for HCI research, presented in 3.4 and 10.2.2, as concerns its substantive and methodological components, in the manner of 14.2.
  - Note the similarities and differences between the methodological concepts of the selected HCI framework and of the General Framework for HCI research.
- Select two of the comparison frameworks from 12.3 that share some of the important common methodological concepts
  - How many of the important common methodological concepts shared by two of the comparison frameworks of 12.3 are also shared by your selected framework?

Hints and Tips

Difficult to get started?

Try reading the section again, while at the same time thinking explicitly about the differences between types of knowledge, especially substantive and methodological, and so types of research needed to acquire each type of knowledge. Note the differences as you go along.

Consider the explicit or implicit framework for its methodological/substantive knowledge content used by your own or others' research, in terms of the General Framework for HCI research, presented in 10.2.2.

Difficult to complete?

Familiarise yourself with the concepts of knowledge and knowledge types, as they are applied in the HCI research (and other) literature.

Note the similarities and differences between the concepts of the types of knowledge identified in the HCI research literature.

Test[1]

- Select one of the frameworks that are compared with the General Framework for HCI research, from 12.3.
- Referencing the framework explicitly and the General Framework for HCI research presented in 10.2.2 from memory only, compare their methodological components. Consider the results of your comparison with the one presented here. Repeat until the results are comparable. Rationalise any differences.

14.3.2 Research Design Scenarios

Research Design Scenario 14.1: Integrating a User-Centred
Design Method with an HCI Framework to Enhance the Methodological
Component of the Former

- Select a user-centred design method, either from the HCI research literature or from 14.2.1, and identify the main concepts.
- Select an HCI framework for research, either from the HCI research literature or from 12.3, and identify the main concepts.
- Integrate the main concepts of the selected user-centred design method with the main concepts of the selected HCI framework for research, such as to enhance the methodological component of the former. Follow the example of Stork (1999) (see 14.2.3).
  - Note that the integration scenario is limited in two ways. First, the concepts of the user-centred design method and the HCI framework for research are limited to only the main concepts. Second, the integration is only conceptualised; it is not operationalised, tested or generalised.

In the light of the selected user-centred design method and the selected HCI framework for research:

1. Were you able to integrate all the main concepts of the selected user-centred design method and the main concepts of the HCI framework for research? If not, why not?
2. Was the balance between the main user-centred design concepts and the main HCI framework concepts for research appropriate? If not, why not?

Research Design Scenario 14.2: Integrating a Structured Analysis
and Design Method with an HCI Framework to Enhance the Methodological
Component of the Former

- Select a structured analysis and design method, either from the HCI research literature or from 14.2.2, but other than MUSE (because used by Stork) and identify the main concepts.
- Select an HCI framework for research, either from the HCI research literature or from 12.3, but other than the framework selected for 14.3.1, and identify the main concepts.
- Integrate the main concepts of the selected structured analysis and design method with the main concepts of the selected HCI framework for research, such as to enhance the methodological component of the former. Follow the example of Stork (1999) – see 14.2.3.
  - Note that the integration scenario is limited in two ways. First, the concepts of the structured analysis and design method and the HCI framework for research are limited only to the main concepts. Second, the integration is only conceptualised; it is not operationalised, tested or generalised.

In the light of the selected structured analysis and design method and the selected HCI framework for research:

1. Were you able to integrate all the main concepts of the selected structured analysis and of the design method and of the HCI framework for research? If not, why not?
2. Was the balance between the analysis and design concepts and those of the HCI framework for research appropriate? If not, why not?

14.4 Notes

1. The test encourages researchers to commit the approaches and frameworks to memory. Such internalisation facilitates their subsequent application.

15

Case Studies for General Framework

The General Framework requires case studies to progress its development. These are of two types – of the framework itself, and of the HCI knowledge acquired with its support by means of HCI research. In turn, these two types of case study can be divided into acquisition and validation case studies. The latter types of case study have yet to be carried out for the General Framework. However, on the basis of case studies reported in the literature, and the validation proposal made here, suggestions are made as to the research needed to conduct such case studies.

15.1 Case Study Requirement

In general, a case study is a particular instance of studying. Such studies may be of different kinds – illustrative, exploratory, cumulative and critical instance. They are used widely in the sciences and engineering to acquire and to validate frameworks and knowledge. They may involve analysis of different kinds – experiments, simulations, tests and surveys. The specific case studies required for the General Framework are research case studies. The latter would report the acquisition and validation of HCI frameworks and the knowledge acquired with their support. It is not possible here, and at this time, to meet this requirement. That remains for longer-term research. What can be done, however, is to use published case studies along with the validation proposal made here (see 11.4) to suggest how such studies might be conducted as part of that future research.

Following Middlemass, Stork and Long (1999), case studies of HCI design knowledge can be successful or unsuccessful. Successful case studies are considered to fall within the scope of the design knowledge being applied. Unsuccessful case studies are considered not to fall within its scope. Thus, successful and unsuccessful case studies together define the scope of the application of HCI design knowledge. Case studies are considered to vary in their definition (that is, how well they are specified), their complexity (that is, how simple or complicated they are), and their observability (that is, the access accorded the validators to the design knowledge itself). Progress requires case studies to increase successively their specification, complexity and observability.

Likewise, HCI research case studies, whether of acquisition/validation or of framework/knowledge, can also be assessed as successful or unsuccessful. The successful research case studies are considered to fall within the scope of the HCI framework or knowledge. The unsuccessful research case studies are considered not to fall within the scope of the framework or knowledge. Thus, successful and unsuccessful case studies together define the scope of the framework or knowledge of HCI research. Research case studies, like case studies of HCI design knowledge application, are considered to vary in their definition (that is, how well they are specified), their complexity (that is, how simple or complicated they are), and their observability (that is, the access accorded the validators to the knowledge itself). Progress requires research case studies to increase successively their specification, complexity and observability.

For example, Carroll et al. (1991) report an illustrative case study of the application of the task-artefact cycle as a framework for HCI research and development. The example concerns the training wheels interface, a reduced-function training environment for a stand-alone text editor. The key feature of the interface is that it blocks the outcomes of inappropriate user actions. Carroll et al. claim that the technique facilitates initial and continuing learning. No separate conclusion is reached concerning the application of the task-artefact cycle as an HCI framework.

The Carroll et al. research case study is one of knowledge acquisition – the knowledge expressed in the training wheels interface, supported by the task-artefact cycle as a framework. The case study is assessed as successful. Stand-alone text editor interactions are considered to fall within the scope of the training wheels knowledge, supported by the task-artefact cycle framework. However, the knowledge and framework are not assessed separately. The case study can be considered to be well defined, moderately complex and highly observable, the researchers being the originators of the training wheels knowledge. The point here is that research case studies need explicit criteria by which to be assessed.

Criteria for the validation of the HCI General Framework for research and the knowledge acquired and validated with its support by HCI research (see 11.2) comprise:

- conceptualisation of framework and knowledge, which is complete, coherent and fit for purpose of
- operationalisation of framework and knowledge, which is complete, coherent and fit for purpose of
- test of framework and knowledge, which is complete, coherent and fit for purpose of
- generalisation of framework and knowledge, which is complete, coherent and fit for purpose.

These criteria can be applied to case studies reported in the literature, with a view to establishing the current state of such studies, and so the need for future research to meet the case study requirement for the General Framework and for other frameworks more generally.

15.2 Meeting Case Study Requirement

The specific case studies required for the General Framework are research case studies. The latter include the acquisition and validation of HCI frameworks and knowledge, supported by explicit frameworks. The resulting four types of case study are considered separately.

15.2.1 Acquisition Case Studies

Acquisition case studies report new frameworks for research or new knowledge acquired by research and supported by existing frameworks. Examples of new frameworks can be found in the assessment of the General Framework against other HCI frameworks (see 12.3). Examples of new knowledge acquired by research and supported, in some cases, by frameworks can be found in the assessment of the General Framework against HCI theories (see 13.3).

15.2.1.1 Framework Acquisition Case Studies

In general, framework acquisition studies are prompted by some change or perceived need. The changes and needs may be of different kinds. For example, the Morton et al. (1979) framework was prompted, according to the authors, by the need to include the behavioural phenomena of people interacting with the novel computing technology of the time, within the scope of the models and methods of cognitive psychology. The aim was to achieve a better understanding of such phenomena. The Shneiderman (1983) framework was also prompted by changes in interactive computer systems enabling users' direct manipulation of the interface. The Long and Dowell (1989) conception was prompted by the appearance and the initial development of different kinds of HCI discipline – craft, applied science and engineering – and also the need to rationalise their structure and relationships. Last, the Carroll et al. (1991) framework was prompted by the need for a programme for HCI. They propose a programme for integrating research and practice. The latter comprises an associated framework – the task-artefact cycle – and a theory – design ratio- nale. The latter is expressed as a detailed description of the history and meaning of an artefact. The Rauterberg (2006) framework was prompted by the need for a scientific language, its definition and its support for consensus for a coherent research line. The latter comprises a framework that triangulates design knowl- edge, the interactive system and empirical validation.

All these case-study examples of framework acquisition constitute new proposals, although they may share some assumptions common to their time, for example, about information processing as a model for human mental behaviour. However, they neither build on each other's work directly nor describe in any detail the origins of the framework in question. Neither do they specify criteria by which the frameworks or the knowledge acquired with their support are to be assessed.

The General Framework is also an example of framework acquisition, but one whose origins are made explicit. The General Framework is based on the Long and Dowell/Dowell and Long (1989) conception for a discipline of HCI and for the design problem of HCI respectively. The conception constitutes the basis for the core framework for HCI, including HCI research (see 10.2.1). The core framework is instantiated in the specific frameworks (see 4.3.2–9.3.2). The latter are then generalised to form the General Framework for HCI research (see 10.2.2). The latter is re-expressed in the form of a general design research exemplar (see 10.2.3) accompanied by a general lower-level description (see 10.2.4).

Applying the criteria for the validation of the General Framework for research, it is concluded with respect to its acquisition that it has been con- ceptualised. The General Framework is considered generally complete with respect to other frameworks, although the completeness is much dependent on the coherence between it and the comparison sets of concepts (see 12.4). However, this does not meet the criteria of being complete, coherent and fit for purpose for the operationalisation of the General Framework or the remain- ing criteria (see 11.2).[1]

15.2.1.2 Knowledge Acquisition Case Studies

Knowledge acquisition case studies may be supported by frameworks or not. The frameworks may be implicit or explicit. Of concern here are case studies of the explicit acquisition of HCI knowledge, supported by explicit HCI frameworks. For example, Timmer and Long (2002) report an acquisition case study, supported by the explicit conception of Dowell and Long (1998), as applied to the domain of air traffic management. The knowledge acquired is expressed in the form of a theory of the operator planning horizon (TOPH). The aim of the theory is to propose a method for expressing the adequacy of operator traffic planning. The aim is to identify instances of ineffective planning, that is, to diagnose design problems. The theory comprises four models – domain, planning horizon, operator planning horizon and horizon effectiveness – in addition to a method for their construction and application. The theory is conceptualised, although the concepts of the framework are not identified individually and no criteria are offered for the assessment of the conceptualisation.

This study is of the kind required by the General Framework. It is a knowledge acquisition study and acquires a theory comprising models and a method. Both are typical forms of HCI knowledge. The General Framework, instantiated as a specific framework, would need to have within its scope such models and methods, and also domains, such as that of air traffic management, which has a long tradition in HCI. To its advantage, the case study would be able to identify its individual concepts and to apply, as appropriate, the complete set of validation criteria for conceptualisation. As for framework acquisition case studies, were the General Framework to be found wanting by validation case studies, its (re)conceptualisation in support of knowledge acquisition would also need a case study as concerns its (re) acquisition.

A further example of a knowledge acquisition case study is reported by Hill (2010). The case study is also of the explicit acquisition of HCI knowledge, supported by an explicit HCI framework. The latter is the conception of Long and Dowell/Dowell and Long (1989) for the discipline of HCI and the design problem of HCI respectively, as applied to the application domain of the Emergency Management Combined Response System (EMCRS). The EMCRS is a complex three-tier command and control system. It was set up in response to a need for better coordination between agencies such as police, ambulance and fire services, when they respond together to disasters. The knowledge acquired is expressed in the form of models, supported by the conception (domain, worksystem and performance). In addition, there is a method, which recruits the models to the practice of design problem diagnosis. Again, as with the Timmer and Long (2002) case study, the theory is considered to be conceptualised, although the concepts of the framework are not identified individually and no explicit criteria are offered for the assessment of its conceptualisation.

The Hill (2010) study, like that of Timmer and Long (2002), is of the kind required by the General Framework. It is a knowledge acquisition study and acquires models and a method for diagnosing design problems. Both are typical forms of HCI knowledge. The General Framework, instantiated as a specific framework, would need to have within its scope such models and methods. However, the domain of Emergency Management Combined Response System does not have a long tradition in HCI and may be challenging for an initial case study. To its advantage, the case study would be able, in addition, to identify its individual concepts and to apply the validation criteria for conceptualisation (see 11.2).[2]

15.2.2 Validation Case Studies

Validation case studies report the confirmation of frameworks for research or confirmation of knowledge acquired by HCI research and supported by HCI frameworks. Examples of frameworks can be found in the assessment of the General Framework against other HCI frameworks (see 12.3). Examples of knowledge acquired by research and supported in some cases by frameworks can be found in the assessment of the General Framework against HCI theories (see 13.3). Validation case studies, however, are notably absent from the HCI literature for both frameworks and knowledge supported by frameworks. The studies referenced here are the exception.

15.2.2.1 Framework Validation Case Studies
In general, framework validation case studies are prompted by the need to confirm the claims made by the frameworks. For example, as concerns the latter, the resultant 'output to designers' of the application of the Morton et al. (1979) framework is intended to provide support for more user-centric design. A case study is required to show that this claim is supported, as it is for the Shneiderman (1983) framework as concerns its claimed support for the design of interactive systems involving direct manipulation interfaces which reduce memory load, and for the Carroll et al. (1991) framework, which claims to integrate research and practice by codifying the knowledge, expressed as claims, implicit in designs. Without case studies, none of these claims can be considered to be supported other than by conceptualisation, as demonstrated by the initial acquisition case studies.

As an example of a putative framework validation case study, Wild (2010) reports the application of the Dowell and Long (1998) conception to the domain of services. He identifies an increase in the importance of, and interest in, services and their associated research. However, Wild argues that this emerging field needs to draw on other disciplines and practices for its development. Although there is a growing body of service-related work by both HCI researchers and practitioners, service researchers themselves seem to be unaware of it.

Wild believes that HCI can make two important contributions to service science. The first contribution is the HCI user-centred mindset and techniques. The second contribution is the HCI concepts and frameworks for understanding the nature of services. His paper exemplifies the latter by way of the application to services of the conception of HCI as cognitive engineering (Dowell and Long, 1998). The application supports Wild's own work of developing a framework relating the different strands of services research. The latter, he argues, can also be used to provide high-level, integrated models of service systems.

This validation case study of the Dowell and Long conception adds another domain of application, that of services, to that of air traffic management, for example. Also, there is no doubt that Wild is correct in identifying the service sector as offering considerable potential for HCI-type research. However, the services sector is only selectively conceptualised by Wild and the concepts are not individually identified. Further, the Dowell and Long conception is only selectively applied. No criteria are offered by which to assess the case study's success. No attempt is made with respect to implementing either operationalisation or test. Further, the claim to generalisation resides in the addition of a single domain of application, that of services. Future case studies of the General Framework would need to make good these shortcomings, and application of the validation criteria (see 11.2) would support such research along with application of the general design research exemplar (see 10.2.3).

A further and more substantial case study of framework validation is reported by Long and Monk (2002). The case study has the advantage over that of Wild, in that the application of the conception of Long and Dowell (1989) is explicit, is generally complete with respect to the latter and reports the detailed mapping of the concepts from the two different domains of application. Long and Monk report a case study in which the framework for HCI as engineering is applied analytically to an instance of telemedical consultation research (Watts and Monk, 1997, 1999) to establish how the former might inform the latter.

Long and Monk consider the case study to be a success. First, they claim that all the concepts in the telemedical research are informally classified by the HCI engineering conception. Second, they claim that the additional concepts of the latter are relevant to informing future telemedical research. In the illustration that follows, the common concepts of the Long and Dowell/Dowell and Long

(1989) conception and the main General Framework concepts are shown in **Boldface**. Classified telemedical concepts are shown in *italics*. The numbering refers to the identification of the telemedical concepts (Watts and Monk, 1998, 1999).

- *Research* (1) – **Research**
- *Telemedical Consultation* (2) – **Knowledge**
- *Work Description* (22); *Ideas* (25); *Knowledge* (30); *Communication Usage Diagrams* (32) – (Substantive) **Knowledge**
- *Method* (20); *Task Analysis* (28); *Scope of Application* (34) – (Methodological) **Knowledge**
- *Field Study* (3); *Interview* (13); *Observation* (14); *Video Analysis* (15) – **Practices**

The Long and Monk conception validation case study is considered a success. However, this is only inasmuch as an additional domain of application, that of telemedicine, is conceptualised in terms of the Long and Dowell (1989) conception for HCI as engineering. Operational and test validation criteria are not addressed. Further, the claim to generalisation resides only in the addition of a single domain of application, that of telemedicine. Future case studies of the General Framework would do well to apply the numbering and mapping schemes of Long and Monk or somesuch, along with the individual identification of concepts. The complete validation criteria would also need to be addressed (see 11.2) and the general design research exemplar would need to be applied (see 10.2.3).

The last case study of framework validation is that of Long and Stork (1994), which illustrates the meeting of the operationalisation criterion, as well as that of conceptualisation. Their long-term research aim is more effective HCI design practice, as supported by general design principles. The validation of the latter by research would offer a better guarantee of the solution of design problems than present design prescriptions, such as guidelines and heuristics. HCI principles require research to develop operationalisations of specific design problems and solutions that are better conceptualised and operationalised than existing ones. The case study reports such a specific design problem operationalisation, supported by the Long and Dowell/Dowell and Long (1989) conception.

The design problem was the failure to maintain desired comfort and costs by an interactive domestic heating system acceptable to the occupants of a house. The latter conception and the General Framework (lower-level) concepts (see 10.2.4) are shown in **Boldface** and their operationalisation in *Italics*. For example, concerning the specific actual domain of application, it has two main **Physical Objects**: 'A' (the house occupant) and the house. 'A' has a **Physical Attribute** of *Temperature* and an **Abstract Attribute** of *Comfort*. The attribute of *Comfort* is related to the attribute of *Temperature* having a range of acceptable temperatures.

The second **Physical Object** is the house, which has **Physical Objects** that are the rooms. The rooms have a **Physical Attribute** of their *Temperature* and **Physical Objects** of the radiators. The radiators have a **Physical Attribute** of their *Temperature*. The *Temperatures* of the rooms are related to the *Temperature* of 'A' and the *Temperatures* of the radiators. The *Temperatures* of the radiators are controlled by an interactive heating system.

The current **States** of the *Temperatures* of the radiators can result in the **State** of the Comfort **Attribute** of 'A' being **Not** comfortable. This comfort state is a task goal and defines the achieved goal of the actual quality by interpretation of the relationships between this attribute and the other attributes in the actual domain of application, that is, of a domestic heating system.

Although the Stork and Long validation case study is a success in the generally complete and coherent conceptualisation of the application domain of domestic heating for the purpose of operationalisation, it makes no attempt to meet the remaining validation criteria of test and generalisation, other than the latter in the form of an additional domain of application. However, these criteria will need to be met by future framework validation case studies of the General Framework (see 11.2), along with the identification of individual concepts and the application of the general design research exemplar (see 10.2.3).

15.2.2.2 Knowledge Validation Case Studies

Knowledge validation case studies may be supported by frameworks or not. The frameworks may be implicit or explicit. Of concern here are case studies of the explicit validation of HCI knowledge, supported by explicit HCI frameworks. For example, Long and Brostoff (2002) report research intended to validate design knowledge in the form of the products of a structured analysis and design Method for Usability Engineering (MUSE; Lim and Long, 1994). The latter provides the framework on which the products or containers of MUSE/C(ontainers) is based (see 14.2.2). MUSE /C, then, constitutes HCI design knowledge supported by an explicit framework – MUSE. In the case study MUSE/C is used to redesign a range of interactive domestic technologies intended to support dementia care in the home. The interactive technologies include hi-fi system, radio, portable audio player, television, video recorder and games console.

The authors consider the case study to be a success. The design products are claimed to be correctly conceptualised and operationalised. An evaluation claims to show the interactive technologies to be more effective following redesign. Difficulties in the MUSE/C application, however, are identified and documented and constitute a requirement for future research and improvement of the method. The validation of MUSE/C, then, can be considered only partial. This conclusion is further supported by the non-inclusion of the validation criteria of completeness and coherence for test and no address of the criterion of generalisation (see 11.2).

This case study, however, is of the kind required by the General Framework, especially in the light of its need for a methodological component (see 14.2). It is a knowledge validation study supported by the MUSE framework, and partially validates an HCI method. MUSE/C is a typical form of HCI knowledge. It is also suggestive as to the potential for the validation of MUSE as a framework. The General Framework, instantiated in a specific framework, would need to support knowledge in the form of such methods, as they apply to the domain of application of interactive domestic technologies, which continue to increase in popularity. The case study would be able also to identify its individual concepts and to apply the remaining criteria of test and generalisation for validation (see 11.2), in addition to the application of the general design research exemplar (see 10.2.3).

A final case study of knowledge validation is reported by Long and Hill (2005). The research aims to validate design knowledge proposed by Timmer (1999) for air traffic management. The design knowledge is expressed as a theory of the operator planning horizon (TOPH). It characterises the adequacy of operator planning, with a view to identifying instances of ineffective planning, that is, diagnosing design problems. The theory comprises four models: domain, planning horizon, operator planning horizon and horizon effectiveness. These models are based on the conception of Dowell and Long (1989), as applied to air traffic management (Dowell, 1998), in addition to a method for their construction and application. The knowledge is applied to an air traffic management simulation to diagnose design problems associated with controller planning horizons. The latter were observed in an en-route sector in the region of Bordeaux, France, characterised by 21 beacons, multiple airways and multiple exits (Debenard and Crevits, 2000).

The case study is judged by the authors to be a success. The design knowledge is claimed to be correctly operationalised, tested and generalised to an air traffic management simulation more complex than that used by Timmer to develop the knowledge initially. However, difficulties with the application are identified and reported. The validation is, thus, considered to be only partial. This case study, however, is of the kind required by the General Framework. The latter, instantiated as a specific framework, would need to support knowledge in the form of such methods, as well as the domain of application traditional to HCI, that of air traffic management. In addition to making good deficiencies such as those reported, the General Framework, supporting an HCI knowledge validation case study, would be able to identify its individual concepts. This would be in addition to the application of the general design research exemplar (see 10.2.3) and the validation criteria (see 11.2).

Conclusion

This concludes suggestions concerning acquisition/validation and frame-work/knowledge case studies as supported by frameworks. All these kinds of case study constitute a way forward for HCI research in general, including the General Framework in particular, to meet the case study requirement.

15.3 Research Practice Assignment

The assignment comprises two sections: General and Research Design Scenario.

15.3.1 General

- Search the HCI research literature, in particular the frameworks referenced in 12.3 and the theories referenced in 13.3, for acquisition and validation framework and knowledge case study criteria not proposed here (see 15.1).
  - Compare and contrast the different criteria.
  - Identify common criterial features.
- Select a framework acquisition case study from the literature not referenced here.
  - Analyse in the manner of 15.2.1.1.
  - List any additional suggestions for future case study research prompted by your analysis.
- Select a knowledge acquisition case study from the literature not referenced here.
  - Analyse in the manner of 15.2.1.2.
  - List any additional suggestions for future case study research prompted by your analysis.
- Select a framework validation case study from the literature not referenced here. Analyse in the manner of 15.2.2.1.

- List any additional suggestions for future case study research prompted by your analysis.
- Select a knowledge validation case study from the literature not referenced here.
  - Analyse in the manner of 15.2.2.2.
  - List any additional suggestions for future case study research prompted by your analysis.
- Why do you think so few validation case studies are reported in the HCI research literature?
  - How might the deficiency be made good?
  - How might your own research contribute to this making good?

Hints and Tips

Difficult to get started?
Try reading the section again, while at the same time thinking explicitly about the different types of case study. Note the differences as you go along.
Consider the explicit or implicit framework used by your own or others' research, as concerns acquisition/validation case studies for frameworks/ knowledge, in terms of the General Framework for HCI research presented in 10.2.2.

Difficult to complete?
Familiarise yourself with the concepts of case study and case study types, as they are applied in the HCI research (and other) literature.
Note the similarities and differences between the concepts of the types of case study identified in the HCI research literature and those proposed here.

Test[3]

- Select a framework acquisition case study from 15.2.1.1 and a knowledge acquisition case study from 15.2.1.2.
- From memory only, list their similarities and differences. Consider why these might be so.
- Select a framework validation case study from 15.2.2.1 and a knowledge validation case study from 15.2.2.2.
- From memory only, list their similarities and differences. Consider why these might be so.

15.3.2 Research Design Scenario

Research Design Scenario 15.1: Framework Acquisition and Validation Case Study

- Search the HCI research literature for, and select, an approach which does not appear among those proposed in 4.2–9.2.
- Apply the following general expression (see 10.1) to the selected approach. The expression indicates the requirement for descriptors and their expansion necessary to characterise an approach.
- The general approach is marked [***] in the text for the descriptor and [*** ...] for its expansion. The descriptor and the expansion together constitute the specification of an approach. Application of the general approach to form a new approach requires the blank descriptors and expansions to be completed by researchers to characterise any new and additional approach.
  - First, a [***] approach to HCI research is a way of addressing the topic or problem of designing [***] human–computer interactions by [***].
    - For example, [*** ...].
  - Second, a [***] approach to HCI research requires the performing of actions to progress that approach to the topic or problem of [***] human–computer interaction.
    - For example, [*** ...].
  - Third, a [***] approach to HCI research requires the evaluating of the success or not of the [***] actions performed by [***].
    - For example, [*** ...].
  - Fourth, a [***] approach to HCI research requires the cumulating of the successes as a way of establishing whether the topic or problem of designing [***] human–computer interactions has been addressed or not.
    - For example, [*** ...].
- Apply the General Framework for HCI research (see 10.2.2) to the newly created approach to create a new framework and so an example of framework acquisition corresponding to the approach, as follows:
  - **Discipline**, as an academic (that is, scholarly) field (that is, branch/subject area) of study (that is, investigation of knowledge as division of information/learning) and
  - **General**, as common (that is, shared) and
  - **General Problem**, as the design (that is, specification) of human–computer interactions and
  - **Particular Scope**, as the design of human (that is, individual/group)–computer (that is, interactive/embedded) interactions (that is, active/

passive) to do something (that is, action/task) as desired (that is, wanted/ needed/experienced/felt/valued) and

- **General Research**, as the diagnosis of design problems (that is, not as desired) and the prescription of design solutions (that is, as desired), as they relate to performance (that is, desired) for the acquisition (that is, creation) and for the validation (that is, confirmation) of knowledge to support practices and
- **General Knowledge**, as guidelines/models/ methods/principles (that is, as acquired and validated by research) and supports (that is, facilitates/makes possible) practices and
- **General Practices**, as trial and error/implement and/then test (that is, supported by knowledge acquired and validated by research).
- Applying the newly acquired framework, as in the application of the General Framework, to the new approach, suggest an illustrative sketch plan for a research project whose aim is to validate the framework and so constitute the basis for a case study of framework validation. The sketch plan should specify the research to be conducted, although only at a high level of description. The latter may restrict the concepts appearing in the acquired framework and so can only be illustrative.
  - The scope of the validation should be two different instances of HCI knowledge, for example, two models, two methods or a model and a method, preferably with which you are familiar.
  - Is the framework able to accommodate both instances of knowledge? Again, the application of the framework can be no more than illustrative, as only some of its concepts are involved.
  - Do your best to include all four superordinate concepts of validation in your plan (see 11.4), as appropriate. In the event that you cannot apply a concept, try to identify the reason.
  - Do your best to include all three superordinate criteria of validation in your plan (see 11.4), as appropriate. In the event that you cannot apply a criterion, try to identify the reason.
  - Finally, consider how your plan might be improved to form the basis for a better validation case study.

15.4 Notes

1. Although case studies are required to meet all the remaining validation criteria for HCI framework and knowledge research, they are not required at present for the conceptualisation of the General Framework, as concerns its acquisition. Its status is

clearly that of having been acquired and in the manner proposed here. However, that status might be changed by two sorts of contingency.

- The first contingency is that, if the General Framework were to be applied to a new approach, not the object of one of the present specific frameworks (see 4.3–9.3), then an acquisition case study would be required for the new specific framework. The case study would need to specify both the new approach (see 2.2) and the associated framework (see 3.4), in the manner shown here.
- The second contingency is that, if the General Framework were to be found wanting by validation case studies, its (re)conceptualisation, should this be required, would also need a case study, as concerns its (reacquisition).

In both these cases, however, the general design research exemplar (see 10.2.3) provides detailed support and indicates the way forward as to how the relevant research case study needs to be conducted and with respect to which validation criteria (see 11.2).

2. Unlike the General Framework as concerns its framework acquisition status, its knowledge acquisition status is at present unacquired. However, if like the General Framework, the knowledge, once acquired, were to be found wanting by validation case studies, its (re)conceptualisation, should this be needed, would also require a case study as concerns its acquisition. However, the general design research exemplar (see 10.2.3) provides detailed support and indicates the way forward as to how the relevant research case study needs to be conducted and with respect to which validation criteria (see 11.2).

3. The test encourages researchers to commit the approaches and frameworks to memory. Such internalisation facilitates their subsequent application.

16

Approaches and Frameworks for HCI Research: Lessons Learned and Lessons Remaining

By way of conclusion, this final chapter brings together the lessons learned and the lessons remaining concerning approaches and frameworks for HCI research. The conclusion takes the form of a proposal for an HCI research programme, which builds on the lessons learned to formulate the lessons remaining. Together they constitute the research programme.

16.1 Lessons Learned and Lessons Remaining

The characterisation of the current state of HCI research concerning approaches and frameworks is expressed in what follows as lessons learned. The latter comprise issues about which there is some current, although limited, agreement (see 12.3 and 13.3). Lessons learned are complemented by lessons remaining, as proposed here for approaches and frameworks. The aim is to make it easier for researchers to build on each other's work and so to advance discipline progress.

The lessons remaining can be considered to be much as the research line proposed by Rauterberg (2006). The line comprises a framework, its triangulation (that is, validation of design knowledge), the interactive system and empirical validation. The lessons remaining can also be considered much as a programme for the specification and implementation of a framework for HCI research and development as proposed by Carroll et al. (1991), and also much as a conceptualisation for a possible discipline of human–computer interaction as envisaged by Carroll (2010). Unfortunately, and by his own admission, a goal, which remained unrealised.

The order of the lessons learned and lessons remaining follows that of the book chapters. This is intended to make it easier for researchers to follow the development of the latter with respect to the former, and also more supportive for researchers to apply the lessons remaining.

16.1.1 Approaches and Frameworks for HCI Research

Lessons Learned

Approaches and frameworks for HCI research are both to be found widely in the HCI research literature (Rauterberg, 2006; Rogers, 2012). Both approaches and frameworks are generally high-level characterisations of research, its products and, to a much lesser extent, how it may be conducted and its results validated. Frameworks are more rigorously specified than approaches.

The lesson learned is that approaches and frameworks appear to serve some common purpose for HCI researchers in supporting their research, but in different ways. Frameworks offer the more rigorous support.

Lessons Remaining

However, approaches and frameworks are not related in the research literature and certainly not systematically. Examples include Kuutti (1996) and Rogers et al. (2011). This is in spite of approaches and frameworks having the same scope of HCI and/or HCI research.

The lesson remaining is that approaches and frameworks for HCI research need to be related, and systematically so (see 2.2 and 3.4). Also, as part of that systematic relationship, frameworks need to be applicable to approaches (see 4.3.5–9.3.5).

16.1.2 Approaches to HCI Research

Lessons Learned

Approaches to HCI research have wide currency in the HCI research literature. Rogers (2012) identifies 19 fields, each of which might be considered to constitute an approach or approaches (see Note 1 in 2.5). Examples include software engineering (Shneiderman, 1983; Lim and Long, 1994) and artist design (Salisbury, 2014; Edmonds, 2018). In contrast to Roger's classification, approaches can also be individual in nature, often associated with particular researchers or even specific publications (Balaam et al., 2015; Mancini et al., 2012).

The lesson learned is that researchers appear to find the high-level description of approach of some use in characterising and thinking about their work, although in an informal manner.

Lessons Remaining

However, individual approaches may have little in common, for example, Cockton (2006) and Harper et al. (2008). They are often implicit, which makes them hard to apply and to develop.

The lesson remaining is that approaches to HCI research need to be specified and implemented explicitly, while remaining informal (see 2.2 and 3.4). The specification needs to support the classification of approaches, according to their common features. It also needs to retain the differences between them. Initial specific approaches need to include innovation, art, craft, applied, science and engineering (see 4.3.2–9.3.2). Additional specific approaches need to be created as required (see 15.3.2).

16.1.3 Frameworks for HCI Research

Lessons Learned

Frameworks for HCI research, like approaches, have wide currency in the HCI research literature. Rogers (2012) identifies 19 fields, each of which might be considered to constitute an implicit or explicit framework or frameworks (see Note 1 in 2.5). Examples include psychology/cognitive science (Morton et al., 1979) and cognitive engineering (Long, 2010). In spite of Roger's classification, frameworks can also be individual in nature, being much associated with particular researchers. (Kuutti, 1996; Olson and Olson, 2000).

The lesson learned is that researchers appear to find the concept of framework a way of characterising and thinking about their work in a more rigorous manner than that offered by approach.

Lessons Remaining

However, frameworks for HCI research differ widely and are largely implicit within frameworks for HCI (Ng, 2002; Vanderheiden, 2008). Further, the frameworks may have little in common, for example, Shneiderman (1983) and Olson and Olson (2000). As a result, their dissemination has been limited to date and their uptake modest. Only the originators, and in some cases members of their immediate research groups, may be involved in dissemination.

The lesson remaining is that frameworks for HCI research need to be specified and implemented explicitly (see 4.3.2–9.3.2). The specification needs to support the common features of frameworks in the form of a common framework – core or somesuch (see 3.4). It also needs to retain the potential for differences between specific frameworks (see 10.2). Initial specific frameworks need to include innovation, art, craft, applied, science and engineering (see 4.3.2–9.3.2), such as to be applicable to research approaches. Additional specific frameworks need to be created as required (see 15.3.2).

16.1.4 Specific Frameworks for HCI Research

Lessons Learned

Specific frameworks for HCI research are to be found throughout the HCI literature (see 12.3). Such frameworks are offered, for example, by science and engineering, as two of the most cited in publications and textbooks (Sharp et al., 2007). Examples of such frameworks include Card et al. (1983), Barnard (1991) and Carroll (2010). They all make reference to both science and engineering in one form or another.

Researchers advance two main lines of argument for the importance of such specific frameworks. First, the frameworks offer a source of additional information to support the conduct of HCI and its research. This is the case made for science frameworks, for example, by Barnard et al. (2000). Second, the specific frameworks offer a source of constraints for the conception of HCI and its research. This is the case made for engineering frameworks, for example, by Dowell and Long (1998).

The lesson learned is that researchers appear to find the concept of specific framework a way of characterising and thinking about their work in a more specific manner than the concept of framework more generally.

Lessons Remaining

However, specific frameworks for HCI research may be expressed only at a high level of description, may differ widely and may be largely implicit within frameworks for HCI (Kuutti, 1996; Olson and Olson, 2000). As a result, dissemination of specific frameworks has been limited to date and their uptake modest. The latter has been mostly limited to the originators and, in some cases, to their immediate research groups. Also, case-study evidence in support of effective uptake of additional information and of compliance with specific framework constraints has been less than convincing.

The lesson remaining is that specific frameworks for HCI research need to be specified and implemented explicitly and at an appropriate level of detail to allow their application to approaches. (see 4.3.5–9.3.5). The specification needs to support the common features of frameworks in the form of a common framework – core or somesuch (see 3.4). At the same time, the differences potentially required by the specific frameworks need to be retained. In addition, initial specific frameworks need to include innovation, art, craft, applied, science and engineering (see 4.3.2–9.3.2), such as to be applicable to research approaches. Additional specific frameworks need to be created as required (see 15.3.2).

16.1.5 General Approach and General Framework
for HCI Research

Lessons Learned

General approaches, in the sense that they support the derivation and specification of a specific approach, such as innovation, art or craft, are not to be found in the HCI literature (see 2.3 and 10.1). Approaches tend to be either high level, for example, engineering, as in the case of Blandford (2013) or low level, for example, application developments, as in the case of research and development projects (Balaam et al., 2015). Neither is general in the sense of concern here.

Frameworks appear widely in the HCI research literature, for example, Rauterberg (2006) and Carroll (2010). However, it is unclear which of these frameworks are general, inasmuch as they support the derivation and specification of specific frameworks, as opposed to the specific frameworks themselves. Dowell and Long (1998), Rauterberg (2006) and Carroll (2010) might be thought to offer the former. Shneiderman (1983), Kuutti (1996) and Olson and Olson (2000) might be thought to offer the latter. However, in neither case is the matter totally clear. Researchers in general advance no clear lines of argument for the importance of such general frameworks. In fact, if anything, such general frameworks are often more criticised than specific frameworks (Rauterberg, 2006; see 10.3). Only a conservative estimate, then, of the existence of the general frameworks of concern here might be thought wise at this time.

The lesson learned is that although researchers make some use of the concepts of approach and framework currently, it is unclear, in their absence, how much use they might have made of the general approach and general framework concepts. The possibility, however, cannot and so should not be excluded. Hence, their retention in the lesson learned.

Lessons Remaining

Since to all extents and purposes they do not exist, general approaches need to be created in the manner of 10.1. As concerns frameworks for HCI research, they may be expressed at a high or low level of description. They may differ widely and may be largely implicit within frameworks for HCI (Morton et al., 1979; Long, 1987). Further, it is not clear that such frameworks are general to frameworks, as opposed to being general to the specific framework that they express.

The lesson remaining is that general approaches need to be created and general frameworks for HCI research need to be specified and implemented explicitly. The latter need to be at an appropriate level of detail, that allows their application to approaches. They also need to support the derivation and specification of further specific frameworks. The specification needs to support the common features of frameworks in the form of a common framework – core or somesuch (see 3.4). It also needs to retain the potential differences required by specific frameworks (see 10.2). General frameworks need to be able to support the derivation and specification of innovation, art, craft, applied, science and engineering frameworks (see 4.3.2–9.3.2), such as to be applicable to research approaches. Additional specific frameworks also need to be derived and created as required (see 15.3.2).

16.1.6 Validating General Approach and General Framework for HCI Research

Lessons Learned

General approaches and general frameworks, such as to support the derivation and specification of specific approaches and specific frameworks respectively, are essentially absent from the HCI literature (see 16.3.5). More specific frameworks for research reported in the literature are limited to acquisition and conceptualisation (Cockton, 2006; Rogers et al., 2011). There are some notable exceptions, which do address some aspects of validation, but only as conceptualisation (Long and Brostoff, 2002; Long and Monk, 2002).

The lesson learned is that acquisition and conceptualisation are required by HCI research.

Lessons Remaining

Validation of general approaches and general frameworks for HCI research is absent from the HCI research literature (Cockton, 2006; Harper et al., 2008). Even if they existed, general approaches and general frameworks, assumed on the basis of the current frameworks, would at best be considered as conceptualised and as acquired (see 11.3–11.4). The lesson remaining is that, as concerns validation, the general approaches and general frameworks would need to be conceptualised, operationalised, tested and generalised, both for their acquisition and their validation (see 11.3–11.4). The superordinate criteria of completeness, coherence and fitness for purpose would also have to be applied for both acquisition and validation (11.3–11.4).

16.1.7 Assessing General Framework against Other HCI Frameworks

Lessons Learned

Informal comparisons of HCI frameworks are to be found in the HCI literature (Ng, 2002; Rogers et al., 2011). These informal comparisons support framework

understanding and development (Blandford, 2013). They also support consideration of the strength and weaknesses of individual frameworks (see 12.2).

The lesson learned is that researchers appear to find such framework comparisons of some use and that the comparisons should, therefore, be encouraged
and continued.

Lessons Remaining

However, the informal comparisons usually fail to make the criteria for the
comparison explicit. They also fail to provide adequate support for the application of the frameworks. Both shortcomings militate against researchers building upon each other's work.

The lesson remaining is that informal comparisons should be transformed
into systematic assessments of general frameworks for HCI research against
other HCI frameworks (see 12.2). Such assessments need to be specified and
implemented generally, but also at the level of individually identified concepts
(Long and Monk, 2002; see 12.3). The assessments should also make explicit
the criteria they apply, for example, completeness, coherence and fitness for
purpose.

16.1.8 Assessing General Framework against HCI Theories

Lessons Learned

Informal comparisons of HCI theories are to be found in the HCI literature
(Nardi, 2002; McCarthy and Wright, 2004). Although informal, such comparisons throw some light on the relationship between frameworks and theories.
As well as supporting assessment of the frameworks, they also support the
relative assessment of the theories with which the former are compared.

The lesson learned is that researchers appear to find such theory comparisons
of some use and that the comparisons should be encouraged and continued.

Lessons Remaining

However, the informal comparisons usually fail to make the criteria for the
comparison explicit. They also fail to provide adequate support for the application of the frameworks.

The lesson remaining is that informal comparisons should be transformed
into systematic assessments of general frameworks for HCI research against
other HCI theories (13.2). Such assessments need to be specified and implemented generally, but also at the level of individually identified concepts (Long
and Monk, 2002; see 13.3). The assessments should also make explicit the

criteria they apply, for example, completeness, coherence and fitness for purpose.

16.1.9 Methodological Component for General Framework

Lessons Learned

All frameworks are primarily substantive (that is, declarative) in nature (Morton et al., 1979; Barnard, 1991; Barnard et al., 2000). It is also true that most frameworks make some reference to practice and methods, if only in passing. Some frameworks, however, make more reference than others (Dowell and Long, 1989; Rauterberg, 2006; Carroll, 2010).

The lesson learned is that such substantive components are basic to the concept of framework.

Lessons Remaining

The substantive component of frameworks, then, needs to be retained. The shortcoming of the methodological component imbalance needs to be made good. The latter would be expected to improve the applicability and so the effectiveness of the frameworks.

The lesson remaining is that a methodological component appropriate for general frameworks for HCI research needs to be specified, implemented, tested and generalised (see 14.2). Design methods of different kinds – user-centred, structured analysis and design, and research structured analysis and design – are available to be used for this purpose. They could constitute the basis on which the more balanced methodological component could be built.

16.1.10 Case Studies for General Framework

Lessons Learned

Case studies of general frameworks for HCI research that support the derivation and conceptualisation of specific frameworks do not exist in the literature. Case studies reported are for more specific frameworks for research. They are limited to acquisition and conceptualisation (Cockton, 2006; Rogers et al., 2011). There are some notable exceptions, which do address some aspects of validation; but only as conceptualisation (Long and Brostoff, 2002; Long and Monk, 2002).

The lesson learned is that acquisition case studies appear to support HCI research.

Lessons Remaining

Acquisition is only part of validation (see 11.2). Conceptualisation is only one of the criteria for validation (see 11.4).

The lesson remaining is that case studies for HCI research need to be specified and implemented for acquisition and validation, for general and specific frameworks, and also for the claims of support for research made by specific frameworks (see 15.2).

16.1.11 Conclusion

The lessons learned and the lessons remaining conclude the research programme, as proposed by this research textbook for approaches and frameworks for HCI research.

16.1.12 Research Practice Assignment

- Consider the list of lessons learned.
  - Is the list complete?
  - If not, then note the omissions and assess them for importance.
  - Identify the lessons learned that also characterise your own research.
  - Provide a rationale for any differences with the list proposed here.
- Consider the list of lessons remaining.
  - Is the list complete?
  - If not, then note the omissions and assess them for importance with the list proposed here.
  - Identify the lessons remaining that you currently follow or you intend to follow in your future research.
  - Provide a rationale for any differences with the list proposed here.

Hints and Tips

Difficult to get started?

Try reading the chapter again, while at the same time thinking explicitly about the concepts of lessons learned and lessons remaining, however they may be described. Include application in the arts or the sciences, in the development of information technology or, indeed, in your own professional or social life.

Describe your research in terms of lessons learned/alternative descriptions before attempting 16.13.

Difficult to complete?

Familiarise yourself with the concept of lessons remaining/alternative descriptions, as they are applied in the HCI research (and other) literature.

Note the similarities and differences between the different concepts of lessons learned/alternative descriptions and lessons remaining/alternative descriptions identified in the HCI research literature.

16.2 Lessons Learned

Researchers might find it easier to complete the research practice assignment (see 16.1.12), concerning the lessons learned, if the latter are listed together as below, rather than interspersed with lessons remaining. The latter order is better suited to their joint consideration. The references and cross-referencing to other relevant sections has been removed for the same reason.

16.2.1 Approaches and Frameworks for HCI Research

The lesson learned is that approaches and frameworks appear to serve some common purpose for HCI researchers in supporting their research, but in different ways. Frameworks offer the more rigorous support.

16.2.2 Approaches to HCI Research

The lesson learned is that researchers appear to find the high-level description of approach of some use as a way of characterising and thinking about their work, although in an informal manner.

16.2.3 Frameworks for HCI Research

The lesson learned is that researchers appear to find the concept of framework of some use as a way of characterising and thinking about their work in a more rigorous manner than that offered by approach.

16.2.4 Specific Frameworks for HCI Research

The lesson learned is that researchers appear to find the concept of specific framework of some use as a way of characterising and thinking about their work in a more specific manner than the concept of framework more generally.

16.2.5 General Approach and General Framework for HCI Research

The lesson learned is that although researchers appear to make some use of the concepts of approach and framework at this time, in their absence, it is unclear how much use they might make of the general approach and general framework concepts. The possibility, however, cannot, and so should not, be excluded. Hence their retention in the lesson learned.

16.2.6 Validating General Approach and General Framework for HCI Research

The lesson learned is that acquisition and conceptualisation are required by HCI research.

16.2.7 Assessing General Framework against Other HCI Frameworks

The lesson learned is that researchers appear to find such comparisons of some use and that the comparisons should, therefore, be encouraged and continued.

16.2.8 Assessing General Framework against HCI Theories

The lesson learned is that researchers appear to find such comparisons of some use and that the comparisons should be encouraged and continued.

16.2.9 Methodological Component for General Framework

The lesson learned is that such substantive components are basic to the concept of framework.

16.2.10 Case Studies for General Framework

The lesson learned is that acquisition case studies support HCI research.

16.3 Lessons Remaining

Researchers might find it easier to complete the research practice assignment (see 16.1.12), concerning the lessons remaining, if the latter are listed together as below, rather than interspersed with lessons learned. The latter order is better suited to their joint consideration. The cross-referencing to other relevant sections has been removed for the same reason.

16.3.1 Approaches and Frameworks for HCI Research

The lesson remaining is that approaches and frameworks for HCI research need to be related, and systematically so. Also, as part of that systematic relationship, frameworks need to be applicable to approaches.

16.3.2 Approaches to HCI Research

The lesson remaining is that approaches to HCI research need to be specified and implemented explicitly, although informally. The specification needs to support the classification of approaches according to their common features, while retaining the differences between them. Initial specific approaches need to include innovation, art, craft, applied, science and engineering. Additional specific approaches need to be created as required.

16.3.3 Frameworks for HCI Research

The lesson remaining is that frameworks for HCI research need to be specified and implemented explicitly. The specification needs to support the common features of frameworks in the form of a common framework – core or somesuch – while retaining the potential for differences between specific frameworks. Initial specific frameworks need to include innovation, art, craft, applied, science and engineering, such as to be applicable to research approaches. Additional specific frameworks need to be created as required.

16.3.4 Specific Frameworks for HCI Research

The lesson remaining is that specific frameworks for HCI research need to be specified and implemented explicitly and at an appropriate level of detail to allow their application to approaches. The specification needs to support the common features of frameworks in the form of a common framework – core or somesuch. At the same time, the differences potentially required by the specific frameworks need to be retained. In addition, initial specific frameworks need to include innovation, art, craft, applied, science and engineering, such as to be applicable to research approaches. Additional specific frameworks need to be created as required.

16.3.5 General Approach and General Framework for HCI Research

The lesson remaining is that general approaches need to be created and that general frameworks for HCI research need to be specified and implemented explicitly. The latter need to be at an appropriate level of detail, that allows their application to approaches. They also need to support the derivation and specification of further specific frameworks. The specification needs to support the common features of frameworks in the form of a common framework – core or somesuch. It also needs to retain the potential differences required by specific frameworks. General frameworks need to be able to support the derivation and specification of innovation, art, craft, applied, science and engineering frameworks, such as to be applicable to research approaches. Additional specific frameworks also need to be derived and created as required.

16.3.6 Validating General Approach and General Framework for HCI Research

The lesson remaining is that, as concerns validation, the general approaches and general frameworks would need to be conceptualised, operationalised, tested and generalised, both for their acquisition and their validation. The superordinate criteria of completeness, coherence and fitness for purpose would also have to be applied for both acquisition and validation.

16.3.7 Assessing General Framework against Other HCI Frameworks

The lesson remaining is that informal comparisons should be transformed into systematic assessments of general frameworks for HCI research against other HCI frameworks. Such assessments need to be specified and implemented generally, but also at the level of individually identified concepts. The assessments should also make explicit the criteria they apply, for example, completeness, coherence and fitness for purpose.

16.3.8 Assessing General Framework against HCI Theories

The lesson remaining is that informal comparisons should be transformed into systematic assessments of general frameworks for HCI research against other HCI theories. Such assessments need to be specified and implemented generally but also at the level of individually identified concepts. The assessments should also make explicit the criteria they apply, for example, completeness, coherence and fitness for purpose.

16.3.9 Methodological Component for General Framework

The lesson remaining is that a methodological component appropriate for general frameworks for HCI research needs to be specified, implemented, tested and generalised. Design methods of different kinds – user-centred, structured analysis and design, and research structured analysis and design – are available for this purpose. They could constitute the basis on which the more balanced methodological component might be built.

16.3.10 Case Studies for General Framework

The lesson remaining is that case studies for HCI research need to be specified and implemented for acquisition and validation, for general and specific frameworks and for the claims of support for research made by specific frameworks.

Postscript

One might be forgiven for wondering what the researchers will make of a textbook written especially for them? Some researchers will no doubt be delighted. They will not be able to wait to get started on the proposed HCI research programme, busily building on their own and each other's work, approach on approach, framework on framework and framework on approach. 'Real HCI research at last,' they will be thinking. 'Now for some discipline progress.'

Other researchers will be more circumspect. They will not be able to wait to get back to research as they know it. 'What's all the fuss about?' the researchers will be thinking. 'HCI, its research and its community are all doing very well, thank you. Anyway, I like designing applications for good user experiences.'

The responses of both groups of researchers are understandable and reasonable by their own criteria. The latter, however, appear to be quite different in the two cases. To complete the circle from the beginning to the end of this research textbook, let us return for a moment to the preface. The growth and diversification of HCI and HCI research will continue apace. Current computing technologies will continue to become more widely accepted. New technologies will continue to be invented. New directions, such as artificial intelligence, robotics, virtual reality and automation, will continue to be developed. In addition, the new computing technologies and directions will engender their own problems with implications for HCI, for example, the editing of social media, the securing of private accounts and the deterring of financial fraud, and also security, the legal responsibility of automated technology such as driverless cars, and the moral censorship of the Internet, to name but a few. All these problems involve human–computer interactions of one kind or another and so also involve their design and research (although other professions and disciplines will also be involved).

The challenges to HCI research will continue and increase as a result. In other words, in 20 years' time or so, researchers will be faced by the same kinds of problem; but even more of them and even more complex ones. How many more academic disciplines, design practices, interdisciplinary overlapping fields and total fields of HCI will the 2030 equivalent of Rogers' 2012 book include? Your guess is as good as mine; but if research continues with business as usual, too many more. And where will that leave HCI discipline progress and the building on each other's work, not to mention the attraction of research funds, both public and private? How will the two groups of researchers and readers of the textbook feel and what will they do about that?

The dilemma resides in how the research of the two groups might be related, while respecting the differences both of the research itself and of the associated rationales. This textbook suggests a way in which this might be brought about. The approach and framework HCI research programme proposed by the textbook offers a common framing for design and research and their relations, including both knowledge and practice. The General Framework (see 10.2.2), the general design research exemplar (see Figure 10.1), as well as the specific design research exemplars (see Figures 4.1–9.1), posit a relationship between design practice research and research practice research (see 14.1). The relation resides in the distinction between user requirements and specific design problems on the one hand and interactive systems and specific design solutions on the other hand. Specific design problems are derived from and validated empirically against user requirements. Specific design solutions are derived from and validated empirically against interactive systems. The design cycle, however, is assumed to include a design process as some combination of specification and implementation, interspersed with iterative trial-and-error cycles. The latter produces an interactive system designed to meet user requirements. Design practice research and research practice research thus both attempt to satisfy one or more user requirements in the form of one or more parts of an interactive system.

However, some researchers may be more engaged in finding specific design solutions, as they relate to interactive systems or their parts, to specific design problems, as they relate to one or more user requirements. These researchers might be considered to be more research practice researchers to whom the greater rigour of a framework is more appropriate. Other researchers may be more engaged in designing interactive systems or their parts, as they relate to one or more user requirements. These researchers might be considered to be more design practice researchers to whom the lesser rigour of an approach may be more appropriate.

The main point is that the General Framework and the general and specific design research exemplars require both types of research and specify the relations between them, in addition to the relations between approaches and frameworks. In this way, the two groups of researchers can pursue their own research preference within the programme proposed by this textbook, while at the same time, they can show how their research contributes to the creation of interactive systems or their parts to satisfy one or more user requirements and so to one another. In this way, the HCI research programme proposed by the textbook may be able to accommodate the aspirations of both groups of researchers. This accommodation is not only by supporting productive communication between them, but by offering them, in addition, a way of building on each other's research.

References

Atwood, M., Gray, W. and John, B. (1996) Project Ernestine: Analytic and Empirical Methods Applied to a Real World CHI Problem. In Rudisill, M., Lewis, C., Polson, P. and McKay, T. (Eds.) *Human Computer Interface Design: Success Stories, Emerging Methods and Real World Context*, 101–121. San Francisco, CA: Morgan Kaufmann.

Bacon, C. and Fitzgerald, B. (2001) A Systematic Framework for the Field of Information Systems. *The DATA BASE for Advances in Information Systems*, 32 (2): 46–67.

Balaam, M., Comber, R., Jenkins, E., Sutton, S. and Garbett, A. (2015) FeedFinder: A Location-Mapping Mobile Application for Breastfeeding Women. In *CHI '15: Proceedings of the 33rd Annual ACM Conference on Human Factors in Computing Systems*, 1709–1718. New York, NY: ACM Press.

Bannon, L. and Bødker, S. (1991) Encountering Artefacts in Use. In Carroll, J. (Ed.) *Designing Interaction: Psychology at the Human–Computer Interface*, 227–253. Cambridge, UK: Cambridge University Press.

Bardzell, J. (2009) Interaction Criticism and Aesthetics. In *CHI '09: Proceedings of the SIGCHI Conference on Human Factors in Computing Systems*, 2357–2366. New York, NY: ACM Press.

Bardzell, J., Bolter, J. and Lowgren, J. (2010) Interaction Criticism: Three Readings of an Interaction Design and What They Get Us. *Interactions*, 17 (2): 32–37.

Barnard, P. (1991) Bridging between Basic Theories and the Artifacts of Human–Computer Interaction. In Carroll, J. (Ed.) *Designing Interaction: Psychology at the Human–Computer Interface*, 103–127. Cambridge, UK: Cambridge University Press.

Barnard, P. and May, J. (1999) Representing Cognitive Activity in Complex Tasks. *Human-Computer Interaction*, 14: 93–158.

Barnard, P., May, D., Duke, D. and Duce, D. (2000) Systems, Interactions and Macrotheory. *ACM Transactions on Human-Computer Interaction*, 7, (2): 222–262.

Barnard, P., Hammond, N., Morton, J., Long, J. and Clark, I. (1981) Consistency and Compatibility in Human-Computer Dialogue. *International Journal of Man-Machine Studies*, 15: 87–134.

Bentley, R., Hughes, J., Randall, D., Rodden, T., Sawyer, P., Sommerville, I. and Shapiro, D. (1992) Ethnographically-Informed Systems Design for Air Traffic

Control. In *CSCW '92: Proceedings of the 1992 ACM Conference on Computer-Supported Cooperative Work*, 123–129. New York, NY: ACM Press.

Blandford, A. (2013) Engineering Works: What Is (and Is Not) 'Engineering' for Interactive Computer Systems. In *Proceedings of the Fifth Symposium on Engineering Interactive Computing Systems (EICS 2013)*, 285–286. New York, NY: ACM Press.

Browne, D. (1994) *STUDIO: STructured User-Interface Design for Interaction Optimisation*. Englewood Cliffs, NJ: Prentice Hall.

Buckley, P. (1989) Expressing Research Findings to Have a Practical Influence on Design. In Long, J. and Whitefield, A. (Eds.) *Cognitive Ergonomics and Human-Computer Interaction*, 166–190. Cambridge, UK: Cambridge University Press.

Card, S., Moran, T. and Newell, A. (1983) *The Psychology of Human-Computer Interaction*. Hillsdale, NJ: Lawrence Erlbaum.

Carroll, J. (1995) *Scenario-Based Design: Envisioning Work and Technology in System Development*. New York, NY: Wiley.

Carroll, J. (2003) Introduction: Toward a Multidisciplinary Science of Human-Computer Interaction. In Carroll, J. (Ed.) *HCI Models, Theories and Frameworks*, 1–9. San Francisco, CA: Morgan Kaufmann.

Carroll, J. (2010) Conceptualizing a Possible Discipline of Human-Computer Interaction. *Interacting with Computers*, 22 (1): 3–12.

Carroll, J., Kellog, W. and Rosson, M. (1991) The Task-Artifact Cycle in Designing Interaction. In Carroll, J. (Ed.) *Designing Interaction*, 74–102. Cambridge, UK: Cambridge University Press.

Cockton, G. (2006) Designing Worth is Worth Designing. In *NordiCHI '06: Proceedings of the 4th Nordic Conference on Human-Computer Interaction: Changing Roles*, 165–174.New York, NY: ACM Press.

Cockton, G. (2014) A Critical, Creative UX Community: CRUF. *Journal of Usability Studies*, 10 (1): 1–16.

Cummaford, S. (2000) Validating Effective Design Knowledge for Re-use: HCI Engineering Design Principles. In *CHI '00 Extended Abstracts on Human Factors in Computing Systems*, 165–174. New York, NY: ACM Press.

Cummaford, S. and Long, J. (1998) Towards a Conception of HCI Engineering Design Principles. In *Proceedings of Ninth European Conference on Cognitive Ergonomics (ECCE9)*, 79–84. York: European Association of Cognitive Ergonomics.

Cummaford, S. and Long, J. (1999) Costs Matrix: Systematic Comparisons of Competing Design Solutions. In Brewster, S., Cawsey, A. and Cockton, G. (Eds.) *Proc. INTERACT 99, Volume II*, 25–26. Swindon: British Computer Society.

Debenard, S. and Crevits, I. (2000) Projet Amanda – *Note Intermediaire*, 1.2 CENA/N12v1/. Paris: Centre d'Etudes de la Navigation Aérienne.

Denley, I. and Long, J. (2001) Multi-Disciplinary Practice in Requirements Engineering: Problems and Criteria for Support. In Blandford, A., Vanderdonkt, J. and Gray, P. (Eds.) *People and Computers XV – Interaction without Frontiers. Joint Proceedings of HCI 2001 and IHM 2001*, 125–138. London: Springer Verlag.

De Souza, C., Barbosa, S. and Prates, R. (2001) A Semiotic Engineering Approach to HCI. In *Extended Abstracts on Human Factors in Computing Systems, CHI 01*, 55–56. New York, NY: ACM Press.

Dinu, V. and Nadkarni, P. (2007) Guidelines for the Effective Use of Entity-Attribute-Value Modeling for Biomedical Databases. *International Journal of Medical Informatics*, 76 (11–12):769–779.

Dix, A. (2010) Human-Computer Interactions: a Stable Discipline, a Nascent Science and the Growth of the Long Tail. *Interacting with Computers*, 22 (1): 13–27.

Dowell, J. (1998) Formulating the Cognitive Design Problem of Air Traffic Management. *International Journal of Human-Computer Studies*, 49 (5): 743–766.

Dowell, J. and Long, J. (1989) Towards a Conception for an Engineering Discipline of Human Factors. *Ergonomics*, 32 (11): 1513–1535.

Dowell, J. and Long, J. (1998) Target Paper: Conception of the Cognitive Engineering Design Problem. *Ergonomics*, 41 (2): 126–139.

Edmonds, E. (2018) *The Art of Interaction: What HCI Can Learn from Interactive Art*. San Rafael, CA: Morgan & Claypool.

Engeström, Y. (1990) *Learning, Working and Imagining: Twelve Studies in Activity Theory*. Helsinki: Orienta-Konsulti.

Gibson, J. J. (1966) *The Senses Considered as Perceptual Systems*. Boston, MA: Houghton-Mifflin.

Gibson, J. J. (1979) *The Ecological Approach to Visual Perception*. Boston. MA: Houghton-Mifflin.

Gilligan, P. and Long, J. (1984) Videotex Technology: An Overview with Special Reference to Transaction Processing as an Interactive Service. *Behaviour and Information Technology*, 3: 41–71.

Glaser, B. and Strauss, A. (1967) *Discovery of Grounded Theory*. London: Aldine.

Gonzalez, V. (2006) The Nature of Managing Multiple Activities in the Workplace. Doctoral Dissertation in Information and Computer Science, University of California, Irvine.

Gregoriades, A. and Sutcliffe, A. (2005) Scenario-Based Assessments of Nonfunctional Requirements. *IEEE Transactions on Software Engineering*, 31 (5): 392–409.

Harper, R., Rodden, T., Rogers, Y. and Sellen, A. (2008) *Being Human – Human-Computer Interaction in the Year 2020*. Cambridge, UK: Microsoft Research Ltd.

Harris, J. and Henderson, A. (1999) A Better Mythology for System Design. In *CHI '99: Proceedings of the SIGCHI Conference on Human Factors in Computing Systems*, 88–95. New York, NY: ACM Press.

Heath, C. and Luff, P. (1991) Collaborative Activity and Technological Design: Task Coordination in London Underground Control Rooms. In *Proceedings of the Second European Conference on Computer- Supported Cooperative Work ECSCW '91*, 65–80. Dordrecht: Kluwer.

Hill, B. (2010) Diagnosing Co-ordination Problems in the Emergency Management Response to Disasters. *Interacting with Computers*, 22 (1): 43–55.

Hill, B., Long, J., Smith, W. and Whitefield, A. (1993) Planning for Multiple Task Work – an Analysis of a Medical Reception Worksystem. In Ashlund, S., Mullet, K., Henderson, A., Hollnagel, E. and White, T. (Eds.) In *Conference on Human Factors in Computing Systems, INTERACT '93 and CHI '93*, 314–320. New York, NY: Amsterdam.

Hill, B., Long, J., Smith, W. and Whitefield, A. (1995) A Model of Medical Reception – The Planning and Control of Multiple Task Work. *Applied Cognitive Psychology*, 9 (S1): S81–S114.

Hutchins, E. (1995) *Cognition in the Wild*. Cambridge, MA: MIT Press.

John, B. and Gray, W. (1995) CPM-GOMS: An Analysis Method for Tasks with Parallel Activities. In *Conference Companion on Human Factors in Computing Systems CHI '95*, 393–394. New York, NY: ACM Press.

Kirsh, D. (2001) The Context of Work. *Human–Computer Interaction*, 6 (2): 306–322.

Kuhn, T. S. (1970) *The Structure of Scientific Revolutions*. Chicago, IL: University of Chicago Press.

Kuutti, K. (1996) Activity Theory as a Potential Framework for Human-Computer Interaction Research. In Nardi, B. (Ed.) *Context and Consciousness: Activity Theory and Human-Computer Interaction*, 17–44. Cambridge, MA: MIT Press.

Lambie, T. and Long, J. (2002) Engineering CSCW. In Blay-Fonarino, M., Pinna-Derry, A., Schmidt, K. and Zarate, P. (Eds.) *Co-operative Systems Design: A Challenge of the Mobility Age*. Amsterdam: IOS Press.

Larkin, J. and Simon, H. (1987) Why a Diagram Is (Sometimes) Worth Ten Thousand Words. *Cognitive Science*, 11: 65–99.

Leontiev, A. (1978) *Activity, Consciousness and Personality*. Englewood Cliffs, NJ: Prentice Hall.

Leontiev, A. N. (1989) The Problem of Activity in the History of Soviet Psychology. *Soviet Psychology*, 27 (1): 22–39.

Life, A. (2018) *User Centred Design*. Birmingham: CIEHF.

Lim, K. and Long, J. (1994) *The MUSE Method for Usability Engineering*. Cambridge, UK: Cambridge University Press.

Long, J. (1987) Cognitive Ergonomics and Human-Computer Interaction. In Warr, P. (Ed.) *Psychology at Work*, 73–95. London: Penguin.

Long, J. (1989) Cognitive Ergonomics and Human-Computer Interaction: An Introduction. In Long, J. and Whitefield, A. (Eds.) *Cognitive Ergonomics and Human-Computer Interaction*, 4–34. Cambridge, UK: Cambridge University Press.

Long, J. (1997) Research and the Design of Human-Computer Interactions or 'What Happened to Validation?' In Thimbleby, H., O'Conaill, B. and Thomas, P. (Eds.) *People and Computers XII: Proceedings of HCI '97*, 223–243. London: Springer.

Long, J. (2002) HCI Is More Than the Usability of WEB Pages: A Domain Approach. In Amadeo, G. (Ed.) *Proceedings of Third USIHC/Fourth Ergodesign Conference*. Rio de Janeiro.

Long, J. (2010) Some Celebratory Reflections on a Celebratory HCI *Festschrift*, *Interacting with Computers*, 22 (1): 68–71.

Long, J. and Brostoff, S. (2002) Validating Design Knowledge in the Home: A Successful Case-Study of Dementia Care. In Reed, D., Baxter, G. and Blythe, M. (Eds.) *Proceedings of the 12th European Conference on Cognitive Ergonomics*, 49–56. York: European Association of Cognitive Ergonomics.

Long, J. and Dowell, J. (1989) Conceptions of the Discipline of HCI: Craft, Applied Science, and Engineering. In Sutcliffe, A. and Macaulay, L. (Eds.) *People and Computers V*, 9–32. Cambridge, UK: Cambridge University Press.

Long, J. and Hill, B. (2005) Validating Diagnostic Design Knowledge for Air Traffic Management: A Case-Study. In Marmaras, N., Kontogiannis, T. and Nathanael, D. (Eds.) *Proceedings of the Annual Conference of the European Association of Cognitive Ergonomics: EACE 2005*, 3–10. York: European Association of Cognitive Ergonomics.

Long, J. and Monk, A. (2002) Applying a Cognitive Engineering Framework to Research: A Successful Case-Study? In McCabe, P. (Ed.) *Contemporary Ergonomics*, 367–371. London: Taylor and Francis.

Long, J. and Timmer, P. (2000) Design Problems for Research: What We Can Learn from ATM-Like Micro-Worlds. In *Proceedings of Travail Humain Workshop*, 197–221, Bretigny, France.

Long, J. and Timmer, P. (2001) Design Problems for Cognitive Ergonomics Research: What We Can Learn from ATM-like Microworlds. *Le Travail Humain*, 64 (3): 197–222.

Long, J. and Whitefield, A. (1989) (Eds.) *Cognitive Ergonomics and Human-Computer Interaction*. Cambridge, UK: Cambridge University Press.

Long, J., Hammond, N., Barnard, P., Morton, J. and Clark, I. (1980) New Technology in the Work-Place: A Method for Identifying Underlying Variables. In *Proceedings of Symposium on Analysis and Health Evaluation of the Workplace*, Portoroz, Yugoslavia.

Long, J., Hammond, N., Barnard, P., Morton, J. and Clark, I. (1982) Introducing the Interactive Computer at Work: The User's Views. *Behaviour and Information Technology*, 2: 39–106.

Lowgren, J. and Stolterman, E. (2004) *Thoughtful Interaction Design*. Cambridge, MA: MIT Press.

Mancini, C., van der Linden, J., Bryan, A., and Stuart, A. (2012) Exploring Interspecies Sensemaking: Dog Tracking Semiotics and Multispecies Ethnography. In *UbiComp '12: Proceedings of the 2012 ACM Conference on Ubiquitous Computing*, 143–152. Pittsburgh, PA: ACM Press.

McCarthy, J. and Wright, P. (2004) *Technology as Experience*. Cambridge, MA: MIT Press.

McGrath, J. (1991) Time, Interaction, and Performance (TIP): A Theory of Groups. *Small Group Research*, 22 (2): 147–174.

Middlemass, J. and Long, J. (2005) A General Model of Human Factors Structured Analysis and Design Methods. In Bust, P. and McCabe, P. (Eds.) *Contemporary Ergonomics*, 361–365. London: Taylor and Francis.

Middlemass, J., Stork, A. and Long, J. (1999) Successful Case Study and Partial Validation of MUSE, a Structured Method for Usability Engineering. In Sasse, M. and Johnson, C. (Eds.) *Proc. INTERACT '99 of Human-Computer Interaction, Edinburgh, UK*, 399–407. Amsterdam: IOS Press.

Morton, J., Barnard, P., Hammond, N. and Long, J. (1979) Interacting with the Computer: A Framework. In Boutmy, E. and Danthine, A., (Eds.) *Teleinformatics '79: Proceedings of the International Conference on Teleinformatics, Paris, France, 11–13 June 1979*. Amsterdam: North Holland.

Nardi, B. (Ed.) (1996) *Context and Consciousness: Activity Theory and Human-Computer Interaction*. Cambridge, MA: MIT Press.

Nardi, B. (2002) Coda and Response to Christine Halverson. *Computer Supported Cooperative Work (CSCW)*, 11: 269–275.

Newman, W. (1984) A Preliminary Analysis of the Products of HCI Research, Using Proforma Abstracts. In Adelson, B., Dumas, S. and Olson, J. (Eds.) *Proceedings of CHI '84 Human Factors in Computing Systems*, 278–284. New York: ACM/SIGCHI.

Ng, K. (2002) Toward a Theoretical Framework for Understanding the Relationship between Situated Action and Planned Action Models of Behavior in Information Retrieval Contexts: Contributions from Phenomenology, *Information Processing and Management*, 38: 613–626.

Nielsen, J. (1993) *Usability Engineering*. San Francisco, CA: Morgan Kaufman.

Norman, D. (1983) Design Principles for Human-Computer Interfaces. In Smith, R., Pew, R. and Janda, A. (Eds.) *CHI '83: Proceedings of the SIGCHI Conference on Human Factors in Computing Systems*, 1–10. New York, NY: ACM Press.

Norman, D. (1986) Cognitive Engineering. In Draper, S. and Norman, D. (Eds.) *User Centred System Design*, 31–61. Hillsdale, NJ: Lawrence Erlbaum Associates.

Norman, D. (2010) The Transmedia Design Challenge: Technology That Is Pleasurable and Satisfying. *Interactions*, 17, (1): 12–15.

Obrist, M., Tuch, A. and Hornbaek, K. (2014) Opportunities for Odor: Experiences with Smell and Implications for Technology. In *CHI 2014 Conference on Human Factors in Computing Systems*, 2843–2852. New York, NY: ACM Press.

Olson, J. and Olson, G. (2000) Distance Matters. *Human-Computer Interaction*, 15: 139–178.

Rauterberg, M. (2006) HCI as an Engineering Discipline: To Be or Not To Be!? *African Journal of Information and Communication Technology*, 2 (4): 163–184.

Redmond-Pyle, D. and Moore, A. (1995) *Graphical User Interface Design and Evaluation (GUIDE): A Practical Process*. Englewood Cliffs, NJ: Prentice Hall.

Rogers, Y. (2012) *HCI Theory – Classical, Modern, and Contemporary*. San Rafael, CA: Morgan and Claypool.

Rogers, Y., Sharp, H. and Preece, J. (2011) *Interaction Design: Beyond Human-Computer Interaction*, 3rd ed. Chichester: John Wiley and Sons Ltd.

Rozanski, E. and Haake, A. (2003) The Many Facets of HCI. In *Proceeding of the 4th Conference on Information Technology Education*, 180–185. New York: ACM Press.

Salisbury, J. (2014) Videogame Engagement as a Process of Seeking Cultural Value. Unpublished PhD thesis. University of London.

Salter, I. (2010) Applying the Conception of HCI Engineering to the Design of Economic Systems. *Interacting with Computers*, 22 (1): 56–67.

Santos, P., Kiris, E. and Coyle, C. (1997) Designing as the World Turns. In *Proceedings of the Conference on Designing Interactive Systems DIS 97*, 315–321. New York: ACM Press.

Scaife, M. and Rogers, Y. (1996) External Cognition: How Do Graphical Representations Work? *International Journal of Human-Computer Studies*, 45: 185–213.

Sharp, H., Rogers, Y. and Preece, J. (2007) *Interaction Design: Beyond Human-Computer Interaction*, 2nd ed. Chichester: John Wiley and Sons Ltd.

Shneiderman, B. (1983) Direct Manipulation: A Step beyond Programming Languages. *IEEE Computer*, 16 (8): 57–69.

Shneiderman, B. (1998) *Designing the User Interface: Strategies for Effective Human-Computer Interaction*, 3rd ed. Reading, MA: Addison-Wesley.

Shneiderman, B. (2010) *Designing the User Interface: Strategies for Effective Human-Computer Interaction*, 5th ed. Reading, MA: Addison-Wesley.

Stork, A. (1999) Towards Engineering Principles for Human-Computer Interaction (Domestic Energy Planning Control). Unpublished PhD thesis, University of London.

Stork, A. and Long, J. (1994) A Specific Planning and Control Design Problem in the Home: Rationale and a Case-Study. In *Proceedings of the International Working Conference on Home-Oriented Informatics, Telematics and Automation*. Denmark: Amager.

Stork, A., Long, J. and Lambie, T. (1999) Is Cognitive Engineering the Way Forward for HCI? In Brewster, S., Cawsey, A. and Cockton, G. (Eds.) *Proc. INTERACT 99, Volume II*, 141. Swindon: British Computer Society.

Stork, A., Middlemass, J. and Long, J. (1995) Applying a Structured Method for Usability Engineering to Domestic Energy Management User Requirements: A Successful Case-Study. In *Proceedings of HCI*, 367–385.

Suchman, L. (1987) *Plans and Situated Actions*. Cambridge, UK: Cambridge University Press.

Sutcliffe, A. and Blandford, A. (2010) Guest Editors' Introduction. *Interacting with Computers*, 22 (1): 1–2.

Teo, L. and John, B. (2008) CogTool-Explorer: Towards a Tool for Predicting User Interaction. In *CHI EA '08: CHI '08 Extended Abstracts on Human Factors in Computing Systems*, 2793–2798. New York, NY: ACM Press,

Timmer, P. (1999) Expression of Operator Planning Horizons: A Cognitive Approach. Unpublished PhD thesis, University of London.

Timmer, P. and Long, J. (2002) Expressing the Effectiveness of Planning Horizons. *Le Travail Humain*, 65 (2): 103–126.

Vanderheiden, G. (2008) Ubiquitous Accessibility, Common Technology Core, and Micro Assistive Technology. *ACM Transactions in Accessible Computing*, 1 (2), 1–7.

Vicente, K. and Rasmussen, J. (1990) The Ecology of Man-Machine Systems II: Mediating 'Direct Perception' in Complex Work Domains. *Ecological Psychology*, 2: 207–249.

Vygotsky, L. (1962) *Thought and Language*. Cambridge, MA: MIT Press.

Watts, L. and Monk, A. (1997) Telemedical Consultation: Task Characteristics. In *Proceedings of the 1997 Conference on Human Factors in Computing Systems, CHI*, 534–535. New York, NY: ACM Press.

Watts, L. and Monk, A. (1999) Telemedicine: What Happens in Teleconsultation. *International Journal of Technology Assessment in Health Care*, 15 (1): 220–235.

Wild, P. (2010) Longing for Service: Bringing the UCL Conception towards Services Research. *Interacting with Computers*, 22 (1): 28–42.

Winograd, T. (1997) From Computing Machinery to Interaction Design. In Denning, P. and Metcalfe, R. (Eds.) *Beyond Calculation: The Next Fifty Years of Computing*, 149–162. Heidelberg: Springer-Verlag.

Woods, D. (1995) Toward a Theoretical Base for Representation Design in the Computer Medium: Ecological Perception and Aiding Cognition. In Flach, J., Hancock, P., Carid, J. and Vicente, K. (Eds.) *Global Perspective on the Ecology of Human-Machine Systems*, 157–188. Hillsdale, NJ: Erlbaum.

Wright, P., Fields, R. and Harrison, M. (2000) Analysing Human-Computer Interaction as Distributed Cognition: The Resources Model. *Human Computer Interaction*, 51 (1): 1–41.

Index

academic discipline, 6, 10, 56, 67, 105, 126
air traffic management, 243, 245
anthrozoology, 89, 95
Apple, 24
    Lisa, 24, 28
    Macintosh, 24
applied
    application, 84
    approach, 83, 86
    case study, 90
    core framework, 86, 90
    design cycle, 88
    design research cycle, 89
    design research exemplar, 83, 85,
        89, 90
    framework, 85
    interactive system, 88
    lower-level framework, 83, 85, 90, 91
    one-to-many mapping, 86
    performance, 94
    specific framework, 83, 90
    specific problem, 89
    specific solution, 89
art
    application, 52
    approach, 44, 46
    core framework, 47
    design cycle, 50
    design research cycle, 48
    design research exemplar, 48
    framework, 47
    interactive system, 52, 53
    lower-level framework, 51
    one-to-many mapping, 47
    performance, 46, 55
    specific framework, 47

    specific problem, 48
    specific solution, 48
arts, types of, 44
Artset, 48
avatar, 50, 52–55

bottom-up strategy, 9, 217, 232
brainstorming, 25, 216
breastfeeding, 65–66, 70–76, 166–167, 201,
    224, 271

case studies, 239
    acquisition/validation, 240
    criteria, 239, 241
    definition/complexity/observability, 240
    framework acquisition, 240
    framework validation, 240, 244
    framework/knowledge, 240
    general framework, 241, 242
    knowledge acquisition, 242
    knowledge validation, 243, 247
    requirement, 239
    types, 239
CHI (computer–human interaction), 3, 4, 28,
    87, 106, 147
codified knowledge, 123, 143
coding – open/axial/selective, 217
conception, 3–4, 13, 16–17, 19, 157, 194,
    242–243, 246, 248, 257
concepts,
    definitional, 47, 67, 86, 105, 126, 146
    extended definitional, 47, 67, 86, 105, 126, 146
    main, 47, 67, 86, 105, 126, 146
core framework, 145, 171, 209, 242
    See also under applied, art, craft,
        engineering, innovation, science